Bluebloods & Rednecks

Discord and Rebellion in the 1830s

D1450359

CHARLES D. ANDERSON

Published by

GENERAL STORE
PUBLISHING HOUSE

1 Main Street Burnstown, Ontario, Canada K0J 1G0
Telephone 1-800-465-6072 Fax (613) 432-7184

ISBN 1-896182-45-3
Printed and bound in Canada

Layout and design by Derek McEwen

General Store Publishing House gratefully acknowledges the assistance of the
Ontario Arts Council and the Canada Council.

Canadian Cataloguing in Publication Data

Anderson, Charles D.
   Bluebloods and Rednecks: Discord and Rebellion in the 1830s

Includes bibliographical references and index.
ISBN 1-896182-45-3

   1. Grenville (Ont. : County)–History.
   2. Leeds (Ont. : County)–History. I. Title.

FC3095.L38A53 1996   971.3'7302   C96-900495-8
F1059.L4A53 1996

First Printing July 1996

Contents

Introduction

MUCH HAS BEEN WRITTEN about the Rebellions of 1837, and this book attempts to add something to the discussion. The focus is on eastern Ontario, specifically the Johnstown District, comprising the counties of Leeds and Grenville and the major towns of Brockville, Gananoque, and Prescott. There is a discussion of events, but the emphasis is on the underlying social and political context that resulted in those events.

During the 1830s, the Johnstown District, and in particular the County of Leeds, became infamous for political violence. Three successive elections were set aside as a result of mayhem at the Poll. A man was killed, his skull crushed, and his killer tried and acquitted by a Brockville jury. In Grenville County, there were further riots. At the close of one election, the Poll Book was stolen, then destroyed. In the aftermath of another, a young Tory was charged with attempted murder. Why did passions run this high? Was it by coincidence only that the Loyal Orange Lodge took root first in Leeds before spreading across the province? Why, for that matter, would Brockville, 150 years later, be famous for a bunch of red necked zealots stomping on the Quebec flag?

The modern political scientists and back-room schemers, who advise governments and politicians on the magic words they should use in election campaigns, now use extensive polling and attitudinal studies broken down into age, religion, monetary, and social status. An attempt is made to apply that methodology to the politics of the 1830s. This book, accordingly, looks at the demography of eastern Ontario in the 1830's as a guide to the political value system of the various groups of people within society.

Canadians currently pride themselves on being a peace loving nation dedicated to the rule of law, democratic principles, and individual liberties. The same might be said of any western democracy. Yet, these principles are not necessarily compatible. South Africa, prior to the emancipation of the non-white population, was governed by the rule of law, but not by the democratic principle of universal suffrage. Democratic principles imply majority rule, but majority rule is often at odds with individual liberties. The character of any nation is largely determined by the manner in which its people have come to terms with these, at times, competing concepts.

Canadians also pride themselves on being distinct from their American neighbours to the south. In Canada, we like to think we have mixed the elements of modern democracy differently than have our American counterparts. The uniquely Canadian melange of values has traditionally given pre-eminence to peace, order and good government. Canada has been the land of the cultural mosaic as opposed to the melting pot. Canadians have prided themselves on collectively caring for one another with extended social programmes, state-funded post-secondary education, and universal health care. The collective good is valued in a manner not understood in the United States where society's emphasis is on individual liberty and the pursuit of happiness.

If Canadians form a distinct society, then that distinctiveness must be found in history. There has been a distinctive Canadian response to historical events which, in a curious dialectic, is both indicative and a principal cause of the unique Canadian mix of social and political traits. The Canadian response to historic events both defines and moulds the Canadian national character.

The first period of Upper Canadian history ended with the Act of Union and the beginning of responsible government in 1841. The rebellions that marked the close of the 1830s and the Canadian response to armed insurrection provide an early example of how Canadians demonstrated that their collective existence would be distinctive. The causes of the rebellion were legitimate. The growing Canadian population chaffed under a system of autocratic government devoid of democratic structure. Most people in the province agreed that fundamental reform was necessary yet, when confronted with a revolution that would obtain that change by force of arms, they recoiled and opted for the status quo. They opted for peace and order. They also opted to remain decidedly different from the United States of America. It was not that they were cowards. Canadians have never had to apologize for a lack of courage but, they would die to preserve a system of government, even if it did not serve their needs, rather than join with men whom they saw as traitors.

This book is an exploration of the ultimate question of that time and place: Why did men die in the cause of rebellion in the political backwaters of eastern Ontario, and, of equal importance, why did that rebellion not enjoy popular support?

CHAPTER I

The System of Government

HE AMERICAN REVOLUTION created two countries: the United States of America and that remaining portion of North America soon to be known as British North America and finally as Canada. When the loss of the thirteen rebellious colonies became inevitable, those dispossessed citizens who had remained loyal to His Britannic Majesty realized that a return to their homes and farmsteads was impossible. Branded as Tories and traitors, their lands and property had been forfeited to the fledgling American government. Their choice was between relocation to Britain or resettlement in a colony still under British control. For the majority, there was no real choice. They lacked the resources to consider a return to England. There was nothing in England for them in any event, except the reasons that had originally caused them to leave. In all, it is estimated that between 35,000 and 49,000 refugees opted to resettle in the various colonies that now make up Canada.[1]

By far the largest percentage of them settled in what was then a part of Nova Scotia, and which soon became New Brunswick, and in that part of Quebec, which, in 1791, became Upper Canada. These areas were an obvious choice for settlement. They were largely devoid of European settlement and could readily absorb the large influx of new settlers. Of equal importance to the colonial administrators in London was the strategic consideration; the Loyalists would provide a barrier of loyal and reliable settlement against future American plans of expansion and aggression.

---

1 Arthur R.M. Lower, COLONY TO NATION, A HISTORY OF CANADA, Longmans Canada Limited, Toronto, 1946, p.46. The estimate is based on statistics gathered in the Report on the Manuscript Lists Relating to the United Empire Loyalists (Public Archives of Canada, Ottawa, 1909).

The Loyalist refugees from central and upstate New York, together with those from Vermont, followed the Richelieu River north to the security of Quebec where they assembled in refugee camps in the Montreal area to await war's end. With the peace of 1783, their bateau brigades left Lachine for the up river settlements of New Johnstown,[2] New Oswegatchie,[3] Kingston, and the Bay of Quinte during the spring of 1784. To the west, other Loyalists from the western American frontier crossed into and began to settle the Niagara frontier. It is estimated that Ontario alone received 10,000 Loyalist refugees.[4]

In the fall of 1783 and early spring of 1784, the British sent out survey parties, first to take an inventory of the land that was suitable for settlement, then to survey the actual lots, concessions, and townships in the areas designated for settlement.

Captain Sherwood, a Loyalist militia officer attached to Jessup's Corps, was a member of the original party that took inventory of the lands along the St Lawrence River. He left Montreal on September 19, 1783, by boat, commanding a party of fellow Loyalist militia men including Lieutenant Solomon Johns, Ensign Elijah Bottum, two men from the King's Rangers, and seven men from the Loyal Rangers.[5] Sherwood noted in his journal that his party was pleased to find that the land to the west of Lake St Francis was, ". . . a deep black mould entirely free from stones, ledges or swamps, the Timber is very thin but grows exceedingly large and Tall, it is a mixture of Beech, Maple, Elm, Basswood, Buttonut (sic), White Oak, Hickory, and some Pine. The land is exceedingly pleasant all along the shore . . ."[6]

The good land extended some twelve miles beyond the old French trading post of Oswegatchie, which they determined ought to be the limit of settlement lands along the St Lawrence River. From there to Lake Ontario, the igneous rock outcroppings of the Canadian Shield, which they could see from the river, precluded farming. While this land did not appear to be suitable for agriculture, it was not without merit. Sherwood commented on the number of "fine islands

---

2 Present day Cornwall.
3 Present day Johnstown, Ontario, across the St Lawrence River from present day Ogdensburg, New York, which was originally known as Oswegatchie.
4 Thad. W. H. Leavitt, HISTORY OF LEEDS AND GRENVILLE, (originally published in 1879 by Recorder Press, Brockville). Facsimile edition printed by Mika Publishing Company, Belleville, 1986, p.14.
5 E. Rae Stuart, "JESSUP'S RANGERS AS A FACTOR IN LOYALIST SETTLEMENT," in THREE HISTORY THESES, The Ontario Department of Public Records and Archives, 1961: p.67, citing Captain Sherwood's Journal in the Haldimand Papers, Public Archives of Canada, B124-50.
6 Ibid.

in the River," and the survey also reported that the mouth of the Gananoque River, referred to as the "Cadarockin" in Sherwood's Journal, was the best mill site imaginable.

The British were satisfied with Sherwood's inventory and determined to settle the Loyalist refugees on the lands identified by him as suitable. The sole impediment to settlement was the occupation of the land by the native population. The native people had generally assisted the British during the Revolutionary War and the British recognized their legal ownership of the land. Their title to the land had to be transferred to His Majesty prior to the actual settlement by the Loyalists.

The British concept of land ownership was foreign to the native people. Land was seen by the natives as a renewable gift to be used and shared by all nations and tribes. Nonetheless, in October of 1783, under the direction of Sir John Johnson, Captain Crawford of the King's Royal Regiment of New York negotiated with one tribe of native people for the purchase of all of the land from Longueuil up the St Lawrence River and along the north shore of Lake Ontario to the Bay of Quinte, and as far inland as a man could travel in one day. In consideration, the native Mississauga people received clothes, ". . . for all the families belonging to them . . . and that those who have not fusees (muskets) shall receive new ones, some powder and ball for their winter hunting, as much coarse red cloth as will make about a dozen coats and as many laced hats."[7] A fair price, one supposes, for most of eastern Ontario and paid to one of many nations and tribes equally entitled.

From the existing Seigneury of New Longueuil, and skipping the swampy and sunken township that became Lancaster, the actual surveying of settlement lands began in what became the Township of Charlottenburg. The survey party then proceeded westerly through the townships of Cornwall, Osnabruck, Williamsburg, Matilda, and into Edwardsburg, Augusta and Elizabethtown. Initially these original eight townships were simply numbered, beginning in the east and progressing westerly.

In the surveying, a baseline was laid out following the general course of the St Lawrence River. The land between this baseline and the river became the broken front concessions of the various

---

7 Ibid., p.70; citing Brig. Gen. G.E. Cruikshank, THE SETTLEMENT OF THE UNITED EMPIRE LOYALISTS ON THE UPPER ST. LAWRENCE AND BAY OF QUINTE IN 1784, Ontario Historical Society, Toronto, 1934, (letter from Sir John Johnson to Gov. Haldimand).

townships. To the north of the base, or first concession line, the remaining concessions were laid out one and one quarter miles apart. Each concession was divided into individual lots of 200 acres each, with suitable road allowances running north and south connecting the concessions. With minor variations, each township consisted of ten miles square containing 100 square miles.

When the front of each township had been surveyed, the beleaguered British prepared to settle their loyal refugees. Each surveyed parcel of land would be drawn by lot and the eligibility of each loyal soldier and refugee to draw land was predetermined by a formula which allotted land according to the military rank of the recipient and number of members in his family. While individuals might question their particular allotment, the system at least had the appearance of consistency, rationality, and fairness.

After drawing their lots, the settlers received location tickets indicating the lots and concessions involved. The land was then marked off as having being disposed of on the township survey and, if the land was properly settled, a grant from the Crown would ultimately be issued.

In a scene repeated across British North America, Loyalist refugees draw their future land by lot from an officer's hat.

NATIONAL ARCHIVES OF CANADA, C-96362.

As the Loyalist settlers began to carve their homes out of the wilderness, their system of government was rudimentary at best. During the period of initial settlement, government was by decree of the military commander. There was no suggestion of any officially sanctioned elective forum. There were no civil courts and there is virtually no documentary evidence of formal, functioning criminal courts during this period. Justice, like the other functions of government, was administered by the military.

There were, however, forms of informal magistrates courts. Justice, rough-and-ready, and somewhat in the drumhead court martial style, was meted out to offenders. There are records of a convicted culprit's feet, following a speedy trial for some minor offence, being fastened between two rails of the judge's fence which served as "stocks," and of a convicted miscreant sentenced to hoe the convicting magistrate's corn and potatoes.[8]

For a time, military rule effectively served the rudimentary needs of the new settlers. They were preoccupied in clearing their fields and attempting to get a crop in the ground in order to stave off the very real prospect of starvation and had little time and less energy to devote to any detailed consideration of the niceties of the constitutional arrangements that governed their settlements.

By proclamation of Lord Dorchester on July 24, 1788, the new Loyalist townships were organized into four districts: Lunenburg, from the western edge of the last Quebec seigneury to the Gananoque River; Mecklenburg, from there to the Trent River; Nassau, onwards westerly to Long Point; and finally Hesse, encompassing the area from Long Point to Lake St Clair. Each district was seen as an administrative unit and a judge and sheriff was appointed for each.

The four original districts of 1788 were renamed in 1792 as the Eastern, Midland, Home, and Western Districts respectively, and counties were created as sub units within each district. In 1798, much of the colony was reorganized by strengthening the county structure and reducing the size of the original districts.

By that time, the continued growth in population made the four original districts too cumbersome for administrative purposes. As a result, the Johnstown District, encompassing both Leeds and Grenville Counties, which included within their boundaries the townships north of the Rideau River, was carved out of the former Eastern

---

8 Marjorie E. Lyons, ELIZABETHTOWN, A TYPICAL ST. LAWRENCE RIVER TOWNSHIP, Queens University M.A. Thesis, 1935, p.50.

District. To the east lay the new, smaller, and more manageable Eastern District encompassing the Counties of Stormont, Dundas, and Glengarry; to the north lay the Bathurst District composed of the newly created County of Carleton together with the County of Lanark; while, to the west lay the Midland District of Frontenac, Lennox, Addington, Hastings and Prince Edward Counties.

As the Loyalist settlers successfully proceeded to establish their new homes, they began to have the time and the inclination to engage in political organization. The era of military rule was passing.

There are records of traditional New England-style town meetings being held in the New Oswegatchie settlement of the Townships of Edwardsburg, Augusta, and Elizabethtown as early as 1785. The Loyalists had brought with them the ideals of majority rule in matters of purely local concern and of consensus petitioning by the local community to the governor in matters exceeding local control. On one documented occasion in 1785, the forty-four heads of families of the Oswegatchie Settlement on the St Lawrence River met at the home of one of their number and formally chose Mr Bryan of the Church of England as their pastor, agreeing to contribute to his maintenance and support.[9]

As the settlements grew, it became apparent that the interests and culture of the new settlers required separation from Quebec. The Quebec Act of 1774, under which Quebec had been absorbed into the British Empire following the conquest, had as its aim an accommodation with the leaders of the French, Roman Catholic, and largely agrarian population of the conquered colony. These aims were not compatible with the needs or expectations of the Loyalist settlers who demanded their traditional rights as British citizens. It was these rights, after all, that had caused them to reject the American Revolution and rally to the British standard. Their traditions were not those of the seigniorial system, but of freehold land tenure. They were familiar with and appreciated the value of habeas corpus, trial by jury, and English Common Law. Perhaps typically of the sentiment of all Loyalist settlers, on December 18, 1786, the new inhabitants of the Oswegatchie Settlement petitioned Sir John Johnson, Superintendent of Settlement, in the following words:

> We most earnestly pray for ourselves and in behalf of the inhabitants of New Oswegatchie that we may have our

---

9 Ibid., at p. 43, citing, A. H. Young, "The Mission Of Cornwall" p.486.

lands by Grants free from any Seigniorial Claims or any other encumbrance whatever, the King's Quit Rent excepted.

That we may be governed by the British Constitution and laws for the support of which and his Majesty's Crown and Dignity we first took up arms in opposition to the American Congress.

That we may be formed into separate counties from Pointe au Baudet upwards having our own Courts, Judges and Civil Officers.[10]

This was not the first time that the British governor had heard concerns expressed by British subjects about the constitutional regime in Quebec.

The English-speaking merchants of Montreal shared the Loyalists' desire for change. Since the defeat of Quebec, the merchants had argued that the wholesale imposition of the British Constitution on the conquered French population would speed their assimilation into the Empire. The British governors had resisted. They were concerned that this course of action would lead to open rebellion by the French population. However, with the influx of Loyalist settlers into the formerly unpopulated western portion of the colony, the government recognized that the current system was unworkable.

The French and the English were two very different peoples, living in two distinct areas, but under one system of government that had been designed solely to accommodate the French. So, in those areas that had become English in language and custom, a new constitutional regime was necessary. In 1791, the Constitutional Act was passed creating the two provinces of Upper and Lower Canada.

Enacted by the British Parliament, with no input from the colonials who were to be governed according to its terms, the Constitutional Act contained the seeds of inequity that would ultimately result in armed insurrection more than forty-five years later.

Sir John Graves Simcoe, the first lieutenant-governor of Upper Canada, was one of the principal architects of the Constitutional Act. Even in 1791, Sir John Graves Simcoe was a social and political anachronism. At a time when England itself was experiencing the beginnings of social turmoil that marked the Industrial Revolution, Simcoe was an ardent and enthusiastic supporter of the monarchy, the aristocracy, a rigid class structure, and the Church of England.

10 Edwin A. Livingston, HISTORY OF NEW OSWEGATCHIE AND THE BLUE CHURCH CEMETERY, Prescott, 1987.

ONTARIO ARCHIVES, S-2145.

The architect of Upper Canada's first constitution, Sir John Graves Simcoe.

Through the Constitutional Act, Simcoe strove to introduce into the raw backwoods of Upper Canada the mirror image of all, in his rather aristocratic view, that was right with England. In this way, he reasoned, there would be no repetition of the excesses of democracy that had run amuck in the former colonies to the south. But Simcoe, the aristocrat, failed to consider the physical realities of the frontier society.

In a colony like Upper Canada, cheap or free land was available to all and anyone capable of working could become a yeoman farmer.

Simcoe failed to realize that, given the opportunity to work their own land, his social inferiors would prefer to do so. The upper class settler therefore found it virtually impossible to attract long-term labourers prepared to work for wages, or a crop share, on land they would never own.[11] To recreate the image of a settled countryside of manicured fields and fences, populated by the local squire or laird and his contented tenant farmers, was simply not possible in Upper Canada. The economics of the new colony dictated that the Upper Canadian farmer would not have to touch his forelock when his betters passed him on the road, as he had been expected to do in England.

There were practical as well as philosophical reasons for the system of government established by the Constitutional Act. In their determination to select an appropriate constitutional regime for Upper Canada, the British considered at length their experience in the loss of their first American empire and resolved not to repeat it. Unfortunately, when they considered the causes of the American Revolution, the conclusions drawn by the Colonial Office were, quite simply, wrong.

The British were convinced that the problems they had experienced with their former colonies were the result of an excess of power in the popular assembly. Democracy in the hands of the colonials was seen as something that could not be controlled by the colonial power. As a result, they were determined to organize Upper Canada in such a manner that the power of the governor, and the social classes on which he relied, would be increased, while the authority of the elected assembly would be strictly limited.[12]

The flow of power and authority established by the Constitutional Act was, accordingly, entirely from the top down. Since Quebec was significantly more advanced in settlement and defence facilities, the governor of Quebec was the superior of the lieutenant-governor of Upper Canada in such matters of common concern as defence, the imposition and collection of customs duties, and the postal service. In all other matters, the lieutenant-governor of Upper Canada was virtually supreme.

His Excellency was the direct representative of His, or Her,

---

11 For anecdotal descriptions of the difficulty in obtaining servants and hired hands in the frontier economy, see Susanna Moodie, ROUGHING IT IN THE BUSH, or, FOREST LIFE IN CANADA, McClelland and Stewart Ltd., New Canadian Library No. 31, 1961.
12 Robert MacGregor Dawson, THE GOVERNMENT OF CANADA, University of Toronto Press, 1948, p. 12.

Britannic Majesty and as such was accountable to and took instructions only from the king, or the king's representatives in the Colonial Office. All major decisions in the colony were made in accordance with general policy established in Whitehall. Those colonial policies were based upon the good of the Empire as a whole, as perceived from the centre of the British universe, London. The interests of fledgling colonies such as Upper Canada and Quebec, and the local desires of their inhabitants, did not play a significant role in that determination.

The practical authority of the lieutenant-governor was increased substantially by the sheer distance of the colony from the mother country. During his tenure, the Lieutenant Governor of Upper Canada was free to interpret his instructions as he thought best. After all, his superiors were at least thirty days away across the North Atlantic. He could be challenged, congratulated, or reprimanded, but only upon his return to London.

While the governor was in complete control of all significant matters in the day-to-day functioning of the province, the Constitutional Act did establish a functioning legislature to provide local input. The legislature consisted of the two usual houses of Parliament. There was an elective Legislative Assembly and a Legislative Council, whose members were appointed at the pleasure of the lieutenant-governor. In keeping with his philosophical orientation, Simcoe held the view that the position of legislative councillor would eventually become hereditary, much like those in the British House of Lords.

In addition to the two houses of Parliament, the Constitutional Act also made provision for an advisory body to provide advice to the governor. This non-elective but potentially powerful body was known as the Executive Council and its members were appointed at the sole discretion of the lieutenant-governor. They provided advice to the lieutenant-governor on issues and at times of his choosing. Their sole significant qualification was the ability to impress the lieutenant-governor with their knowledge and wit sufficiently to obtain and maintain their appointment. Since all significant power was vested in the lieutenant-governor, and by definition the members of the Executive Council had his ear, these men were clearly the most powerful in the country.

The Legislative Assembly, as the lower house of Parliament was called, was elected by the popular vote of eligible voters at public elections held at times and locations fixed by the lieutenant-governor. The franchise was by no means universal, however all British male subjects owning freehold land in the county with an assessed value of 40 shillings, or a minimum of £5 in town, were eligible to vote. By 1818, to be eligible to assume a seat in the Legislative Assembly, the elected member had to establish assets totalling a minimum of £80 sterling.[13]

The lieutenant-governor began the electoral process by dissolving the legislature, issuing the writ for the election, and appointing the returning officer for each constituency in the province.[14] The location of the poll or polls in each constituency was established by executive decree. The lieutenant-governor had uncontrolled discretion in selecting the number of polls in each riding and their location. Theoretically, this allowed the executive the discretion to determine local needs, and to locate such polls as were necessary in locations most convenient to the population. However, any system based on uncontrolled discretion invites abuse and examples of abuse were legion. Polls could be, and often were, located in areas of the riding calculated to assist the candidate favoured by the lieutenant-governor. Voters from an area known not to favour the candidate supported by the authorities would be forced to travel for miles to vote. They would then enter a community that was a hotbed of support for the candidate favoured by the establishment, and be obliged to fight their way to the poll in order to exercise their franchise.

To compound the potential for abuse, voting took place by public declaration and not by secret ballot. The returning officer oversaw the erection of the hustings in the main square, or principal intersection of the village selected as the site for a poll. This was usually no more than a makeshift raised platform constructed out of rough-sawn lumber and protected from the elements by an even rougher roof. It was on the hustings that candidates were formally nominated and, having accepted their nomination, were called upon to exhort their supporters to come up and vote for them. It was also on the hustings that each elector who wished to vote had to declare his support vocally for the candidate of his choice. Their vote, once announced, was duly recorded by the returning officer or his assistant. Suffice it to say, this public act of voting was open to physical abuse, intimidation, and violence.

---

13 60 Geo. III, cap. 9.
14 The standing instructions to the Returning Officer for the riding of Leeds dated 1808 is appended as SCHEDULE A.

Elections usually lasted a week. Ordinarily, each candidate maintained a headquarters at the poll, often at the tavern operated by his principal supporter in the village. At the headquarters, deals could be struck, promises made, favours dispensed, and strategy devised and altered as the election progressed. Each candidate maintained scores of scrutineers who challenged the right to vote of anyone suspected of supporting the opposing candidate, and intimidated and bullied any voter who insisted on voting for the opposition.[15]

Initially, the Assembly consisted of sixteen members elected from the original nineteen counties. By 1816, the number of members had risen to twenty-six. In 1820, each county with a population of 1,000 was given one member and any county with a population in excess of 4,000 was entitled to two members. This ratio was also applied to towns. Applying this formula, the Legislative Assembly of 1820 contained forty members and, by 1836, the Assembly had a total membership of sixty-nine. During the 1830s, the electors of the Johnstown District had a total representation in the Legislative Assembly of five members; Leeds and Grenville Counties each had two members, while Brockville elected its own representative.

The 1830s was a time when the concept of political parties was still in its infancy. There were groupings of like-minded individuals in the Legislative Assembly who shared a similar approach to issues of common concern, however, these groupings had not yet reached anything approaching party affiliation as we now understand the term. As Lord Durham noted in his analysis of the political situation prior to the rebellions, the quarrels of the 1830s created ". . . not two but several parties; each of which has some objects in common with some one of those to which it is opposed. They differ on one point, and agree on another; the sections, which unite together one day, are strongly opposed the next."[16] Nonetheless, by the 1830s, two general groupings were emerging in the Legislative Assembly: the Tories who, in general, supported the lieutenant-governor, his council, and the economic and social elite of the province, and the Reformers.

Then as now, those referred to as Tories were conservative in thought. They tended to support the status quo in matters of political

---

15 Edwin C. Guillet, PIONEER DAYS IN UPPER CANADA, University of Toronto Press, 1973, p. 163.

16 Gerald M. Craig, ed., LORD DURHAM'S REPORT, McClelland and Stewart Limited, Toronto/Montreal, 1963, p. 77.

philosophy and saw in society an overriding need for structure. They identified a need for social class and position and, of course, defined themselves as superior to some other class, group, or individual. In general terms, they sided with the governor and his chosen advisors in the Executive Council and expected to assume positions of social and economic superiority within the existing social order. Their leaders aspired to positions of authority, which could only be obtained with the active co-operation of those already in authority. Each person in the social order dispensed favours to those who were below him in status and sought favours from those who were superior.

On economic issues, the Tories tended to support the financial interests of the elite in the towns and blossoming cities, as opposed to the interests of the common settler struggling to make a success of his new farm. The Tories favoured large economic projects, such as the creation or enhancement of roads or canals linking the major settlements and allowing the export of Upper Canadian products to the world beyond the provincial boundaries. They sought to advance the general economic interest of the province and were eager to expend public funds to do so.

The local farmers did not see these public works as having any significant benefit. They were not concerned with efficient means of exporting cash crops of square timber and wheat. Their concern was with local roads to ensure only that they could get their harvest to a local mill in the fall. They objected strenuously to any increases in taxation for major projects which did not have any immediate positive effect on their local concerns. In fact, the majority were subsistence farmers who had no funds to pay taxes.

The Reform politicians saw themselves as the defenders of local interests. They opposed taxation, railed against the position of the banks and favoured local schools. They opposed the expenditure of pubic funds on more august institutions such as King's College at York, which by reason of cost was necessarily reserved for the sons of the rich. They vehemently opposed the favoured position of the established Church of England and, in particular, the clergy reserve system on which it relied. The Reformers were anti-establishment, rather parochial in outlook, and not content with the social, political and economic status quo. Most importantly, Reformers favoured democratic institutions through which their collective voice would be heard.

The central feature of the political system, from the arrival of the first Loyalists in 1784 up to the implementation of the modern concept of responsible government in the mid 1840s, was its total unresponsiveness to the popular will. Authority rested with the lieutenant-governor. He administered Upper Canada through a mixture of personal opinion and formal British colonial policy, and whether the Legislative Assembly was dominated by Tories who supported his views or by Reformers, who did not, the lieutenant-governor could and did ignore any course of action prescribed by them with which he disagreed. The actions of the Assembly were in large part irrelevant to the functioning of the administration.

The Legislative Assembly could initiate legislation and was, in that regard, quite prolific. No legislation, however, became law until it was also passed by the Legislative Council, assented to by the Crown, represented by the lieutenant-governor, and proclaimed in force by him. There was no recognition in practice, or in law, of the superiority of the elected Assembly over the appointed council. Nor was there any recognition of the concept that legislation once passed by the Legislature ought to be signed and proclaimed in force by the governor. The Legislative Council was free to reject any legislation presented to it by the Assembly and the members of the upper house of Parliament did so with alacrity. The Legislative Assembly, accordingly, was reduced to little more than a debating society, busily passing legislation that would never become law.

At best, the executive equated the legislative programme of the Assembly as statements of the popular will, since it did reflect the majority view of the elected representatives. Bills of the legislature had no more of a persuasive effect on the course of government than petitions circulated and signed by the citizens of a community urging a particular course of action.

On those occasions when a particularly reform-oriented Assembly was returned by the electorate, the disagreements between the Assembly and the Legislative Council became most pronounced. In the legislative sessions of 1829 and 1830, when the Assembly was dominated by active Reformers, fifty-three bills duly passed by the Assembly were rejected by the Legislative Council and did not become law. These bills included such diverse subjects as: the abolition of primogeniture in estate matters, repeal of the civil list which had provided salaries for civil servants since 1816, legislative amendments to the marriage laws authorizing religious dissenters to perform marriage ceremonies, the exclusion of judges from eligibility to sit on either the Legislative Council or Executive Council, and the prohibition of appointed sheriffs from sitting in the Assembly.[17] These legislative initiatives may have expressed the will of the people, and they certainly enjoyed the majority support of their elected representatives, but they did not conform to the legislative intentions of the lieutenant-governor or his appointed Councils. They would never become the law of Upper Canada.

The Legislative Assembly was impotent. It could not materially affect government policy.

In the British parliamentary tradition, the Commons has control over the Executive through its exclusive authority to approve or reject money bills. Applying that tradition to Upper Canada, one would expect that the Legislative Assembly would have been able to exert some control over the lieutenant-governor simply by refusing to authorize the expenditure of public money.

The lieutenant-governor, however, did not require funds from the legislature in order to function, as the government derived its greatest source of revenue from the sale of Crown lands. All of the vast land area of the province was held by the Crown. It was available for grant or sale on terms that the lieutenant-governor, in his discretion, deemed advisable and the revenue derived from the sale of these Crown lands belonged to the Crown absolutely, free of any control from the colonial legislature. The lieutenant-governor was thereby supplied with a source of revenue more than sufficient to run the government without reference to the legislature. With these funds he was able to administer the province, independent of any control of the legislature. During the entire period from 1828 to 1830, the revenue from the sale of Crown lands was more than sufficient to fund the entire provincial government.[18]

Prior to the Rebellions of 1837 and 1838, the revenue from Crown lands caused the greatest source of friction in the province. The British Crown claimed absolute control over these funds on the theory that, in a new country, the land belongs to the colonizing government. Therefore, it was not unreasonable to presume that the colonizing mother country, and not the small number of colonists

17 Aileen Dunham, POLITICAL UNREST IN UPPER CANADA 1815 - 1836, McClelland and Stewart Ltd., 1963, p. 118.
18 Ibid., p. 118.

who happened to be the first arrivals, should control the public land for future immigrants.[19] In practice, however, absolute control over the land and the resulting revenues by the lieutenant-governor removed the possibility of any effective control by the people of the province over any aspect of their government.

The Legislative Assembly of Upper Canada fought a continuous but losing battle for control over the proceeds of the sale of Crown lands. Their purpose was twofold. They, of course, sought control of the funds, which could then be administered for the good of the province, as they understood it. Of even more importance, however, was the control over the lieutenant-governor they would immediately achieve once they obtained control over the purse strings.

On the municipal level, the authority of the governor, his advisors and functionaries, was equally intrusive. Following the initial period of martial law, justices of the peace sitting in quarter sessions administered local government.

Any two justices of the peace could assemble the freeholders of their township for the purpose of seeing to the election of tax assessors and collectors, the overseer of highways, poundkeepers, and town wardens. While the freeholders of the township had a say in the selection of tax collectors and the like, the far more significant function of actually setting the local tax rate was within the sole purview of the appointed justices. Similarly, it was the role of the justices of the peace in quarter session to appoint and supervise the treasurers for the district, to build and supervise roads, to build the gaol, court house and other public buildings, and to grant licences for everything from the operation of taverns and ferries to the right of non-Church of England clergymen to solemnize marriages. In fact, farming was about the only activity the government did not actively control.[20]

Licences for such lucrative occupations as that of innkeeping were renewed yearly. In theory, this would allow the justices of the peace within the community the opportunity to reassess the quality of service offered by the licence holder. In practice, it allowed the local power elite to review the personal loyalty, gratitude, and political orientation of the licence holder on a yearly basis. If the licence holder was unco-operative, the justice could simply terminate his livelihood by refusing to renew his licence.

Decisions as to who would be allowed to operate what do not

19 Ibid., p. 35.
20 Ibid., p. 34.

appear to have met any objective criteria of approval other than cronyism and family ties. Concepts of conflict of interest were non-existent. In 1801, for example, Joel Stone, then a justice of the peace, was awarded the right to operate the ferry across the Gananoque River on the only direct road between Montreal and York.[21] Those persons, however, who did not conform to the social and political views of the local elite were quickly frozen out.

The lieutenant-governor had sole discretion in the appointment of and length of term for justices of the peace. These significant positions of local power enabled the office holder to establish his own power base by dispensing patronage at the local level. At the same time, a justice of the peace who fell out of favour with his superiors could have his position quickly terminated.

The first General Quarter Sessions of the Peace for the old Lunenburg District in eastern Ontario was held at Osnabruck on June 15, 1789. In all, ten justices of the peace attended and two of those represented the Oswegatchie settlements in Augusta, Edwardsburg, and Elizabethtown Townships. Two recent appointees were well known and wealthy Loyalists, Ephraim Jones and Justice Sherwood. As well, nine of the twenty-four grand jurors had been summonsed from these three most westerly townships of the district.[22]

By 1800, other well known Loyalists from the Oswegatchie area of settlement, already leaders in their community, had been appointed as justices of the peace. They included Solomon Jones, the former surgeon's mate of Major Jessup's Corps of Loyalist militia, Joel Stone, the founder and leading merchant of Gananoque, William Fraser and Hugh Munroe. These men ran the local government, determined who could engage in government-controlled activities and formed the nucleus of the future Tory party in the Johnstown District. Notably absent from this group are the names of future reformers, such as Buell, even though they enjoyed comparable military rank and social status.

In conclusion, Upper Canada, at the time of the rebellions of the late 1830s, was governed by a political structure rife with the potential for patronage, favouritism, and graft. The Constitutional Act imposed a social pyramid where each person within the system owed their political allegiance to their superior and, in turn, handed out favours to their inferiors. An individual's success depended upon his ability to placate the interests of those to whom he owed his success.

---

21 Leavitt, p. 58.
22 Lyons, p. 53.

It was a system wherein the lives of those not included in it, were constrained by it. It was a system that generated, by necessity, fierce loyalties and deep and abiding hatreds. It was a system that had the trappings of democratic structures, but which categorically refused to respond to the needs of anyone other than the lieutenant-governor and those who could attract his favourable attention.

It left those individuals ostracized by the system, and who chose to dissent, with no legitimate means to express their concerns, or influence political decisions. They were frozen out of the political process.

People who are frozen out of the political system, and who recognize the impotence of legitimate political protest, tend to turn to extra-political and often violent forms of action. That truism explains part of the dissatisfaction that brought the Province of Upper Canada to the brink of revolution in 1837.

By the time of the rebellions of the late 1830s, the political situation in Upper Canada had become intolerable. Upper Canadian society had polarized to such an extent that a radical minority intent on reform saw armed rebellion as the only effective means of political expression, while the loyal majority equated any suggestion of reform with treason. This polarization was the inevitable result of a closed society composed of different political and economic groups in which only the views and aspirations of one group were allowed expression.

Theoretically, society had been organized to ensure the continued colonial association of Upper Canada with imperial Britain. Practically, the result of the constitutional regime was an oligarchy in which all power had been placed in the hands of the few at the top of the social pyramid. All others were effectively excluded from any meaningful participation. Those who perceived themselves as being excluded opted for reform. Those who perceived their exclusion, and recognized that there could be no meaningful reform without wholesale changes to the political system, became radical reformers. Those who perceived the need for radical reform as the most important thing in their lives took up arms.

CHAPTER II

The People Governed: the Loyalists, the Americans and the Irish or the Good, the Bad, and the Ugly

*P*EOPLE PERCEIVE SPECIFIC political issues in different ways. Some see the issue under consideration through rose-coloured glasses, while their equally intelligent neighbours see the same issue through what must be the dark black glass of the bottom of a bottle. Social psychologists have long noted that people who share a common heritage, religion, family background, and group experience tend to share a common attitudinal base. Similar experiences lead to shared attitudes and those attitudes form the lenses through which specific issues are perceived. The concept is made more complex, however, by the fact that individuals tend to belong to numerous groupings whose values often conflict.

Political groupings tend to occur around constellations of shared perceptions. Successful political parties or movements manage, either by design or accident, to attract adherents of several groups of the electorate to their cause precisely because the general concepts which they espouse are accepted as desirable by those diverse groups. When analyzing the specific issues of an election campaign, the members of these various satellite groups view the issues through the same conceptual lenses and tend, accordingly, to arrive at a common, supportive conclusion.

During the 1830s, there was a widely held recognition of a need for political reform. The early reform movement tended to focus its concerns on specific issues, which were little more than symptoms of the fundamental problem. The underlying difficulty was structural, resulting from the lack of responsiveness on the part of those in control of the power structure to the popular will. The thrust of meaningful reform was, accordingly, the movement toward responsible government. Integral to the movement was the concept that the executive branch of government ought to be responsible to the mass of the electorate. The corollary to this concept was the inevitable lessening of the authority of the monarch and the imperial connection.

The political genius of those in power was their ability to move the issue away from a consideration of their unresponsiveness and unpopularity to a consideration of loyalty and Upper Canada's connection to Britain and the monarchy. They successfully equated loyalty to themselves and the existing power structure with loyalty to more fundamental values. Opposition to the status quo meant opposition to the existence of the state itself, and the quest for reform meant treason. With the issue defined in this fashion, the defeat of reform was inevitable.

Denied political success and branded as traitors, the majority of Reformers retreated to the relative security of the status quo. A few accepted the substance of the label, but subjectively transformed the characterization of themselves so that, in their own minds, they were not traitors but patriots. They opted for rebellion. They remained a minority. If they had understood the social and economic context of their time, they would have realized that the defeat of radical reform in the 1830s was as inevitable as the conflict itself.

Approximately 33,000 people lived in Johnstown District during the late 1830s.[1] Of this total, approximately 55% were classified as native Canadians of British origin, 25% were naturalized Canadians of Irish birth, 7.5% were naturalized Canadians of English and Scottish birth, while some 5% were naturalized Canadians of American birth.[2] These four principal groups shared a common language and culture. They were predominantly Protestant, though of various denominations, and all shared a political and philosophical attachment to the British parliamentary system. There were, however, significant differences in their collective and group experiences, their economic positions, and in their political beliefs and expectations.

---

1 Donald Harman Akenson, THE IRISH IN ONTARIO, A STUDY IN RURAL HISTORY, McGill-Queen's University Press, Montreal and Kingston, 1985, p. 388, Appendix C. The Census of 1842 of the Johnstown District shows a total population of 33,019 for the entire District.
2 Ibid.

THE LOYALISTS

United Empire Loyalists and their descendants comprised the majority of those classified as native-born Canadians of British background. These original settlers were the pre-eminent social and political group of the 1830s, in terms of influence, power, and prestige. Initially, they formed a self-contained society, alone in the new settlements in the wilderness, cut off by inadequate systems of transportation from the more established settlements of Montreal, Quebec City, or Halifax, let alone Mother England. They had been the first to wield axes against the forest, to experience and endure the Canadian winter in hastily constructed log shanties, and to scratch a crop among the blackened stumps of their recently cleared fields.

There was no denying the fact that they had suffered greatly, not only in the fledgling settlements of Upper Canada, but in the former Thirteen Colonies from which they had fled. By the 1830s, a Loyalist myth had become institutionalized in Upper Canadian society based on the political exodus from their former homes in the United States, military service on the side of the King during the Revolution, and their subsequent suffering in establishing the new colonies. The myth that only Loyalists had suffered privation, that all Loyalists had been dedicated to the preservation of the monarchy during the American Revolution, that they willingly accepted suffering and new homes in Canada rather than submit to a republican government, and that as a result only Loyalists could be trusted, permeated Loyalist communities. In a patronage-based society where favours resulted from the whims of the executive power, the Loyalists themselves internalized and repeated the myth to legitimize the favoured treatment that they felt entitled to receive from the government.

The Loyalist Myth, with some justification, was entrenched in the minds of successive colonial governors. As early as 1784, the British Prime Minister, Lord North, in correspondence to Sir Frederick Haldimand, the Governor of Quebec, noted that the, ". . . Loyalists surely had some claim to our affection . . . They have exposed their lives, endured an age of hardship, deserted their interests, forfeited their possessions, lost their connections and ruined their families in our cause."[3] These were people who, from a British point of view, were dependable and deserving of support.

It is difficult to generalize about the actual political motivation

---

3 Public Archives of Canada, HALDIMAND PAPERS, letter from Lord North to Sir Frederick Haldiman, 1784.

of these people. Their reasons for refusing to join the American Revolutionaries were as diverse as their personalities.[4] Some common themes, however, emerge when analyzing the background of the Loyalist settlers, and this is particularly true of the settlers in the Johnstown District. Virtually all had served in Jessup's Corps of Loyal Americans during the war and had been recruited in the Upper Hudson and Mohawk Valleys of upstate New York.

It is clear that some Loyalists had simply miscalculated and backed the wrong political horse. As the political debate intensified in colonial America, and even as hostilities began, many people could not imagine a British loss to the ill-equipped and poorly trained American patriots. In a calculated move, they chose to throw in their lots with the sure British winner. So certain were the farmers of upstate New York of a British victory that Ebenezer Jessup and his brother, Edward Jessup, the leaders of Loyalists who ultimately found their way to the Johnstown District of Upper Canada, were able to recruit their regiment by promising to reward recruits with portions of their land once victory was obtained.[5]

The Jessup brothers obviously saw their leadership and recruitment of the regiment as an investment. They were confident that their labours on behalf of the Crown would be rewarded once the revolutionaries were put in their place. With equal confidence in the strength of British arms, the local farmers and artisans who rallied to the British standard failed to consider the possibility that if the British lost, the Jessups would have no lands and would be unable to fulfil their promises.

American persecution drove other Loyalists into the British ranks. These people had wished to remain neutral in a time when neutrality was no longer an option. The American revolutionaries, through their Committees of Safety, attempted to coerce recalcitrant members of their communities into conformity with the aims of the revolution. In many instances, their threats and acts of physical violence had precisely the opposite effect. "It was the very pressures by which the Whigs attempted to coerce the rest of the population into conformity with their wishes, however, which aroused the opposition of countless ordinary people and turned them into

---

4 Leonard Woods Larabee, CONSERVATISM IN EARLY AMERICAN HISTORY, Cornell University Press, Ithica, New York, 1948, includes a chapter on The Tory Mind, which provides a social psychological analysis of the reasons for the political decision to side with the British.
5 Stuart, p. 30.

Loyalists."[6] Estimates show that persecution, far from having the desired effect from the American point of view, actually created one half of the "King's friends."[7]

Many of these people cared very little for politics. As talking turned to fighting, however, neutrality ceased to be an option. The developing American majority of patriots, as represented by the local Committees of Safety, soon maintained that those who did not actively support the revolution were opposed to it.

Perhaps typical of this sort of Loyalist refugee was the McLean family who were forced from their home in New York. They fled northward into Quebec as refugees and ultimately settled with the majority of Jessup's Rangers in the Johnstown District, drawing land in the first concession of Elizabethtown.[8] Alexander McLean, a Scottish silk weaver and strong adherent of the Church of Scotland, immigrated to Harpersfield, New York, in 1774. He and his family arrived in America as part of the congregation of the Rev. John Witherspoon, just in time to become embroiled in the violent politics of the revolution. It seems that McLean played no active role in the revolution. It is clear, however, that his political views were not acceptable to his new community and its Committee of Safety. As the revolution began, his home in Harpersfield was plundered and his family was driven out. They resettled in a neighbouring community only to be driven out once more. It is reported that, in one year, the family was driven out of nine communities. Finally, the McLeans sought refuge to the north, in the secure British colony of Quebec.[9]

Illustrating the divisive nature of the American Revolution, the Reverend John Witherspoon, who had led McLean and his family across the wide Atlantic to America, did not share the McLean feeling of loyalty to King George III. John Witherspoon wholeheartedly adopted the radical politics of his new home and was a signatory to the Declaration of Independence.

The fact that some Loyalists who had hoped for neutrality were driven into the Loyalist camp does not explain the very real choice made by others to actively support the King. Social standing does not appear to be determinative. Some Loyalists, including some of those

6 W. G. Shelton, "THE UNITED EMPIRE LOYALISTS: A RECONSIDERATION," DALHOUSIE REVIEW 45 (1965) p. 5-16.

7 Lorenzo Sabine, BIOGRAPHICAL SKETCHES OF THE LOYALISTS OF THE AMERICAN REVOLUTION, 2 vols. (Boston) 1864. vol.1, p. 78.

8 Lot 23 in Concession 1 of the County of Leeds as recorded in the Registry Office for the County of Leeds, Province of Ontario.

9 Leavitt, p. 102.

who ultimately settled or received significant land grants in the three townships of Edwardsburg, Augusta, and Elizabethtown in the Johnstown District, were of the American upper class prior to the revolution. But, to an equal or greater extent, many of the leaders of the republican movement for independence were also upper class and wealthy, including Thomas Jefferson and George Washington. Some of the Loyalists, even in the wilds of the New York frontier, were men of substance. The Jessup brothers, Edward and Ebenezer, for example, held vast tracts of land in Albany, Charlotte, Essex, Warren, Hamilton, and Herkimer Counties in upstate New York, which they controlled from the family's log mansion in the Glen's Falls area of the Hudson River, known at the time as Jessup's Landing.[10] Of even greater significance were the vast holdings of Sir John Johnson along the Mohawk River. Not everything was abandoned on the flight north to Canada. The people of property did bring much of their portable wealth with them. The wealthier of the backwoods Loyalist refugees, who ultimately settled along the St Lawrence River, also brought with them twenty-six black slaves.[11]

The record reveals that the Loyalists were a social and economic cross-section representative of the general population. Following the Loyalist exodus from the United States, the British government entertained claims for losses sustained by them as a result of their loyalty. Many Loyalists simply did not bother to file a claim. This may be partially explained by personal difficulties in obtaining any form of documentary proof, as some Loyalists escaped persecution with little more than they could carry. Land deeds and other proofs of title were simply left behind, buried, or destroyed, and were not available to establish ownership. For the vast majority, however, it is apparent that no claims were filed simply because these people had owned nothing of substance in the United States. They had lost no property and, accordingly, were not entitled to compensation.[12]

Statistically, it appears that a significant majority of Loyalists belonged to groups which made them minorities in their particular communities.[13] These included practising Presbyterians in the Baptist South, Quakers and Mennonites in Pennsylvania, merchants in agricultural areas where trade was looked down on, frontiersmen in settled areas, or farmers in frontier areas, such as the majority of

---

10 Stuart, p. 15.
11 Stuart, Appendix E, p. 140.
12 Shelton, p. 253.
13 W.H. Nelson, THE AMERICAN TORY, Oxford, 1961, p. 91.

Jessup's Corps. As members of minorities, these citizens had traditionally looked to the authority of their king for political protection from the democratic excesses of their neighbours. The thought of majority rule held little comfort for them.

Finally, however, the choice of supporting the patriot cause in revolution, or of remaining loyal to King George III and Britain, remained an individual one. Often it was influenced by the decision of opinion leaders in the community, like Sir John Johnson, who possessed huge estates with entire settlements and valleys of families accustomed to dependence on them for a livelihood. Once the decision was made to support one side or the other, the individual involved quickly recognized the stake that they had in the outcome. Those who had chosen, or who were forced into the British camp, rallied to arms and acquitted themselves with distinction and courage during the hostilities.

None other than John Adams, one of the leaders of the revolutionary movement and later president of the new republic, observed that as much as one-third of the population of the Thirteen Colonies had favoured the British cause, while another one-third had favoured the revolution. Another estimate indicates that approximately half as many Americans enlisted in the British Army as in the Continental Army.[14] In any event, more than fifty Loyalist American units formed to fight on the British side of the war before its conclusion.[15] Their goal was to turn back the tide of history and restore what they believed to be rightful British constitutional rule to the American colonies. In that, they failed. With gentleman Jack Burgoyne's disastrous defeat and surrender to the leather stockings at Saratoga, a battle in which many of the future Loyalist settlers of Johnstown District participated, their fate and that of their families was sealed. The ultimate British surrender at Yorktown and the Peace of 1783 ceding the Thirteen Colonies to their American inhabitants was only a matter of time. For those who had opted for Britain and their king, the wilds of Canada awaited.

In what was to become the Johnstown District, and finally the United Counties of Leeds and Grenville, the refugee boats began to pull into the north shore of the St Lawrence River in the spring of 1784 carrying the disbanded militia families of Sherwood, Jones,

---

14 Shelton, p. 253.
15 J. M. S. Careless, CANADA: A STORY OF CHALLENGE, MacMillan of Canada, Toronto, 1963, p. 109.

Buell, Clow, Cole, McLean, and so many others.[16] They had passed the latter years of the war in the refugee camps in and around Montreal and, after Saratoga, had occasionally been assigned to do specific military duties. But, more often than not, they simply waited - either for battle or for peace.

Following the peace of 1783, they left the camps at Sorrel, Yamaska, Vercheres, and St John and mustered to Lachine for the journey up the St Lawrence to the proposed new settlements. Those Loyalists affiliated with Jessup's Rangers were assigned to townships numbered 6, 7, and 8 (later named Edwardsburg, Augusta, and Elizabethtown), and lands in the Bay of Quinte area west of Kingston. Some, when given the opportunity, chose to relocate along the coast of the Bay of Chaleur in north-eastern New Brunswick. Most, however boarded the bateaux for the journey up river into the unknown.

They left Lachine with near-military precision: four or five families to each bateau, twelve bateaux to a brigade, each brigade under the control of an appointed conductor who knew the St Lawrence River, its shoals, and its rapids. Ultimately, they pulled ashore at New Oswegatchie, the name originally given to the entire new settlement on the St Lawrence, and proceeded to draw their land by lot. Then, armed only with the barest of essentials, they set off again to locate their chosen lots and commence the arduous task of carving a farm home out of the wilderness. Within fifty years, the virgin forest would be transformed into a settled agrarian community. Their success in conquering the wilderness laid the foundation for Canada.

All of the Loyalist settlers of New Oswegatchie were associated with Jessup's Rangers. By and large, they had been recruited in the Upper Hudson and Mohawk River Valleys of New York. They shared a common British colonial background forged on the American frontier. They knew all about the hardships of life on the frontier. The officers of this corps, following the military practice of the time, owed their positions to their social status and not to their military ability. Any actual military proficiency was a happy coincidence.

An officer of rank in one of His Majesty's Militia Companies was a gentleman who had the financial resources to recruit and outfit a regiment. The lesser officers had family connections or sufficient independent resources to be of significant assistance to their social and financial superior who would actually raise and command the regiment.

---

16 A complete list of the original settlers is contained in Appendix B, taken from E. Rae Stuart, JESSUP'S RANGERS AS A FACTOR IN LOYALIST SETTLEMENT, The Ontario Department of Public Records and Archives, 1961.

The leading families of the new Loyalist settlements were composed of the officers of the regiments. Many of these refugees remained people of considerable wealth even after the revolution. Aside from whatever portable wealth they brought with them, the officers also received larger grants of land on their arrival. While land was drawn on a lottery system to ensure equality of opportunity of all settlers, rank determined the quantity of land that each was entitled to draw. Each field officer was initially entitled to 1,000 acres, each Captain to 700 acres, each subaltern to 500 acres, each non-commissioned officer to 200 acres, while each private soldier, drummer, and Loyalist civilian received 100 acres. Women and children drew fifty acres each.[17] It was apparent from the outset that an economic class structure of some form was inevitable. In many cases, the officers and their descendants continued to be the opinion leaders of the community into the 1830s and beyond.

By the 1830s, the dominant families in the Johnstown District included: the Buells who, with the Howards, led the reform coalition in the County of Leeds; two families of Sherwoods, who dominated the legal profession and the judiciary; and two separate Jones families. With the notable exception of the Buells, virtually all of the socially significant Loyalist families sat solidly in the Tory camp. In many cases, their wealth and position depended upon their relationship with the power elite surrounding the governor. They understandably supported the status quo.

Justus Sherwood, founder of one of the Sherwood families in Canada, was born in Connecticut. By 1774, he had settled at New Haven, Vermont, which at the time remained part of the colony of New York, and, up to the commencement of the revolution, he served as proprietor's clerk in the village. At the start of the war, he fled to Canada and lived at St John on the Richelieu where he obtained a commission as Captain, under Lieutenant Colonel John Peters in the Queen's Loyal Rangers. During the war, he saw service both as a spy and, for a time, as commander of one of the blockhouses at Dutchman's Point. By the end of the revolution, Sherwood was a Captain in the Loyal Rangers, the newly merged Loyalist militia force under the command of Major Edward Jessup. Ultimately he obtained his grant of land in the New Oswegatchie settlement and resided in

---

17 Public Archives of Canada, HALDIMAN PAPERS, B. 126, 70. Leavitt in his HISTORY OF LEEDS AND GRENVILLE, at p. 17, indicates that the initial land allotment was a grant of five thousand acres to every field officer, three thousand acres to each captain, and two thousand acres to each subaltern, while the private soldier received a grant of two hundred acres. No source is given.

the vicinity of the Blue Church, in the Township of Augusta, for the remainder of his life.[18]

Sherwood was a man of position and substance in the new community and became one of the first members of the Legislative Assembly. He had two sons, Samuel and Levius Peters Sherwood, both of whom received their early education from the Reverend John Strachan and made their careers at the bar and bench of the courts of Upper Canada.

In public affairs, Levius Peters Sherwood had the more illustrious career. He was elected to the Legislative Assembly as the member for the County of Leeds in 1822. In 1825, he was named the Speaker of the House and, despite his duties in the legislature, he remained active in local politics and government. In July 1822, he was appointed to the land board for the Johnstown District. In April 1825, he was named as one of the three trustees for St Peter's Church (Church of England) in Brockville and was active throughout his life on the local board of education.[19] His career in law developed apace and, in 1825, he received an appointment to the Court of King's Bench. His position as a Puisne Judge necessarily detracted from many aspects of his local interests, not because of the concepts of judicial independence and neutrality, which were in their infancy, but simply because of time constraints.

Thomas Sherwood, a former subaltern in the 84th Regiment who had later served in Jessup's Loyal Rangers, was the patriarch of the other Sherwood family. Prior to the outbreak of hostilities, Sherwood had farmed in the Fort Edward area of upstate New York, not far from Saratoga where Burgoyne had been forced to concede the defeat of his invincible British troops to the upstart Americans. As the war began, he made his way up the Mohawk Trail, through Lake George, Lake Champlain, and down the Richelieu River towards Montreal. Crossing into Canada at St John's, he enlisted in the British regiments then being formed. The revolution tore Sherwood's family apart. His two brothers took up the patriot cause of freedom from British rule and saw service as officers in the Continental Army. Sherwood, on the other hand, found active duty in the British Secret Service. He operated throughout the Thirteen Colonies recruiting potential

---

18 Stuart, p. 43, fn. 33, citing H. H. Noble, "A Loyalist of the St. Lawrence" in Ontario Historical Society, PAPERS AND RECORDS, XVI, 34-36. See also Leavitt, p. 72.

19 Robert L. Fraser, ed., PROVINCIAL JUSTICE, UPPER CANADIAN LEGAL PORTRAITS FROM THE DICTIONARY OF CANADIAN BIOGRAPHY. University of Toronto Press, 1992, pp. 185 - 187.

Loyalist soldiers for the various British militia units. In 1779, he finally evacuated his family to Canada and was appointed a subaltern with Jessup's Corps. As the defeat of the British became inevitable, Sherwood was engaged as a surveyor by Sir John Johnson to prepare the new townships for the arrival of his fellow Loyalist refugees.[20] He ultimately drew land in the first and second concessions of Elizabethtown and became a leading citizen of the new community.[21]

Thomas Sherwood was made a Captain in the First Regiment of the Leeds Militia and was appointed one of the original justices of the peace. He died in 1826 leaving behind him a well-established family including his son, Adiel Sherwood, who became a colonel in the Leeds Militia, and was, at various times, Paymaster of the Eastern and Johnstown Districts, Treasurer of the Johnstown District, Commissioner of Branch Roads, Member of the Land Board, Clerk of the Crown for the District, Sheriff for the District of Johnstown, and Returning Officer for many of the tumultuous elections of the 1830s. On the local scene, Sheriff Adiel Sherwood was a man to be reckoned with.

The history of the founding members of the two Jones families to settle in the Counties of Leeds and Grenville is similar to that of the Sherwoods. Ephraim Jones, the Canadian patriarch of the Jones family of Augusta Township, was residing comfortably in the Mohawk Valley at the commencement of the revolutionary hostilities. Like the other Loyalists in the area, Jones headed north for Canada as the war began and was sufficiently connected with the British that he procured an appointment as Commissary of Supplies. Thereafter, he was known to all as "Commissary Jones." At the conclusion of the war, he travelled up river from Montreal to the Brockville area where he took land in the vicinity of Maitland.[22]

Ephraim Jones had a total of eight children, all of whom would do exceedingly well in the new colony. The sons - Charles, William, Jonas, and Alpheus - all of whom had received the benefit of an education at the hands of the Reverend John Strachan, and an introduction from childhood into the upper classes of Upper Canadian society, became community leaders. Jonas Jones transcended the local area and became a significant figure on the provincial stage. The daughters – Charlotte, Lucy, Sophia, and Elizabeth - solidified the gains made by the family over the years by

20 Infra, p. 2.
21 Leavitt, p. 18.
22 Ibid., p. 183.

marrying well: Charlotte to Levius Peters Sherwood; Lucy to Dr Hubble of Brockville; Sophia to Andrew Stuart, Sheriff; and, most importantly, Elizabeth to Henry Boulton of Toronto, a leading member of Canadian society. By the late 1830s, the family of Ephraim Jones was in the ascendancy.

The other principal Jones family had settled the Hudson River Valley prior to the outbreak of the revolution. The family consisted of a widow and seven sons who owned extensive tracts of land opposite Fort Edward, New York. In 1776, all of the sons joined the newly formed corps of Jessup's Loyal Rangers. They saw action at Saratoga and thereafter along the frontier of Canada. Of the seven brothers, three settled along the banks of the St Lawrence, while the remaining four opted for lands on the Atlantic coast.

Solomon Jones served as the Surgeon's Mate in Jessup's Corps and settled in the vicinity of Maitland in the Township of Augusta. David Jones lived with his brother Solomon, largely in seclusion, following the murder and scalping of his fiancee by a war party of American-allied Indians during her flight to Canada. The death of this poor unfortunate young Loyalist woman, Jane McRea, became a *cause celebre* and is the sort of tragically romantic tale from which the Loyalist myth and folklore grew. Daniel Jones, another of the seven sons, settled in Elizabethtown Township following the war and died there in 1820, by which time his family, too, had become leaders in Brockville society.[23]

The overwhelming majority of leading Loyalist families became ardent supporters of the Tory cause. The Buells were the exception. From the time of their arrival with the first bateaux, the Buells espoused the cause of reform. William Buell Sr was born at Hebron,

---

23 Stuart, p. 69, fn. 30, citing information taken from Judge H. S. Macdonald's "The U.E.L.'s of the Old Johnstown District," Ontario Historical Society, Papers and Records XII, 28 (Toronto,1914).

See also the tombstone of Daniel Jones erected by his grandson in the Brockville Cemetery the inscription on which reads: "In memory of Daniel Jones Esq. A United Empire Loyalist, one of seven brothers, five of whom were British Commanding officers in the revolutionary war.

"No man ever possessed a warmer attachment to the government of his own country, for love of which he abandoned his home of two thousand acres with valuable improvements near Glen Falls in the Province of New York, for the forests of Canada, settling upon the land, now the west half of Brockville in 1784.

"Gifted with a strong and superior mind, he was a leading spirit among the foremost of the many accomplished and distinguished Loyalist gentlemen, who in their fidelity to british institutions forsook their homes in the rebellious provinces, and took up their abode in the wilderness, now comprising the United Counties of Leeds and Grenville."

Connecticut, in 1751.[24] His father, Timothy, had been a prosperous merchant owning a sawmill and probably a store.[25] One must assume that, by the start of the revolution, the Buells had relocated to the Mohawk or Hudson River Valleys since William left for Canada following the traditional route, the Mohawk Trail - north by way of Lake George, Lake Champlain, and the Richelieu River. Once in Canada, he immediately enlisted in the militia and was present at Burgoyne's disastrous defeat in the forest at Saratoga. If the family had been still living in Connecticut when war commenced, Buell's field of action would have centred on the coast and his road to the British lines would have led him to New York City and not north to Montreal. In any event, he did receive an ensign's commission in the King's Loyal Rangers and served with the militia regiments for the duration of the revolution. During the war, he saw active service, both as a dispatch courier and as a quartermaster. On two occasions while travelling with British dispatches, he was captured by the enemy but, on each occasion, he managed to escape. With the end of hostilities, Buell was demobilized as a lieutenant.[26]

In 1782, while in the refugee camp at St John on the Richelieu, he met and married Martha Norton; they ultimately had nine children. In the spring of 1784, the Buells travelled up the St Lawrence River with the bateau brigades of Loyalists. He drew land which subsequently became the site for the Town of Brockville. William's father, Timothy Buell, chose to remain in Montreal, where he died in 1789. Timothy's last will, drawn in 1786 and probated on his death, provided a bequest to his wife, Mary, of ". . . the whole part in the Dutch and English saw mills."[27] The bequest confirms that the Buells were a family of property. In addition, since no such mills existed in the British colonies in which Mr Buell had an interest, it can only be surmised that he was referring to property that he had owned in pre-revolution America. It is apparent that Timothy Buell had not relinquished hope of a restoration of his property in the United States of America, or perhaps he thought that there still might be a chance for the restoration of British authority in his former home.

While Timothy Buell remained in Montreal, the balance of the family travelled with William to the Township of Elizabethtown, and

---

24 Leavitt, p. 181.
25 Ian MacPherson, MATTERS OF LOYALTY: THE BUELLS OF BROCKVILLE 1830 - 1850, Mika Publishing, 1981, p. 13.
26 Leavitt, p. 181.
27 Lyons, p. 64.

it was William Buell who assumed the leadership role within the extended family.

William Buell was a man of some substance, even on his arrival in Elizabethtown. His sons, William Buell Jr, and Andrew Norton Buell, would play important roles in the political wars of the first half of the 1800s. William Buell Jr carried the candidate's banner for reform throughout the 1820s and 1830s when, with his perennial running mate, Matthew Howard, he enjoyed considerable success. In addition, he assumed the ownership of the Brockville newspaper, The *Recorder*, which also espoused moderate reform.

The Buells, however, did remain equally dedicated to the concepts of loyalty, family, gentility, and order. They found it impossible to advocate or condone tactics of reform which fell outside that which was permitted under the existing constitution. Since the Constitution of 1791 precluded meaningful methods of popularly induced change and reform, their agitation was reduced to mere rhetoric ultimately supportive of the status quo. In short, the Buells in their newspaper, and in their political actions on the hustings, spoke of reform, but they spoke politely. That tradition began with William Buell Sr of whom it was said, "Mr Buell was upright and honest, and very kind to the poor. He was generous in his character, liberal in his politics and highly respected."[28]

Reference to Buell's liberal politics did not, during Buell's lifetime, equate to membership in a political party. There were none. To be liberal in the first half of the nineteenth century meant that one was open-handed and generous, as well as open-minded. However, it also refered to Buell's long-standing opposition to the existing power structure, including his political opposition to the other leading Loyalist families.

The senior William Buell died at his home in Brockville on August 8, 1832, at the age of eighty-one.

During the fifty years between their arrival in the untamed wilderness of Upper Canada and the rebellions of the 1830s, the Loyalists transformed the countryside. By 1830, there existed farms, towns, mills and a developing local industry. In economic terms, the Loyalists had done well. In addition, the Loyalist Myth was indelibly etched on the consciousness of the entire province. There was, of course, enough truth in the myth of their bravery and defence of the monarchy and British way of life to make it acceptable and believable.

---

28 Leavitt, p. 181.

In an unspoken agreement with the colonial administrators, it was expected, certainly by the leading Loyalists themselves, that they would receive preferred treatment at the hands of the government. It was their birthright in a bargain paid for in blood. And, up to the 1830s, that bargain had been honoured.

Every success that the Loyalists had experienced since their arrival in the new colony was a result, in whole or in part, of an exercise of discretion by the lieutenant-governor or his underlings in their favour. Exercising the prerogative of the Crown, the lieutenant-governor had granted them their land to farm. The lieutenant-governor determined, by granting licences, which of them would have the opportunity to become millers, innkeepers, ferry operators, or to develop mines and foundries. This experience was totally at odds with that of their American counterparts in the United States where individual action, unfettered by governmental interference, was the norm. In relation to any predilection to political attitudes, one would expect that the Loyalists would support the executive branch of government; partly because of habit, partly because of the perception that all benefits necessarily flowed from the government, and partly because the Loyalists themselves had, by then, internalized their own myth of loyalty.

THE AMERICANS

In the 1830s, the demographic group closest to the Loyalists in life experience and heritage comprised those Americans who, for a variety of reasons, had emigrated from the United States of America to Canada in the years following the revolution. They shared with the Loyalists an understanding of all that was involved in homesteading along the wilderness frontier. They shared as well a common culture, the English tradition of Common Law, an understanding of parliamentary democracy as it had evolved to that time, and the English language. They lacked, however, the "red badge of courage," which had been won by the Loyalists during the American Revolution by their early commitment to the cause of Britain and the monarchy. As a result, they were often objects of suspicion by the government and by their Loyalist neighbours.

The first lieutenant-governor of the newly created colony of Upper Canada, Sir John Graves Simcoe, recognized that a lack of settlers impeded the success of the new colony. The Loyalists, in and of themselves, were simply not numerous enough to constitute a viable colony. Simcoe strove to encourage the emigration of colonists from the British Isles to rectify this situation. At the same time, however, he recognized the difficulties of wholesale emigration from Britain, which was at war with Napoleon. The population of Britain was fully engaged in either direct military service, or in industry and agriculture then operating at full capacity in support of the war effort. Since emigration from the British Isles was impractical, Lieutenant-Governor Simcoe reasoned that immigrants must come from the only other significant source of English people - the newly independent United States of America.

Simcoe instituted a policy that actively encouraged American emigration to Upper Canada. He did so even though, mere years before, Britain had been engaged in mortal combat against these same Americans who had turned their backs on Britain and their king during the revolution. In advancing this policy, Simcoe was taking an obvious risk. He was inviting Yankee republicans into his northern Garden of Eden. To many, this appeared an invitation to disaster, comparable to the invitation of the Trojan horse into the city of Troy, or of the non-eunuch into the harem as keeper of the virgins. Yet the policy fit with Simcoe's belief in the inherent superiority of British institutions.

Simcoe was one of those who could not conceive of the success of democracy as envisaged by the Americans. He believed that the American concept of democracy was nothing more than mob rule, the result of which must be anarchy. By creating in Upper Canada a society based on sound British principles, the break-away colonies to the south would soon seek readmission into the Empire. Upper Canada, as the obviously superior society, had nothing to fear from immigrants from the United States. In many ways, these immigrants were refugees from the anarchy of republicanism in the same way as the Loyalists had themselves been refugees. To Simcoe's mind, they ought to be welcomed.

Virtually all subsequent lieutenant-governors of Upper Canada, and certainly all leading Loyalists, including the members of the Executive Council, took the opposite view. They saw the growing block of American immigrants as a threat to the security of the province. This perception became increasingly pronounced as the problems inherent in the system of government caused the province to move inexorably to rebellion in the late 1830s. The opinion of R.B.

Sullivan, a member of the Executive Council, as expressed to Sir George Arthur, was typical. "In this country unfortunately," he wrote, "the settlement of American citizens has been too much permitted and encouraged, and thus in the bosom of this community there exists a treacherous foe."[29] The Reverend John Strachan rarely let pass the opportunity to rail against the American immigrants. He feared that the Americans brought with them, not only republican ideas, but a religious base which Strachan perceived as antagonistic to the established church. Strachan did not trust Americans; he hated American Methodists.

Susanna Moodie, in her memoir of life in the wilds of Upper Canada in the 1830s, provides anecdotal evidence of the habits and traits of the American immigrant from the perspective of the upper-class British immigrant.[30] She noted, her nose in the air, that these people were loud, uncouth and untrustworthy. The sort of people, in short, who refused to accede to the wishes and demands of their betters of which she, of course, was one. Perhaps these comments establish nothing more than the basic Americanism of these people. They were, like the vast majority of Upper Canadians of the time, including the United Empire Loyalists, fundamentally of the new continent. The concept of class subservience, which Mrs Moodie expected to see copied from her English experience, had not totally survived the ocean crossing. The upper classes in Canada attempted to emulate British custom and fashion; the lower orders refused. The province would remain essentially North American in custom until the massive immigration from the British Isles of the 1830s.

These late arrivals from the United States were first and foremost North Americans. As North Americans they were pragmatists; chosing to be monarchists or republicans as the occasion required.[31] The opinions and prejudices of Reverend Strachan and his fellow members of the Executive Council notwithstanding, these new settlers were not doctrinaire in their political beliefs. They had willingly traded the doctrines of liberty, equality, and the pursuit of happiness, which were trumpeted south of the border, for cheap land in Upper Canada. They did not share any English notion of class structure. They wore their egalitarianism on their sleeves and saw

---

29 C. R. Sanderson, ed.,THE ARTHUR PAPERS, VOL. 1, Toronto, 1957, p. 134.
30 Susanna Moodie, ROUGHING IT IN THE BUSH, OR, FOREST LIFE IN CANADA, McClelland and Stewart Ltd., New Canadian Library No. 31, Toronto, 1962.
31 Arthur R. M. Lower, CANADIANS IN THE MAKING, Longmans Canada Limited, 1958, p. 157.

themselves as the equal of anyone. They had not come to Canada as a result of any conviction as to the inherent superiority of the British government as envisioned by Governor Simcoe. Neither, however, were they a subversive fifth column as feared by the Loyalist elite. Richard Cartwright of Kingston assessed their admission to the colony and influence on the politics of Upper Canada for Lieutenant-Governor Hunter as follows:

> I will not disguise from your Excellency the opinion which I have always entertained, and on every proper occasion expressed, that this ought never to have been permitted. I am not, however, inclined to impute to such of them as emigrate to this Province either hostile or treacherous views, but it would be an error equally to suppose that they are induced by any preference they entertain for our government. They come probably with no other intent than to better their circumstances by acquiring lands upon easy terms.[32]

Along the St Lawrence frontier, despite the War of 1812 and the continual expression of anti-American attitudes, the population always maintained close ties with the Americans across the river. It was not uncommon for the wealthier Loyalist families to have business interests in the United States, but those interests never prevented them from railing against the threat of American influences and wrapping themselves in the Union Jack. The new residents of Upper Canada, who had arrived from the United States either during or after the revolution, frequently crossed and recrossed the border to visit family and friends left behind.

The Wells family, which settled in the Prescott area some four years after the initial Loyalist migration, provides an example of American immigration. William Wells, of New Chester, New Hampshire, emigrated to Upper Canada in 1787, at age nineteen. He settled first near Mallorytown, but subsequently relocated to the Maitland area in the Township of Augusta along the banks of the St Lawrence River. He retained close ties throughout his life with friends and relatives in the United States. In 1799, he returned to New Hampshire long enough to marry and brought his new wife back to Upper Canada. His ties to the United States, however, did not interfere with his allegiance to the military interests of Upper Canada.

---

32 C. E. Cartwright, ed., LIFE AND LETTERS OF THE LATE HONOURABLE RICHARD CARTWRIGHT, Toronto, 1876. p. 95.

He was actively engaged in the local militia during the War of 1812 and, on one occasion, was taken prisoner by a band of American cavalry that had ventured across the St Lawrence River on the winter ice to capture Wells in his own home. In accordance with the practice of the time, he was released on his "parole of honor not to serve or act in any capacity against the United States until legally exchanged."[33]

He had eight children: four daughters and four sons. Ruth, who married George Longley of Maitland, the Member of the Legislative Assembly for Grenville from 1828 to 1832;[34] Sally, who married George Mallock, a Brockville lawyer who was appointed to the bench in 1842; Maria and Frances, both spinsters who remained in Maitland; Horace, who entered the lumber trade in the Ottawa Valley, went broke and moved to the United States; Isaac Brock who, like his father, married an American and then became the collector of customs at Maitland; and William Benjamin Wells, the radical Reformer and member of the Legislative Assembly for the County of Grenville.[35]

William Benjamin Wells played a pivotal role in the politics of the 1830s. Educated as a lawyer, Wells studied under the expatriate American and leader of the Reform forces in Upper Canada, Marshal Spring Bidwell. It is a matter of speculation as to whether Wells selected Bidwell as his mentor, due to a pre-existing interest in reform politics, or, conversely, that Bidwell by example, strength of personality, and argument, caused his student to adopt the politics of reform as his own. In any event, W.B. Wells became a force to be reckoned with in the Johnstown District, both as a self-professed radical Reform politician and as a newspaper publisher in Grenville County. On his call to the bar of Upper Canada, he returned to Grenville County and practised law in Prescott. For a time, he also operated the Prescott newspaper, the *Vanguard*, which, unlike Buell's *Recorder*, was an outspoken advocate of radical Reform politics.

The Reform platform on which Wells based his political career was obviously acceptable to the electors of Grenville County. Wells was twice returned as the Member for the Legislative Assembly during

33 Queen's University Archives, Kingston, Ontario, WELLS FAMILY PAPERS, Undertaking of Lt William Wells given at Ogdensburg N.Y., February 9, 1813.

34 Longley was the leading citizen of Maitland, but something less than an ideal husband. In a letter dated March 11, 1835, Ruth's sister Sally wrote, ". . . Longley does not put himself out much for either wife or child, his business must be attended to - he left the day after the child was born and was away from home 10 or 12 days, no person thought she would survive a part of the time however she struggled through." Queen's University Archives, WELLS FAMILY PAPERS.

35 Queen's University Archives, Kingston, Ontario, WELLS FAMILY PAPERS, J. B. Wells, "A Short Sketch of the History of William Wells and his Family," dated Maitland, April 20, 1895.

the 1830s. It is equally clear, however, that his family paid a price socially for his involvement in Reform politics. As the decade wore on, the leading Loyalist Tories shunned Wells and his family, despite their wealth and position. In a letter, dated March 4, 1835, one of the girls wrote to her brother, William B. Wells. She complained that there had been a large ball in Brockville:

> . . . but as I was the only one in the family that had an invitation I would not go. Malloch never gave me an invitation to go with him and if he had I should not have gone . . . Frasers, in Brockville have held a large party, not long since - the whole country was asked but our family. The old Doctor was there dancing on one foot all night but I do not mind we will have one in the spring when you come down and wont ask them . . . that will spite.[36]

The Wells family prospered in their adopted new home despite their political views and American origin. Their experience was by no means atypical. In effect, they made their wealth in an area with minimal governmental control. Many of the other American immigrants were farmers who similarly required and received little assistance from the government. They simply purchased land, either from a land jobber who, because of his favoured connection with the government had acquired large land grants and was now engaged in resale for profit, or directly from the government at the going rate when land was available. They were entitled to no preferred status. But land in Upper Canada was available at a cheaper price than in the United States and, as a result, many Americans were attracted north.

The attitude of the government towards the American immigrant became evident whenever one of these new settlers was obliged to ask the authorities for any concession or consideration. Abel Stevens, an American immigrant who established the first settlements in the Townships of Bastard and Burgess in the County of Leeds, quickly discovered the practical effect of the unofficial suspicion against new American immigrants.

Stevens had immigrated to Ontario from Vermont in 1793. His brother, Roger Stevens, had been a Loyalist who had served in Jessup's Corps under the immediate command of Captain Justus Sherwood. On one occasion during the war, Abel had intervened and assisted his

---

36 Queen's University Archives, WELLS FAMILY PAPERS, letter to W. B. Wells, at Toronto, dated March 4, 1835.

Loyalist brother in escaping from the Americans. He, however, had remained in Vermont and it is clear that if he held any Loyalist views, he was able to keep them entirely to himself. It was not until 1793, some ten years after the end of hostilities, that Abel Stevens emigrated to Canada in response to Lieutenant-Governor Simcoe's open invitation to Americans to do so, which had been widely circulated in Vermont. He surveyed the new province and chose to settle in the Township of Bastard, in north Leeds. The next year he returned to Vermont and led nine families north to his new settlement.

Over the years, Abel Stevens was responsible for the immigration and settlement of over 100 families and was responsible for the establishment of settlement in a significant portion of the county.[37] He quite rightly felt entitled to consideration from the government as a valued member of Upper Canadian society. In 1798, Stevens petitioned the lieutenant-governor for permission to develop the newly discovered iron ore body at the great falls of the Gananoque River, now known as the village of Lyndhurst. The request was denied. Undaunted, Stevens continued to encourage new settlers and petitioned for land. The government again refused. In relation to the Stevens settlements, the government would make grants of land only to the actual settlers. There would be no overall grant to Stevens and no recognition of his leadership role.

He then joined with Matthew Howard, a Loyalist comrade-in-arms of his brother, and constructed a road through the bush to Kingston Mills. The road was built to provide proof of his sincerity and ability, and to establish the feasibility of his iron mine and foundry proposal. Despite his efforts, Stevens was again denied permision to develop the iron. The contest over who would be granted the right to develop the iron deposits on the upper Gananoque became an exercise in duplicity and double-dealing, with the prize going to the individual who impressed the government with his actual ability to do the work coupled with the support of the political elite.

Ultimately, the rights to the ore and permission to develop the site were granted to Wallis Sunderlin.[38] Sunderlin was an American who had been brought into the project by Ruel Kieth, Stevens' new associate. At the same time that Stevens was negotiating with the government on his own behalf, he sold the iron rights to Matthew

---

37 Ruth McKenzie, LEEDS AND GRENVILLE: THEIR FIRST TWO HUNDRED YEARS, McClelland and Stewart Limited, Toronto, 1967. p. 49.
38 McKenzie, pp. 49, 50.

Wing. When Sunderlin arrived from Vermont with Ruel Kieth to open the mine and foundry, they found Wing in possession with no authority from the government. When the government discovered that Wing was proceeding to develop the area without authority, all possibility of approval for his or Stevens' proposals was doomed. Sunderlin then obtained the support of several of the well-known Tory elite and received a grant of the mineral rights, water power, and land sufficient to manufacture enough charcoal to make the iron.[39]

Stevens was a Baptist which also brought him into conflict with the authorities. In 1793, Lieutenant-Governor Simcoe had seen to the enactment of legislation confining the legal solemnization of marriages to the clergy of the Church of England. In a petition to Simcoe dated May 16, 1796, Stevens explained his role as a Baptist elder. He noted that he did not wish to interfere with any other denomination, but wanted the same rights for Baptists. "Particularly we pray that those which are . . . Elders in any Baptist Church in this Province shall be fully empowered to administer the ordinance of Marriage."[40] Simcoe, unimpressed, refused. In July 1800, he put the same concern to the justices of the peace at the quarter sessions and applied for permission to marry members of his congregation. The request was again denied.[41] Given the terms of the Marriage Act at the time, the justices took the position that they had no authority to grant the request even if they so desired.[42]

The next year, there was an unsubstantiated allegation that Vermonters might be involved in a conspiracy to manufacture small arms for use in a rebellion against His Majesty.[43] Abel Stevens, the upstart American immigrant, was charged with sedition.

The period prior to and immediately following the War of 1812 was a time of open discrimination against Americans. In 1810, Solomon Jones received instructions from the office of the lieutenant-governor advising that ". . . the Lieutenant Governor cannot approve of any person to be a teacher of any of the public schools who is not a British subject."[44] One can only assume that Abel Stevens, for real or imagined offences and despite his many talents, had become *persona non grata* to the power structure at the local and provincial level. One

---

39 Brigadier General E. A. Cruikshank, THE ACTIVITY OF ABEL STEVENS AS A PIONEER, Ontario Historical Society Papers and Records, vol. 31, Toronto, 1936, p. 56.
40 Ibid., p. 64.
41 Lyons, p. 59.
42 Cruikshank, p. 88.
43 Ibid., p. 78.
44 Ibid., p. 80, citing Jones Papers, Ontario Archives.

must assume that his Americanism, together with his religious beliefs, had a great deal to do with this obvious lack of support.

THE IRISH

The Irish were the third demographic group of significance in the politics of the 1830s in the Johnstown District. In some respects, the Irish might be considered as a sub group of immigrants from the British Isles. The Irish, however, had several distinctive cultural and attitudinal traits that impacted on their political behaviour. In addition, the Irish warrant separate consideration simply because of their numbers.

The raw census data from the first provincial census completed in 1842 provides graphic evidence of the impact of Irish immigration on the Counties of Leeds and Grenville. Proceeding along a back concession of Elizabethtown Township, the census taker came upon eleven homes where every adult was Irish by birth. The twelfth home was that of a Canadian. The home next door contained three Scots residing with two Irish born. Proceeding down the concession, the next twenty-four houses were Irish.[45] That concession was typical of the developing back country throughout the district.

The trickle of immigrants from the British Isles, which began after the Napoleonic Wars, became a flood after 1820 and the population of Upper Canada rose dramatically.[46] In 1824, the total population of the province was 151,000 people. By 1851, the population had increased to 952,000 people - an increase of more than 600% within a period of thirty years. In the Counties of Leeds and Grenville, the census reports show that the population roughly doubled between 1816 and 1824, and redoubled by 1835. By the time the full census of 1842 was completed, the combined population of all of the townships in the Johnstown District was 33,019 people. Of this total, 10,984 people had been born in the British Isles, the vast majority of those in Ireland. Reverend John Strachan, writing to a friend in September of 1832, gave an indication of the magnitude of the immigration funnelling through Montreal. "The stream of emigration has been very great this season," he wrote, "upwards of 50,000 have already landed at Quebec; and 4/5 of this number directed their course to Upper Canada."[47] In the Johnstown District,

---

45 Lyons, p. 92.
46 Lower, p. 209.
47 J. L. H. Henderson, ed., JOHN STRACHAN DOCUMENTS AND OPINIONS, Carleton Library Number 44, p. 129.

the census of 1842 confirms the numerical superiority of the Irish immigrants. In that census, there were 10,984 British born in the Counties of Leeds and Grenville and of those British born, 8,531 were of Irish origin.[48] This represents fully 78% of the British immigrants and 26% of the total population.

These Irish immigrants were in large part homogeneous in outlook and came closer than any other group to forming a unified voting block. They shared an almost universal subjective world view. First and foremost they were Protestant. Turning to the census data of 1842, the total population reporting adherence to Roman Catholicism amounted to 4,130 people, which represented only 12% of the total population. If it is assumed that all of the French Canadian population, some 753 people, were Roman Catholic, then the number of non-French Roman Catholics is a maximum of 3,383 people. Of these, a significant number must have been other than Irish and, in particular, the Highland Scots. It is variously estimated that of the Irish immigrants, the Protestants outnumbered the Roman Catholics by two-to-one in the County of Leeds,[49] or that these Irish immigrants were 75% Protestant.[50]

The Irish brought with them the concept of sectarian violence and the innate feeling of being a favoured yet threatened minority. The Irish Protestant was a member of the numerical minority in Ireland. Nonetheless, they totally dominated the Roman Catholic majority who were subjected to Protestant rule and authority.

Britain and, in particular, Ireland had a long history of virulent anti-Catholic discrimination. The Penal Laws, passed between 1697 and 1727 by the Irish Parliament, from which Roman Catholics were excluded, took away the electoral franchise of all Roman Catholics in Ireland and precluded Catholics from holding virtually any office or profession from that of Lord Chancellor down to gamekeeper. A Roman Catholic could not be educated at a university, marry a Protestant, be the guardian of a child, own land, or even possess a horse exceeding £5 in value.

Old prejudices inevitably die a long death. In Britain, Catholic emancipation, which allowed Roman Catholics to sit in parliament and hold offices, other than that of Lord High Chancellor and Lord Lieutenant of Ireland, only became law in the dying days of the Duke of Wellington's government, which fell in 1830.

48 Akenson, Census data 1842.
49 Akenson, p. 26.
50 Lower, p. 189.

*A later portrait of Ogle R. Gowan, the deceitful, conniving,
unscrupulous, unprincipled, and hugely successful founder
of the Loyal Orange Lodge in Upper Canada.*

It was the English monarchy and the British Constitution which ensured the supremacy of the Protestant minority over the Catholic majority. Needless to say, the Protestant Irish were ultra-loyal to the British Crown and Constitution. It was the Crown and the Constitution that had established their inherent superiority over the Catholics and which provided the rationale for their dominance. Finally, the Irish Protestants brought with them to Upper Canada political and social organization, in the form of the Loyal Orange Lodge, and an appreciation of the value of physical intimidation in the political process.

It is impossible to commence a discussion of the political attitudes of the Irish in Leeds and Grenville Counties, and their role in the political wars, without introducing Ogle Robert Gowan.

Gowan was the undisputed leader, manipulator, and representative of the Irish settlers in Leeds and Grenville. He arrived from County Wexford, Ireland, in 1829, and settled in the Township of Escott, approximately fifteen miles to the west of Brockville. Ostentatiously, he called his home Escott Park. Within two years, he had established the Loyal Orange Lodge as an organized political force with himself at its head. In addition, he had procured the nomination and stood for the Legislative Assembly as one of the Tory candidates for Leeds County. He was unsuccessful in that initial political campaign of 1832 but, with it, he began a remarkable political career that lasted for the next thirty years.

Gowan owed his political success to his innate knowledge of the needs, fears, and aspirations of his Irish constituents. In addition, he was a political master at forging alliances, when necessary, with other interest groups whose views were not inimical to those of his Irish base. The record shows Gowan to have been deceitful, conniving, unscrupulous, unprincipled, and most importantly, hugely successful.

Gowan recognized that the principal concern of the new settlers was land. The immigrants obtained their farm lots from the usual sources, but Gowan was instrumental in obtaining the official deed and Crown Grant for them.[51] In an electoral system in which proof of land ownership was a prerequisite for the franchise, Gowan's efforts on behalf of the Irish settlers not only helped them, but assured him of their electoral support.

The Irish wanted power, or at least access to it, such as they had enjoyed in Ireland. They looked at the power structure in Upper Canada, as it existed on their arrival, and recognized that the Loyalists

---

51 Akenson, p. 172.

formed the power elite. It was also apparent that the Loyalists would not readily relinquish or share their control of the province with the Irish. By the same token, the Irish Protestants, who in Ireland formed a society separate from the Catholic majority based upon their loyalty to the Crown and the Constitution, were shocked to observe the influences of Americanism in the new province. The Loyalists, as well as the more recent American immigrants, had business and social ties with their neighbours in the republic to the south. To the minds of the ultra-loyal Irish, many of their actions and attitudes bordered on treason. Subliminally, they reasoned that their religion and their loyalty had ensured their privileged position in Ireland and ought to do the same in Canada. Any suggestion of American republicanism was seen as a threat to their very existence.

Gowan founded, organized, and used the Loyal Orange Lodge as his vehicle to political power. The Lodge was an offshoot of the denominational Protestant Christianity of Ireland. By the time of the rebellions in Upper Canada, Orangeism was the single most powerful organization in the province. The network of Orange Lodges became the cutting edge of red-necked Toryism throughout the province. Orangemen provided the muscle and organization to secure electoral victory for those of its members chosen to run for office, or for those non-members whose candidacy the Lodge endorsed.

As the Loyal Orange Lodge began to develop as a political force, both old-line Loyalist Tories, and those favouring Reform, shared a common misconception that they would dominate any alliance that they might form with Gowan and the Orangemen. The Irish shared some areas of common concern with the Reformers. There was a commonality of interest between the struggling back concession settler of Irish origin and his non-Irish neighbour. Both were ill-served by the political process of the time and all sought redress. In correspondence to his brother William, then one of the Reform members of the Legislative Assembly, Andrew Norton Buell mused about the possibility of an alliance between the old Reformers and the Orangemen after William Lyon Mackenzie's expulsion from the Assembly in late 1833:

> I see Gowan has condemned the Assembly for their conduct . . . Gowan seems coming round to the liberal side & perhaps, with a little management,

might be brought fully over . . . What would you think of a Union between the Canadians and Irish and allowing G. (Gowan) to go in at the next Election under strong pledges.[52]

The suggestion came shortly before Buell and the Reformers were physically mauled - and politically humiliated - by the Irish and Orange bully boys. The very suggestion indicates a total lack of appreciation of the fundamental political motivation of the Irish. To the Irish, there could be no alliance with traitors! The traditional call of loyalty to the British Crown and Constitution was far more compelling to the Irish than their immediate economic self-interest.

Gowan's political path to power obviously lay in an alliance with the old-line Loyalist Tories. Like the Reformers, the Loyalist Tory families were initially convinced that they would dominate the alliance with the Orangemen. Sheer numbers and the ability of Gowan to maintain the Irish as a solid block of support soon proved that the Loyalists would not be able to do so. The politics of the period is, in part, a study of how Gowan and the Irish rose to ascendancy.

Orangeism had its origins in eighteenth century Ireland where the Protestant minority had, through the laws of the Protestant ascendancy, been able to dominate totally the Catholic majority. Protestants were very much aware of the inherent frailty of their position. All of their power arose as a direct result of their connection to England, the Constitution, and the Crown. They were, accordingly, fanatic in their loyalty. Any attempt by the Catholic majority to challenge the established order was seen as a direct threat to the Protestant minority and was ruthlessly suppressed. It was in this political climate that the Orange Lodge was established, much as the Ku Klux Klan would be 100 years later in the United States.

The first recorded Orange Lodge was formed to assist in the bloody suppression of a local revolt by Catholics in the village of Loughall in 1795. The organization married the tradition of armed gangs of Protestant bully boys to the organizational model of Freemasonry. Each Lodge formed a cellular group based on the immediate neighbourhood. The local Lodges were loosely tied together into county, district and, ultimately, an overriding national command. There were, of course, the internal rankings

---

52 Public Archives of Canada, WILLIAM BUELL PAPERS, MG24 B75, letter from Andrew Norton Buell to William Buell, dated December 12, 1833.

and various levels of membership, together with secret signs, passwords, and elaborate rituals based upon a worship of God and the monarchy. Such ceremonies provided the internal justification for the external demonstrations of violence and suppression of the Catholics.

From its inception in Loughall in 1795, the organization spread like wildfire throughout the Protestant community in Ireland. By 1798, the year of the major Catholic rising, it was sufficiently entrenched to be of significant assistance to the British authorities in the suppression of the rebellion. The successful Orange response to the "Rising of '98" resulted in a long-term alliance between the British government and the Orange Lodge. From that time forward, each would look to the other for succour and support.

The military carried the seeds of Orangeism throughout the British Empire and, ultimately, to British North America. Officers and men reassigned from Irish garrisons, where they had adopted familiarity with and membership in the Orange Lodge, soon arrived in Canada. A lodge was in existence in Halifax as early as 1799, in Montreal by 1800, and in the Ottawa Valley by 1803.[53] The town of Perth, Upper Canada, had been settled by discharged British troops in 1816 and, by 1827, the community had an established Orange Lodge that attracted not only Irish, but also the non-Irish to its membership.[54] By the time that Ogle Robert Gowan arrived in Brockville in 1829, there were large numbers of settlers both aware of and sympathetic to the Orange Lodge. Gowan's genius was to convert that critical mass of actual and potential Orange adherents into an organized national body and to exploit that organization for his personal political purposes.

Shortly after his arrival in the Johnstown District, Gowan organized an Orange meeting at the court house in Brockville. In response to his invitation, three Orange delegates from Montreal, several from Perth, and a large contingent from Brockville and the surrounding villages responded and met with Gowan on January 1, 1830. Gowan procured his own appointment as the Deputy Grand Master of the Lodge in British North America. The role of Grand

---

53 Cecil J. Houston and William J. Smyth, THE SASH CANADA WORE: A HISTORICAL GEOGRAPHY OF THE ORANGE ORDER IN CANADA, University of Toronto Press, p. 16.
54 Ibid., p. 18.

Master was reserved for the Duke of Cumberland, which added prestige and credibility to the entire order.

The organizational model followed that in existence in Ireland. Each Lodge would be focussed on the local community. There would be supervision based on the township, the county Grand Lodge and, ultimately, a provincial and all-British North American command. The model of community, township, and county organization proved so successful that the Tories adopted it as their own once the domination of the Tory party by the Orangemen was complete; the modern Progressive Conservative Party in the United Counties of Leeds and Grenville continued this basis of organization well into the twentieth century.

The growth of the Lodge was phenomenal. In the three years following the inaugural meeting organized by Gowan, ninety-one Lodges were formed. Most of these Lodges were within the counties of Leeds, Grenville and Lanark.

Several factors account for the phenomenal success of the Orange Lodge in eighteenth century Upper Canada. First, and perhaps most importantly, was the numerical strength of the immigrant Irish population. These people were familiar with Orangeism as both an organization and a philosophy. In a philosophical sense, they had already internalized the Orange values of ultra-loyalty together with a hatred of all that they subjectively classified as treasonous, whether treasonous ideas, people, or conduct.

Upper Canada was not subjected to the institutionalized anti-Catholicism of Ireland, yet the attitudes that bred discrimination and suspicion remained. In the early repression, following the initial Mackenzie Rebellion in December of 1837, the Roman Catholic population in Perth was immediately under suspicion for no other reason than their religious affiliation. Father John McDonnell, the parish priest, and 277 of his parishioners felt it necessary to declare their loyalty openly:

> We . . . have heard with deep regret, that we are suspected of being disloyal. We here solemnly declare, that the said suspicion, is most unjust and false . . . we love and venerate our Young Queen and Her Government; and that we are ready to join with her other subjects to put down any

Rebellious attempts that may be made to sever the connection of this Colony from Great Britain and Ireland.[55]

The growth of the Orange Lodge, despite Gowan's public expressions to the contrary, added to the traditional suspicion and hatred of Roman Catholics.

At some points in his political career, Ogle R. Gowan openly solicited Catholic votes. To win a political campaign by forging a temporary alliance with Catholics, however, was an entirely different matter than accepting them as equals. Gowan was anti-Catholic to the very essence of his being. He defined people by their religion. To identify someone as being Catholic was sufficient in Gowan's eyes to disqualify them from consideration for any post of authority. In discussing the merits of the appointment of John Neil as an officer in the Leeds Militia, Gowan wrote to the commanding officer, Charles Jones:

> I must say in justice and truth, that I consider him a Loyal, Honest and Industrious man, of good character, and the worst I ever heard against him, was that his Father was a Roman Catholic . . . you can however dispose of the matter as you think proper.[56]

Neil was a member of the Orange Lodge of Lansdowne. This was rather faint praise from the deputy grand master of the Lodge in British North America.

On the local level, the Lodge provided a social network and refuge for the back concession settler and farmer. Here was a place where the "lads" could gather, drink, socialize amongst friends and neighbours, and feel that one's ideas were important. It was Gowan's genius to forge these latent desires into an effective social and political machine. The members of the Orange Lodge became his foot soldiers in the political wars of the 1830s. He used them not only to organize his supporters for the hustings, but also as his bully boys to intimidate and physically attack the opposition.

---

55 Colin Read and Ronald J. Stagg, ed., THE REBELLION OF 1837 IN UPPER CANADA, A COLLECTION OF DOCUMENTS, Toronto, The Champlain Society, 1985, p. 265. Public Archives of Canada, Correspondence of the Provincial Secretary's Office, vol. 9, file 1257, enclosed in Anthony Leslie to John Joseph, Perth, 22 December 1837.
56 Public Archives of Canada, CHARLES JONES PAPERS, MG24 B7, pp. 1-67, Charles Jones Papers, correspondence of Ogle R. Gowan to Charles Jones, dated July 17, 1832.

CHAPTER III

The High Church and Tory System

THE STATED GRIEVANCES of the Reformers prior to the rebellions of the late 1830s were many and varied, but all of those specific grievances shared a common root. They were natural outgrowths of the economic and political organization of society.

Upper Canada in the 1830s contained an anomalous mixture of attitudes. On the one hand, the individual settler was self-made, exhibiting all of the characteristics of the rugged individualist. He and his family had cleared the land, planted, tended, and harvested their crop in the fall. If for whatever reason the crops failed, they had no one to look to for support but themselves. Yet this family of rugged individualists resided in a community in which the government and the political elite valued, not the rugged individualist, but class, genealogy, background, and position. The North American value system typified by the rugged individualist found itself in an unhappy marriage with the class consciousness of the old country.

In any situation, based upon the immediate family and the purely local community, it was the North American system which dominated. However, whenever the government of the day was called upon to exercise its discretion in preferment, either for the appointment of individuals to positions of authority, for grants of land or licences, or even for grants and favours to groups, associations, and religious denominations, it was the English class system of the old country which dominated. Superimposed on this transposed English

---

1 Arthur R.M. Lower, COLONY TO NATION, A HISTORY OF CANADA, Longmans Canada Limited, Toronto, 1946, p.46. The estimate is based on statistics gathered in the Report on the Manuscript Lists Relating to the United Empire Loyalists (Public Archives of Canada, Ottawa, 1909).

class system of preferment, were the religious and ethnic prejudices of the time. The social ideal was the upper-class English gentleman – the sort of person who belonged to the Church of England and who supported the status quo, the monarch, and the constitution.

An individual's acceptance into society, and his place within it, was ordinarily determined by the degree of his deviation from the ideal. To worship in the Kirk of Scotland, since it was the established church in Scotland, was clearly more acceptable than belonging to some dissenting Protestant denomination, while that in turn was more acceptable than adherence to Roman Catholicism. To offer political support to the Tory cause was infinitely more acceptable than to question the status quo and seek political reform.

The families that did well and grew rich in the new province were those which met the criteria for social acceptability and who were able to attract and maintain the favour of the lieutenant-governor and his advisors. In the Brockville area, it was the Sherwood and Jones families – in particular the family of Ephraim Jones – who were most successful in that regard.

In 1784, when the Loyalist settlers arrived, the Jones family was by no means dominant. Ephraim, or Commissary Jones as he was known for his role as quartermaster with the Loyalist troops, had served in Jessup's Corps, but not in a leadership role. Ephraim Jones, however, recognized implicitly the value system of the new province and within that value system he and his progeny excelled. Jones, along with many of the other upper-class Loyalist families, saw that all of his sons received, not simply a rudimentary education from a local grammar school, but training suitable for entrance into the elite of provincial society. They would study under Reverend John Strachan. Strachan, soon to become the leading Tory advisor to a succession of Lieutenant Governors and head of the Church of England, commenced his career in Upper Canada as a teacher engaged in the education of the children of the elite. At a time when typical settlers had a great deal of difficulty providing adequate clothing for their children, let alone even rudimentary formal educational instruction, the Jones and Sherwood children had the advantage of private boarding schools.

When Sir John Graves Simcoe made his inaugural visit to the Johnstown District, it was Ephraim Jones and others who broke a trail for him through the cold January snow. Simcoe's trip through the settlement on his way to York allowed Jones to demonstrate his allegiance, hospitality, and gentlemanliness. The occasion provided an opportunity for him to demonstrate that here in the wilderness of the townships of Augusta and Elizabethtown was a man cut of the right cloth. In her diary, Lady Simcoe noted:

> We set off at 8 and met two Mr. Jones, who were coming to request the Governor not to undertake the journey yet. When they found him determined to proceed, they said they would go also, to beat the way and to hasten our journey; they took us into their lighter carriages or we never should have got on, the snow was so heavy. We stopped at another Mr. Jones where there was the largest fire I ever saw; he also set out to beat the road and so did several other people.[1]

Of the sons of Ephraim Jones, Alpheus obtained an appointment as the collector of customs at Prescott, a highly respectable government position. Prescott, at the time, was a significant port and the centre of the forwarding trade. It provided Alpheus Jones with a yearly income of £300 sterling[2] and, more importantly, it provided him with the social status that went with the highest civilian government position in the community. He confirmed his status in Prescott when he built a magnificent, five-bay, Georgian, dressed-stone structure in the Adamesque style, with neo-classical side lights and an elliptical fanlight surrounding the central door and portico in 1820.[3] The first floor theme was repeated by the fenestration on the second floor. This was not the home of some minor government functionary. This was the home of a gentleman.

Alpheus Jones' personal correspondence further confirmed his position as the unofficial representative of the executive in the community. People wrote to Jones on their own behalf, and on behalf of their children, seeking his intercession with the government to obtain either dispensation for some real or imagined wrong or for some preferment.

Charles Jones became the most successful businessman of the

---

1 John Ross Robertson, ed., SIMCOE DIARY, Toronto, 1911, p. 268, entry for 23 - 26 February 1795.
2 APPENDIX TO JOURNAL of the HOUSE OF ASSEMBLY of UPPER CANADA, Fifth Session, Thirteenth Parliament, p. 40.
3 Local Architectural Conservation Advisory Committee of Prescott, 1982.

Ephraim Jones children and continued his father's close relationship with the lieutenant-governor and the power elite. In addition to his personal business interests, Charles also served as the colonel in command of the Second Regiment of the Leeds Militia. He owned extensive mills at Jones' Creek and elsewhere in and around the Johnstown District. In addition, he was the resident expert in the county at buying property and business establishments at sheriff's sales once the original owners had gone broke. His reputation in business was one of ruthlessness; in cultivated society, he was received as a true gentleman.

Charles' brother, Jonas Jones, became one of the provincial power elite: a member of the judiciary, from time-to-time a holder of elective office and, most importantly, a member of the Executive Council. Like all of his brothers, Jonas Jones received his early education from Reverend Strachan. He went on to study law and developed a legal practice in the Johnstown District.

By the time of Gourlay's travels through the District in 1818, Jonas Jones was already seen as a leading Tory and was honing his skills as a debater. Gourlay was a rabble-rousing Scot who provided the first effective opposition to the established order. He was a worthy debating opponent. Later, Jones was elected to the Legislative Assembly, initially as the representative for Grenville and latterly for Leeds, where he opposed the voices of reform then emerging in the Legislative Assembly. The Reformers argued for an increase in Legislative authority at the expense of the power of the lieutenant-governor. Jones was an articulate voice against the cause of any reform and just the sort of representative that the lieutenant-governor would rely on for advice. Jonas Jones had learned the lessons that had been taught to him by his father and Reverend Strachan. Only the well connected got ahead in Upper Canada. And only those who demonstrated an ability and desire to maintain the status quo could develop a network of properly connected friends.

By the 1830s, the system of preferment and advancement based on social status and favouritism had become endemic. William Lyon Mackenzie, the jingoist of reform, first coined the moniker "Family Compact" in reference to the aristocratic group of cronies, friends, and relatives who by that time constituted the social and political elite of the province. The designation captured the imagination of the populace. They may not have known who comprised Mackenzie's so-called Family Compact, but they knew with the certainty of practical experience that they were excluded from it. In the Brockville *Recorder*, a newspaper of moderate reform, an anonymous Irish immigrant expressed an opinion in a letter to the editor shared by the editor, William Buell, himself. The Irishman deplored what he saw as an attempt to import into Upper Canada a class system similar to that which was then tearing Britain apart. He noted the growing strength of what Mackenzie referred to as the Family Compact and commented:

> The most prominent members of this system can be found in a few individuals trained up and disciplined by an ecclesiastic who for years was literally their school master (an obvious reference to Strachan) . . . He sits at the ear of His Majesty's Representative like a serpent at the ear of Eve in Paradise.[4]

Within the political elite that Mackenzie referred to as the Family Compact, the Reverend John Strachan was pre-eminent. He dominated the early religious, social, and political development of Upper Canada, and was the undisputed leader of the social and political elite. Very little of substance occurred in Upper Canada without Strachan's knowledge and endorsement. The issue of clergy reserves, religious preference, and the political development of the province is inexorably linked to his political philosophy and power. To the Reformers, Strachan was indeed the viper who "sits at the ear of His Majesty's Representative like a serpent at the ear of Eve in Paradise." To the Tories, he was the spiritual and temporal voice of reason.

John Strachan was born on April 12, 1778, into a respectable but far-from-wealthy Scottish family. His father favoured young John's entry into trade. His mother, however, wanted one of her children to enter the ministry and John, her youngest child, was her last hope. Mrs Strachan's view prevailed and it was decided that John Strachan would receive a liberal education to prepare him for a career in the church. At considerable expense and sacrifice to the family, young Strachan began his studies at King's College in Aberdeen. While his academic career was in its infancy, Strachan suffered the loss of his father who died in an industrial accident while setting off a blast of dynamite. Strachan's correspondence to his friends concerning the event revealed a personality that would be far better suited to the future political

METROPOLITAN TORONTO REFERENCE LIBRARY, J.ROSS ROBERTSON COLLECTION, T-15000

John Strachan Archbishop of Toronto and leading member of the Family Compact. He sat "at the ear of His Majesty's Representative like a serpent at the ear of Eve in Paradise."

battles of Upper Canada than to the ministry. Strachan showed himself to be the ultimate pragmatist. His concern was not for the loss of a beloved parent, nor for the effect of his father's death on his mother and the balance of the family, but with his loss of financial support and how that would impact on his education and career. "In him I depended for everything;" wrote Strachan, "in his death my hopes were buried, my prospects of finishing my education destroyed."[5]

The manner in which Strachan dealt with the economic difficulties following his father's death revealed other facets of his

4 BROCKVILLE RECORDER, October 11, 1833.
5 Henderson, ed., JOHN STRACHAN DOCUMENTS AND OPINIONS, p. 4, Strachan's autobiography written when he was twenty-two.

character. Strachan was both stubborn and determined, and those qualities saw him through. At age fifteen, Strachan began to teach to supplement his income, then drastically reduced by the death of his father. In this manner, he was able to continue his education and ultimately graduate from King's College at Aberdeen with his Masters Degree in Arts.

In 1799, in order to advance his prospects and station in life, he decided to emigrate to Upper Canada, by way of the United States, and accepted a teaching position under the patronage of Richard Cartwright in Kingston, paying a yearly stipend of £80.

On surveying the political and economic realities of Upper Canada, Strachan calculated that his optimum career lay in the ministry and not in teaching. Religion was to be a career and not a vocation, so he looked for the denomination that would best advance his personal and secular well-being. He cared not a wit about doctrinal matters. In 1802, he wrote that his, ". . . understanding (was) that a great proportion of the most respectable people of Montreal were connected with the Presbyterian Church, or at least could be connected with it, were the clergymen agreeable."[6] Strachan, of course, was of the opinion that he was just the sort of individual who would be agreeable to those respectable people of Montreal, and he actively solicited for the position through his Kingston patron, Richard Cartwright, and others of influence.

When the opportunity of an appointment as a Presbyterian minister did not materialize, Strachan began to cast about for alternatives. He was not prepared to continue indefinitely as a lowly teacher and, in October of 1802, he wrote to a friend that he, ". . . considered going to the States where if I do not think I can easily succeed it is probable I shall recross the Atlantic."[7] His prospects brightened when a vacancy materialized within the ministry of the Church of England.

The British government at the time subsidized four clergymen in Upper Canada and, late in 1802, Richard Cartwright managed to procure one of these positions for his protege. It was a welcome Christmas present. By the spring of 1803, Strachan's conversion to the Church of England was complete. In Quebec City, he received the sacrament of Holy Communion according to the rites of the Episcopal Church from the Reverend John Stuart. It was the first time

---

6 Ibid., p. 23, letter from Strachan to Blackwood, September 21, 1802.
7 Ibid., p. 23, letter from Strachan to Brown, October 23, 1802.

ever, in any church, that Strachan had received the sacrament of Holy Communion. One can only wonder what a profound Christian experience this must have been for him, since his personal papers do not deal with the religious importance of the ceremony, but only with the launching of his new carer. On May 22, 1803, he was consecrated a deacon in the Church of England by Bishop Jacob Mountain of Montreal. Within the year, he began his priestly career with an appointment to the parish of Cornwall, Upper Canada.

In addition to his religious functions, Strachan continued to teach. Amongst his students were the privileged children of the elite of Brockville and area whose families had sufficient funds for their tuition and board in Cornwall. The sons of Ephraim Jones – Alpheus, Charles, and Jonas – were all students of Strachan in Cornwall,[8] as were the Sherwoods and others. By 1812, when Strachan moved on to York, virtually all of the second generation of the leading families in the eastern part of the province had received at least some instruction from him. Undoubtedly, Strachan's developing political thought had a significant influence on their young minds. Of even more importance, Strachan remained in constant contact with his former students as they rose through the ranks of society. In a dialectic of power, Strachan used their growing power to support his own, just as they used their association with Strachan to establish their credentials in the class-conscious society of Upper Canada.

Strachan continued to prosper. In Cornwall, he married the widow of Andrew McGill, the former fur trading czar, most influential citizen in either Upper or Lower Canada, and founder of McGill University. Not only would the new Mrs Strachan provide her husband with an introduction to the upper echelons of society from a base of social equality, she also had an income from the McGill estate of £300 per annum.

In 1812, he accepted a new position in what was then the village of muddy York. At the time, Cornwall was the more advanced of the two settlements. Strachan, however recognized that the potential of York, as the new capital of the province, would far exceed that of Cornwall. For a young man intent on furthering his career, York provided obvious advantages that Strachan would not miss, including an increase in his ecclesiastical salary at his new parish. In addition, he assumed the headship of the Home District Grammar School at York. Strachan's star was in the ascendancy.

---

8 Leavitt, p. 98.

By the 1830s, the Reverend John Strachan, now Archbishop of Toronto, was the leading member of both the Legislative and Executive Councils. The lieutenant-governor invariably sought his advice on issues of substance. Strachan had arrived. In a society based upon patronage and currying favour with one's betters, Strachan had become one of the betters, if not one of the best. So adept was he at currying favour that even the names of his children were calculated to please. Rather than follow the traditional Scottish practice of giving the first born male child the Christian name of the mother's father, his oldest son was named James McGill Strachan, after his wife's first husband, while his second son, George Cartwright Strachan, was named after his old mentor, Sir Richard Cartwright.

The man who had chosen the ministry as a profession that could provide secular advancement, and who selected the Church of England as his denomination for the same reason, became the leading proponent of religious favouritism. Similarly, the man who at one time had toyed with the possibility of emigration to the United States if he could not ensure a sound career in Upper Canada had, by 1830, become almost pathologically anti-American.

In 1833, Mackenzie, in a pamphlet published primarily for the British market, identified some of the principal office holders in Upper Canada. He included in his list the family ties that bound the various members together. The leading Tories of the Johnstown District played a significant though not dominant role. He argued that it was beyond dispute that, ". . . the government of Upper Canada is a despotism," and went on to remark that:

> When I left Upper Canada last year some of the offices, sinecures, and pensions of the government were divided as follows:-
> 1. D'Arcy Boulton, senior, a retired pensioner, £500
> 2. Henry, son to No. 1, Attorney-General and Bank Solicitor, £2400.
> 3. D'Arcy, son to No. 1, Auditor-General, Master in Chancery, Police Justice &c. Income unknown.
> 4. William, son to No. 1, Church Missionary, King's College Professor, &c. £650.
> 5. George, son to No. 1, Registrar of Northumberland, Member of Assembly for Durham, &c. Income unknown.
> 6. John Beverly Robinson, brother-in-law to No. 3, Chief

Justice of Upper Canada, Member for life of the Legislative Council, Speaker of the Legislative Council, £2000.

7. Peter, brother to No. 6, Member of the Executive Council, Member for life of the Legislative Council, Crown Land Commissioner, Surveyor general of Woods, Clergy Reserve Commissioner, &c. £300

8. William, brother to Nos. 6 and 7, Postmaster of Newmarket, Member of the Legislative Assembly for Simcoe, Government Contractor, Colonel of Militia, Justice of the Peace, &c. Income unknown.

9. JONAS JONES, brother-in-law to No. 2, Judge of the District Court in three districts containing eight counties, and filling a number of other offices. Income about £1000.

10. CHARLES, brother to No. 9, Member for life of Legislative Council, Justice of the Peace in twenty-seven counties, &c.

11. ALPHOUS (sic) , brother to Nos. 9 and 10, Collector of Customs, Prescott, Postmaster at Prescott, Agent for Government Bank at Prescott, &c. Income £900.

12. LEVIUS P. SHERWOOD, brother-in-law to Nos. 9, 10, 11, one of the Justices of the Court of King's Bench, income £1000.

13. HENRY, son to No. 12, Clerk of Assize, &c.

14. John Elmsley, son-in-law to No. 12, Member of the Legislative council for life, Bank Director, Justice of the Peace, &c.

15. Charles Heward, nephew to No. 6, Clerk of the District Court, &c. Income £400.

16. James B. Macauley, brother-in-law to Nos. 17 and 19. One of the Justices of the Court of King's Bench, Income £1000.

17. Christopher Alexander Hagerman, brother-in-law to No. 16, Solicitor general. £800.

18. John McGill, a relation of Nos. 16 and 17, Legislative Councillor for life. Pensioner, £500.

19. and 20. Allan and George Crookshanks, connexions (sic) by marriage of 16 and 17, legislative Councillors for life, the later President of the Bank. £500.

21. HENRY JONES, cousin to Nos. 9, 10 &c., postmaster at Brockville, Justice of the Peace, member of Assembly

for Brockville. income unknown.

22. Wm. Dummer Powell, father of No. 24, Legislative Councillor for life, Justice of the Peace, Pensioner. Pension £1000.

23. Samuel Peter Jarvis, son-in-law to No. 22, Clerk of the Crown in Chancery, Deputy Secretary of the Province, Bank Director, &c. Income unknown.

24. Grant, son to No. 22, Clerk of the Legislative Council, Police Justice, Judge Home District Court, Official Principal of Probate Court, Commissioner of Customs, &c. Income, £675.

25. William M. brother to No. 23, High Sheriff Gore District, Income from £500. to £800.

26. William B., cousin to Nos. 23 and 25, High Sheriff, Home District, Member of Assembly. Income £900.

27. ADIEL SHERWOOD, cousin to No.12, High Sheriff of Johnstown, and Treasurer of that district. Income, from £500 to £800.

28. GEORGE SHERWOOD, son to No. 12, Clerk of Assize.

29. John Strachan, their family tutor and political schoolmaster, archdeacon and rector of York, member of the Executive and Legislative Councils, President of the University, President of the Board of Education, and twenty other situations. Income on an average of years, upwards of £1800.

30. Thomas Mercer Jones, son-in-law to No. 29; associated with No. 19, as the Canada Company's agents and managers in Canada.

This family connexion rules Upper Canada according to its own good pleasure, and has no efficient check from this country to guard the people against its acts of tyranny and oppression.[9]

The wages paid to the political elite were exorbitant. To place the salaries referred to by Mackenzie in context, the typical wage for farm labour was four shillings per day in harvest or one bushel of wheat. Women earned a maximum of five shillings per week. A pound of butter sold for one shilling and three pence.[10]

9 William Lyon Mackenzie, SKETCHES OF UPPER CANADA AND THE UNITED STATES, London, 1833, p. 377. The names of those members identified by Mackenzie as belonging to the Family Compact who resided in the Johnstown District are in capitals.
10 Glenn J. Lockwood, KITLEY 1795-1975, p. 47, citing the Gourlay Report on the Township of Kitley, compiled in 1818.

The Family Compact as identified and popularized by Mackenzie was nothing more than the apex of a society based on the British concepts of inherited class and status. At the lower levels were the local functionaries, such as the Justices of the Peace, who despite the growth of elected police boards in municipalities, continued to exert significant authority. They, in turn, were appointed on the advice and recommendation of individuals above them in station, power, and influence. The gentlemen of the Johnstown District, and in particular the second generation Sherwood and Jones boys, were able to deport themselves in such a way that they were recognized as upper class and worthy of acceptance as equals by the best of Upper Canadian society. Their marriages and those of their siblings further cemented their social, political and business ties to the provincial elite.

Those who were at the apex of the social pyramid that dominated the political and economic life of society did not dispute the existence of an elite in Upper Canada. To them there was nothing startling about the existence of an elite, nor ought its existence be hidden. In their opinion, society needed an elite. Speaking on their behalf, the lieutenant-governor, Sir Francis Bond Head, argued that this was nothing more:

> . . . than that 'social fabric', or rather fortress, within which the British yeoman, farmer, and manufacturer is enabled to repel the extortionate demands of his labourers; and to preserve from pillage and robbery the harvest of his industry after he has reaped it! . . . The 'family compact' of Upper Canada is composed of those members of its society who, either by their abilities and character have been honoured by the confidence of the executive government, or who, by their industry and intelligence, have amassed wealth. The party, I own, is comparatively a small one; but to put the multitude at the top and the few at the bottom is a radical reversion of the pyramid of society which every reflecting man must foresee can end only by its downfall.[11]

Any objective analysis, however, would have revealed that there

11 Sir F. B. Head, A NARRATIVE, London, 1839, pp. 464-5.
12 H. William Hawke, HISTORIC GANANOQUE, Mika Publishing, Belleville, 1974, p. 13.

was more than industry and intelligence or abilities and character at issue. In selecting candidates for any position in the civil service of the province, or in determining who should rise to a rank of some superiority in the local militia, ability played an unimportant role in comparison to family background and patronage.

As early as 1803, Joel Stone, the founder of Gananoque, wrote to the Executive explaining that he was not prepared to serve as the collector of customs in that village. "I therefore have not yet Executed or sent forward the said bond, in hopes that His Excellency will be kind enough to appoint some other person to serve in this office here." wrote Stone. Then, significantly, he added, "Pray give me leave to recommend my son in my stead. William Stone about 23 years of age, he has no military allowance, I will assist him and consider myself fully answerable, in every respect that he shall punctually discharge the Duties of that office."[12]

Stone, like Ephraim Jones, clearly understood and benefitted from the existing system. He was an early Justice of the Peace and had used his influence in the past to obtain large grants of land and milling rights along the Gananoque River. It was, accordingly, not in the least out of the ordinary for him to suggest to the lieutenant-governor that his son be appointed as the Collector of Customs in his place and employ as an argument in support of his appointment the fact that the young man did not have a military pension. Here was a young gentleman from a solid upper-class family who required a government position in order to finance properly his inherited station in life. Singularly absent from the discussion is the concept of individual merit or ability to perform the job.

Associations and social clubs played a significant role in consolidating groups and factions in the society of the 1830s. Obviously, the Loyal Orange Lodge was a dominant force in society and was the significant organization among the Protestant Irish and other Protestants of the middle and lower classes. In part, the appeal of the Orange Lodge to the back concession farmers can be explained by their familiarity with earlier associations.

The earliest and most influential of these associations was the

---

13 Lyons, p. 44, citing John Ross Robertson, HISTORY OF FREEMASONRY, vol. I, p. 307.

14 SCHEDULE C contains a complete list of the members in attendance at a meeting held in 1786 at the home of Thomas Sherwoood, and recorded as the first entry in the Minute Book of the New Oswegatchie Lodge, all of which is taken from Marjory E. Lyons' Thesis.

15 Lyons, p. 65.

Freemasons which came to Upper Canada with the Loyalists. Initially, the refugee Masons met under the authority of a travelling warrant dated May 7, 1783, issued by the American parent Lodge to "a lodge in His Majesty's Loyal American Regiment."[13] By 1786, all ties with the American Freemasons had been severed and the Freemasons of the New Oswegatchie settlement were meeting under the authority of a new warrant issued by the Grand Lodge of England.

The membership list of 1786 contains a cross section of the new society,[14] and the Lodge very clearly exercised significant control over its members. One meeting dealt with the sharp dealing of one of the Lodge members against another. The minutes of the meeting recorded that:

> . . . brother Campbell has not behaved with that rectitude and honesty, which becomes a man professing Masonry; and hereby order that he shall pay brother Larne 7/6 (7 shillings and 6 pence) which is his just due, and that he shall clear up the aspersions which Larne says he cast on him . . .

Campbell was suspended for a six month period, following which:

> . . . if it appears that he has refrained from the slippery actions which he has been guilty of, he will be permitted to resume his seat as a member of this Lodge.[15]

In many ways, the militia of Upper Canada, at least so far as the officer ranks were concerned, played the same role in society as the voluntary associations. The militia provided the officer with an opportunity to socialize, solidify a network of socially advantageous comrades, and demonstrate his personal importance to the community. To the private soldier, militia service was an obligation imposed by the state and participation was usually less than enthusiastic.

The Militia Act provided for compulsory military service in the local militia unit by all men between the ages of sixteen and sixty, excepting only conscientious objectors and foreign aliens. In times of peace, the duty was not particularly onerous. The militia was assembled for only one full day in June of each year and, in one day, the officers could do little with the troops other than take the roll and announce the promotions that had taken place during the year. Uniforms were an odd collection of cast-offs and homespun, and even

---

16 Public Archives of Canada, CHARLES JONES PAPERS, MG24 B7, letter dated 16 December 1837, Bytown, from Geo. Baker to Charles Jones.

Drilling the militia.

arms were scarce. It was a day out for the men which was either welcomed or cursed according to the state of their crops and the weather. The thought of sacrificing a fine day of haying for King and Country must not have seemed a fair trade in times of peace, when militia day provided little more than an opportunity for their officers to parade about in their dress uniforms, shout orders, and pretend they were on Lord Wellington's staff.

The officers, however, obtained a great deal of local prestige from their participation on behalf of Her Majesty. To be an officer in a militia unit was often an introduction to the provincial power structure. There was, accordingly, significant competition for appointments to the various officer ranks, and these methods were filled following the usual criteria: family position, social rank, and power.

Initially, leadership in the county militia was determined by the rank of the individual in the militia units of the British forces of the Revolutionary War. In Grenville County, accordingly, Edward Jessup was the commanding officer, while in the County of Leeds, James Breakenridge commanded. As the original Loyalist leaders became too old to serve, new leaders were selected and these new men invariably reflected the shifting influence among the leading families. By the time of the Rebellions of the late 1830s, Charles Jones of Brockville, one of the sons of Ephraim Jones, was the senior colonel for the County of Leeds, the officer commanding the Second Regiment of the Leeds Militia, and was the ranking officer for all of eastern Ontario.[16]

The military career of Levi Soper provides another example of how the shifting power structure of the Johnstown District affected militia rank. Soper was one of the old and respected settlers of the County of Leeds; he was also a vocal supporter of the Reform cause. Initially, he had settled in the Township of Kitley sometime before 1798,[17] and was in possession of a Crown Patent for his land by 1802.[18]

In September of 1823, Levi Soper, who at the time held the rank of major in the 2nd Regiment of the Leeds Militia, received an order commanding his attendance for militia service. The order had been issued by Captain John Weatherhead, who had been promoted to the

17 Lockwood, p. 8, citing a report prepared by Abel Stevens dated 14 February 1798, listing the settlers of Kitley Township.
18 Leavitt, p. 118.
19 Public Archives of Canada, CHARLES JONES PAPERS, MG24 B7, letter from Levi Soper to N. Coffin, Adjutant General, dated 26 Sept 1823.
20 Public Archives of Canada, CHARLES JONES PAPERS, MG24 B7, letter from N. Coffin, Adjutant General, to Charles Jones, dated 15 October 1823.

rank of major of the Regiment. Soper, who had no advance knowledge of the promotion of Weatherhead, was apoplectic. He immediately wrote to the provincial adjutant general and submitted his resignation. In view of ". . . the faithful and vigilant discharge of my duties at all times as a militia officer and particularly during the late war," wrote the old warrior, "I humbly trust I have committed no breach in manifesting that spirit necessary for every officer in support of his rank and dignity. And beg you will lay before his Excellency the Lieutenant Governor this as my humble request of his allowing me to resign."[19]

Coffin, the adjutant general, immediately wrote two letters to Charles Jones as the officer in command of the Regiment. Officially, he wrote Jones advising that he had received Soper's correspondence and requesting a report on the merits of accepting or rejecting the resignation. He then added a far more interesting private note. "My Dear Colonel," he wrote, "The poor fellow (Soper) was under the necessity of employing some one to write his letter, but it appears he did not let his friend see how he wrote Regiment under his signature." Soper had signed his letter of resignation in his own unschooled hand below which he had added in an even shakier hand "2 Ridgmint L Militia." "Surely," continued Coffin, "that is sufficient to convince the poor man that he is not qualified to be a field officer."

Coffin, however, doubted that the lieutenant-governor would accept the resignation; it might set a bad example. "My best respects to Mrs. Jones," he concluded.[20] It was apparent that Soper's ability to write fluently and deport himself as a gentleman was far more important than his ability to lead men into battle.

As always, in Upper Canada, there was a political subtext to any government appointment and the military was not exempt. Politics, as always, played a dominant role. The militia did not exist in a vacuum, rather it was an integral part of a politicized society and the same criteria for advancement applied. Soper was not only largely illiterate, he was also a known supporter of the Reformers. It was understandable then that Jones would prefer a Tory supporter in a position of authority.

Jones himself was subject to political pressure when selecting his officers. In July of 1832, at a time when Ogle Robert Gowan was helping Charles Jones' brother Jonas with his election preparations, he wrote to Charles Jones offering gratuitous advice with a veiled threat that the Irish were:

> . . . in a state of rebellion against the appointment of the 3
> Howards and 2 Sopers as officers in your Regiment. My
> own opinion is that whoever advised the step it was highly
> impolitic and perhaps intended to prejudice your brothers
> nomination.[21]

The message was clear. The Jones could have Gowan's help in the election, but they would have to pay for it.

These anecdotes indicate a society that was organized from the top down along class lines. To those in the elite, this was the natural order of things. One looked after one's own, and thereafter dispensed favours to those in the lower orders. The lower orders in society were pleased to receive the largesse of their social superiors and in turn dispensed their own patronage to those below them. This was the Tory system of the time. The elite could not conceive of a successful society being organized in any other way. It was not surprising that those persons who benefitted from the system would fight tooth and nail against any significant reform.

During the period of settlement and early development, the persons who were at the bottom of the social pyramid had neither the time nor the energy to consider their political position. Further, the rigours of the early colonial period enforced a level of economic democracy as all members of the growing communiFty worked to establish themselves in their new homes. By the 1830s, the social distinctions between the elite and the common settler were obvious. The reasons for those distinctions were equally obvious. Those at the bottom now had the time to look at their betters and, when they did so, they were not satisfied with the explanation of Sir Francis Bond Head and the members of the Family Compact that this was the way things were and ought to be. They sought reform.

---

21 Public Archives of Canada, CHARLES JONES PAPERS, MG24 B7, letter from Gowan to Charles Jones, dated 17 July 1832.

CHAPTER IV
The Grievances

*B*Y THE 1830S, the internal stresses inherent in Upper Canadian society were causing widespread popular discontent. Boils were beginning to appear on the body politic and, denied legitimate political expression, the forces of reform erupted in rebellion. In a society such as existed in Upper Canada, it is hardly surprising that a segment of the populace became disillusioned to the point of armed rebellion. It is more surprising that the rebellions did not enjoy popular support.

The typical farm family working their hundred acres, the labourer in the town, and even the small shopkeeper were ill-served by the High Church and Tory system. This was government by the favoured few, for the favoured few, at the expense of the majority. This majority did not understand, nor were they interested in, discussions concerning theoretical issues such as the political organization of society or the merits of responsible government. They focused their attention, instead, on more immediate issues.

They objected to the failure of the province to assist in the mundane aspects of their lives. They lived with inadequate roads, inequities in the school system, a banking system that did not meet their needs, interference in their religion, excessive taxation, and the exorbitant expenditure of public funds on an elitist civil service. As the decade wore on, the situation was exacerbated by the growing recession and by the growth of the reform movement around the world.

Of all the various issues, nothing caused more public rancour and ill will than the attempt on the part of the colonial administration to impose on the people of Upper Canada the Church of England as the established, state-sponsored church. As an integral part of the plan to encourage and develop the British connection in the new colony of Upper Canada, the Constitutional Act of 1791 made express provision for clergy reserves. In each township, land equal to one-seventh of the value of all land granted was to be set aside or reserved to provide a source of revenue, ". . . for the support and maintenance of a Protestant clergy."[1] Any subsequent rent or profit arising from the clergy reserves was similarly to be used to maintain and support the Protestant clergy. These provisions were a source of constant friction and irritation until they were ultimately abandoned in the mid-nineteenth century.

The various denominations scrambled for their share of public support and argued continually over which of them ought to be included within the ambiguous definition of "protestant clergy." The theology of some denominations precluded them from accepting any state aid. They argued that the funds from the reserves ought to be spent on schools and other non-religious public bodies. To these denominational voluntarists, and to the members of those denominations otherwise excluded from public support, the fundamental issue of why one denomination ought to be favoured over another remained unanswerable.

To the authors of the Constitutional Act, the intent of the provision for clergy reserves had been obvious. Britain had an established church, the Church of England, which enjoyed state support from public funds. The framers of the Constitutional Act saw the established church as a vital element of a stable society. Sir John Graves Simcoe was not in the least interested in religious doctrine. He was a snobbish, but practical upper class English civil servant charged with the governance of His Majesty's new province. In his view, and that of his superiors in Whitehall, the Established Church would strengthen the bonds of loyalty to England and to the monarchy. A strong and vital Church of England would further tie the population of the province to the system of government that the monarchy represented. "I must beg leave to promise," Simcoe wrote, "that I am decisively of opinion, that a regular Episcopal establishment, subordinate to the primacy of Great Britain, is absolutely necessary . . ." This was particularly true in Upper Canada, a ". . . colony (that) is peculiarly situate amongst a variety of republics . . ."[2]

---

1 The Constitutional Act, 31 George III, c. 31.
2 J. M. Bliss, ed., CANADIAN HISTORY IN DOCUMENTS, 1763-1966. Ryerson Press 1966, p. 34., letter from Simcoe to Portland dated 30 October 1795.

To Simcoe the reason for an established church was obvious: ". . . every establishment of church and state that upholds the distinction of ranks, and lessens the undue weight of democratic influence, ought to be introduced."[3] The Established Church of England, with an episcopal structure and the King at its head as Defender of the Faith would reinforce in the minds of the inhabitants of the province their allegiance to the mother country and to the King.

The religious and social doctrine of the church reinforced the concepts of order, obedience, and subservience. The Church preached a doctrine of the subservience of the masses to those of rank and provided religious sanction to the class structure.

> What is it that makes the poor man take it for granted that ten chimneys smoke in my palace while he dies of cold – that I have ten changes of raiment in my wardrobe while he is naked – that on my table at each meal there is enough to sustain a family for a week? It is religion which says to him in another life I shall be his equal, indeed that he has a better chance of being happy there than I have.

wrote Napoleon Bonaparte, expressing the political thinking of the upper classes on both sides of the English Channel.[4]

In all probability, Simcoe never considered that the clergy of any denomination other than the Church of England would be considered as entitled to support. Certainly his comments referred only to the Church of England. However, Upper Canada contained innumerable denominations and sects, none of which were prepared to allow the ambiguous wording of the Constitutional Act stand unchallenged.

To the head of the Anglican establishment, Reverend Strachan, there was no doubt that the term "Protestant Clergy," as used in the Constitutional Act, ought to refer to the clergy of the Church of England and no other. "Indeed the enactments in the 31st Geo. c. 31 (the Constitutional Act) making provision for the Protestant clergy are all descriptive of the Church of England and no other church . . ."[5] he argued. Strachan was even opposed to the recognition by the civil authority of the religious sacraments of the other Protestant denominations.

Initially, only marriages solemnized by properly constituted

---

3 Ibid.
4 Alec R. Vidler, THE CHURCH IN AN AGE OF REVOLUTION, 1789 TO THE PRESENT DAY, Penguin Books, London, 1961, p. 19.
5 Henderson ed., p. 105, letter from Strachan to Rt Hon Thomas Frankland Lewis, MP, dated 1 February 1830.

priests who conducted the ceremony according to the rites of the Church of England were recognized as valid. Baptists and other dissenting Protestant churches could marry their adherents, but those ceremonies were not recognized as valid by the civil authority. This could have profound effects on such issues as the entitlement to the property of a deceased spouse.

Practically, restrictions such as these could not work. Even if the population was prepared to adhere to the Church of England, there were simply not enough clergy to service their needs.

In his attempt to freeze out all other denominations, and preserve the primacy of the Church of England, Strachan was fighting a rear guard action and ultimately a losing battle. In 1819, the role of the Church of England as the established and state-sponsored church of the province was dealt its first blow. The first successful challenge came from the Auld Kirk of Scotland.

The Kirk was the Established Church of Scotland, and in Scotland it received state support in much the same fashion as the Church of England did in England. The law officers of the Crown determined that since the Kirk of Scotland enjoyed these privileges in Scotland, its clergy must be entitled to share in the support offered by the clergy reserve system in Upper Canada. Logically, the argument was irrefutable, but Strachan saw it as the thin edge of the wedge. "If therefore, the clergy of the Kirk of Scotland be let in, there is no denomination of Dissenters should not also be admitted . . . which appears altogether absurd," he wrote.[6]

By 1828, the Select Committee of the British House of Commons reported that the revenue from the clergy reserves ought to be divisible amongst all Protestant clergy. To Strachan this was dangerous nonsense.

> That the Canadas might be attached to the parent state by religious as well as political feelings was the intention of the great William Pitt, when in framing their constitution he provided for the religious instruction of the people. For it was well known to this illustrious statesman that almost all the episcopal clergy and their congregations remained during the American Rebellion loyal and faithful to the King.[7]

---

6 Ibid.
7 Ibid., p. 157, from "Observations On A Bill For Uniting The Legislative Councils And Assemblies" by John Strachan, 1824.

While the Church of England could be depended upon to foster loyalty, the same apparently could not be said about other denominations.

> The policy of depriving our Church of this single future advantage (the revenue from the clergy reserves) may well be questioned, when it is considered that her clergy are the only religious teachers over whom the Government has any control. Indeed the teachers of all other denominations . . . are for the most part from the United States.[8]

To the Archdeacon of Toronto, there was nothing more potentially subversive than the American influence in matters of religion.[9]

Strachan argued that the dissenting Protestant denominations, and in particular the Methodists, had provided religious succour to the American revolutionaries in the past and ought not now be trusted in Upper Canada.[10] Further, in a rather circuitous argument, he noted that the clergy of the Church of England were the only Protestant clergy subject to any control by the government. With its episcopal structure, whereby the government appointed the clergy, there was some truth to Strachan's argument. The government, however, would instantly assume some control over the clergy of the dissenting Protestant religions just as soon as they began to provide them with funding. By providing funding, the government would acquire the control that comes with the threat of withdrawing that public support.

As the decade wore on and the religious infighting intensified, it became apparent that Reverend Strachan and the political elite had lost the argument in both the arena of public opinion and amongst the political planners in Britain. Nonetheless, funds from the clergy reserves remained for the sole support of the Church of England, the Kirk of Scotland, and a few other designated denominations until the Durham Reforms following the rebellions.

Strachan continued to preach that the Church of England alone could encourage loyalty and dependability among the people, but as that argument became less persuasive, he began to stress in the alternative that the privileges afforded his church were not substantial in any event. State support for the Church of England did not prevent other denominations from freely exercising their own religion, it

---

8 Ibid., p. 98, from "Observations of the Provision Made for the Maintenance of a Protestant Clergy," by John Strachan, London, 1827.
9 Ibid., p. 157, from "Observations On A Bill For Uniting The Legislative Councils And Assemblies," by John Strachan, 1824.
10 Ibid., p. 98, from "Observations of the Provision Made for the Maintenance of a Protestant Clergy," by John Strachan, London, 1827.

simply assisted his. Adherents of other denominations accordingly had no legitimate grounds for complaint. After all ". . . if of the Established Church he (the Upper Canadian) has the same privileges as at home (in England); and if of a different denomination he has the same liberty."[11]

In Ontario generally, and certainly in the Johnstown District comprising the counties of Leeds and Grenville, adherents to the Church of England were a minority even among Protestants. In the census data of 1842, adherents to the Church of England in the Johnstown District numbered 9,111 people out of a total population of 33,019. This represented only thirty per cent of the population. Anglicans were a favoured minority enjoying privileges denied to members of other Protestant denominations. The Reverend John Strachan could rationalize the favoured position of his church any way he wished. The fact remained that to the adherent of the non-Church of England denomination, the favoured position of the Church of England was a blatant irritant. To attempt to rationalize to the seventy per cent majority that they, through the state, ought to support the minority denomination was a futile exercise. The fact that these people, who represented the majority in the province, were free to worship in their own church at their own expense was no consolation.

The religious history of eastern Ontario was typical of the province, in that the Church of England did not predominate. Glengarry County, in the most easterly part of the province, was settled in 1804 by Roman Catholic Scottish Highlanders under the leadership of Reverend Alexander Macdonell. By temperament and design, Macdonell, who became the first Catholic Bishop of Upper Canada, was a Tory. He sought to advance the cause of Catholicism by continually demonstrating the loyalty of his flock to the colonial governors. In many respects, his strategy was successful. From time to time, Macdonell received *ex gratia* support from the government for Catholic clergy and to establish Catholic schools and he ultimately was invited to join the Executive Council.

In the early years of settlement, the denominational choice of Protestant immigrants was more often the result of an available church, or preacher, than any doctrinal difference.[12] Once a denominational choice was made, however, the adherents took their religious

---

11 Ibid., p. 73, from "A Visit to the Province of Upper Canada in 1819" written by John Strachan, and published under the name of his brother James Strachan in 1820.
12 S. D. Clark, CHURCH AND SECT IN CANADA, Toronto, University of Toronto Press, 1940, p. 167. The point is made that denominational choices amongst protestants were often determined by availability rather than doctrinal choice.

differences seriously. It was an age of denominational differences. There were three branches of Presbyterianism and three branches of Methodism. There was every sort of Protestant Christian from Baptists and Congregationalist, through Quakers, Tunkers, and Shakers.

The earliest permanent, full-time minister in Brockville and area was the Presbyterian (as opposed to the Kirk of Scotland or Free Presbyterian), Reverend Smart. By the sheer power of his presence,

Reverend William Smart arrived in Brockville in 1811 as a Presbyterian missionary and stayed as the community's pastor until his death thirty-eight years later.

the Presbyterian Church dominated the other denominations in the early days of settlement in the Brockville area.[13]

Reverend Smart arrived in Elizabethtown on October 7, 1811.[14] His mission field was the entire Johnstown and Eastern Districts, an area from the border of Lower Canada to Gananoque and from the St Lawrence River north to Perth. Many families, such as the Buells of Brockville, became Presbyterian simply because Reverend Smart was the only minister available to them. The Buells had nominally been Episcopalian in their pre-Revolution American home. They, however, supported Reverend Smart and became leaders of the local Presbyterian congregation, in part due to the absence of an Episcopal preacher.

In the Johnstown District, Augusta Township contained the original home of Barbara Heck and her family, the founders of Methodism in North America.[15] Methodists, by 1830, far outnumbered Anglicans. In the province as a whole, Methodists were the largest Protestant denomination and the established church saw them as its greatest threat. The Methodist circuit rider, carrying his Bible in his saddle bag, rode the blazed trails through the wilderness bringing the love and fear of God to the people. Their intellectual leader, and the editor of the principal Methodist newspaper, the *Christian Guardian*, was a young preacher by the name of Egerton Ryerson.

The Reformers at first thought that they had found a kindred spirit in Ryerson, but their goals differed from his. Mackenzie and the Reformers sought social and political reform; Ryerson sought to advance the cause of the Methodist Church. The inevitable break came soon after Ryerson visited England and met with the leading British Reformers. He was shocked by the men he met and on his return to Upper Canada he labelled them all Godless republicans. No longer would the Reformers in Upper Canada receive any support from Ryerson.

While emotional issues dominated the debate, the clergy reserves had tangible negative effects on the developing communities. Reverend Strachan and the Tories argued that the land held in the clergy reserves provided opportunities for settlers who lacked the financial resources to purchase land outright.[16] In correspondence reminiscent of the world view of Sir John Graves Simcoe, Strachan

---

13 Akenson, Census of 1842.
14 Leavitt, p. 27.
15 The house is described and a photograph is provided in THE ANCESTRAL ROOF, DOMESTIC ARCHITECTURE OF UPPER CANADA, by Marion Macrae, Clarke Irwin Co. Ltd. 1963, pp. 17, 18.
16 Akenson, p. 160.

noted that ". . . the Clergy Reserves are in most instances preferable to a grant of 100 acres; consisting always of 200, a settler, who has got his grant adjacent, may, at the expense of $7.00 per annum, have a farm of 300 acres."[17]

It was true that clergy reserve lands were made available at modest rents and that the immigrant settler from the British Isles was used to a system of tenant farming. It was also true that these lands provided short term advantages to some settlers. Nonetheless rented land had little appeal in Upper Canada. The immigrant settler was not interested in remaining a tenant farmer as he had been in the old country. They were in search of better lives and, given the opportunity, the immigrant farmers invariably elected to improve farms of their own. They were extremely reluctant to expend labour on land that they would never own. The clergy reserves remained, in large part, unoccupied and undeveloped.

It was in the interest of the settler to have the entire township in which he lived developed. Since landowners were responsible for the repair of roads immediately adjacent to their properties, a fully settled township meant that there would be decently maintained roads. If there were sufficient farms in the community then there would be sufficient crops to support a local mill and other services. Setting aside one-seventh of all the available land interfered with this goal and worked to the detriment of the community.

The practical difficulties associated with the clergy reserve system were not the only problems occasioned by the land policies of the colonial administration. From the inception of the colony, His Majesty's government viewed land as a commodity to reward loyal subjects according to their rank and position. Land was something that the Government of Upper Canada had in abundance and, even though it cost the government nothing, it was the one commodity that every immigrant wanted.

Those persons with access to the lieutenant-governor became most adept at obtaining significant land grants. These same opportunities, obviously, were not made available to the average settler. In 1797, each member of the Executive Council received, ex gratia, a grant of six thousand acres as a reward for their public service.[18] Examples of individual favouritism are legion. D'Arcy Boulton, a member of the Executive Council, and his immediate

---

17 Henderson ed., p. 73, from "A visit to the Province of Upper Canada in 1819."
18 Dunham, p. 22.

family received 16,000 acres over the years. George Stanley Boulton alone received 3,700 acres, while Abraham Nelles, a member of the Legislative Council, received 5,500 acres in 1823, and a further 1,200 acres in 1828.[19] In 1836, William Lyon Mackenzie, the firebrand leader of the Reform forces, noted in his "Seventh Report on Grievances" that the concern was not that the law had been broken in any way by the granting of huge tracts of land to the favoured few. The problem was that there were no legal restrictions on the right of the lieutenant-governor to grant land to whoever, and in whatever quantities he deemed appropriate.[20]

The original townships along the St Lawrence River were quickly filled with Loyalist settlers from the initial migration. As a result, land in great quantities along the front was not available for subsequent grants. The townships to the rear of the district, however, do provide examples of the general land-granting policies of the government.

In Kitley Township, located directly north of Elizabethtown, the Honourable William Dummer Powell, then Chief Justice of Upper Canada, received a grant of two thousand acres in 1797. Hazelton Spencer, a Major in the British Regular forces, was favoured with a grant of 1,200 acres. Similarly, John Cumming of Kingston received a grant of 1,400 acres, while William Walters, one of His Majesty's printers from York, received 1,000 acres.[21]

Of more significance, Sir John Johnson, the former Laird of the Mohawk Valley, Superintendent of Indian Affairs, and former Loyalist Commander of the Royal Greens, for whom the Johnstown District was named, received a grant of 1,534 acres on the east side of the Gananoque River. In addition, he received all of Amherst Island to the west of Kingston and, to the east, all of Howe Island in the St Lawrence River. However, as Sir John was also the seigneur of Argenteuil, giving him ownership of the entire Township or Seigneury of Argenteuil in Quebec, he had no intention of occupying his Upper Canadian holdings. Sir John obtained the Crown patents for his land grants in the Counties of Leeds and Frontenac in 1802, which, in 1824, he transferred to his sister who ultimately sold the lot.[22]

The personal history of Joel Stone, the founder of Gananoque, provides another illustration of governmental favouritism in the

---

19 Robert E.Saunders, "WHAT WAS THE FAMILY COMPACT?" Ontario History, vol. 49, 1957.
20 Akenson, p. 162, indicates that the discretion to grant free land ended in 1827.
21 Lockwood, p. 7.
22 Akenson, p. 66.

Johnstown District. Stone, a successful Yankee pedlar who had opted reluctantly for King George III, arrived in Gananoque in 1789 as the recipient of a 1,100 acres grant on the west side of the Gananoque River. In 1792, he had the confidence to petition the Crown for an entire township and, in 1799, he petitioned the government for still more land. Both of these petitions were refused, but the very act of making the request proves the point. Land in large quantities was available for the asking, provided that the person making the request was sufficiently connected to the government and was deemed sufficiently worthy.

These enormous land grants were destined to remain vacant for long periods of time. Their absentee owners had invested nothing in their acquisition, yet they invariably held onto it until such time as they could realize, through its sale, sizeable profits. However, land only increased in value when it became a part of a viable, settled community with roads, mills, schools, and shops. This state of affairs resulted in retarded growth and community development. Lord Durham delineated the magnitude of the problem in his 1837 report when he noted that virtually half of all of the surveyed land in the province was held either by the church as clergy reserves, or by recipients of grants to the favoured few.[23]

The 1830s were further marred by a general economic malaise. Money had always been a rare commodity in the province and most trade was carried on by barter. The farmer would bring his cash crop of grain, potash, or timber to town and exchange it for cloth, tools, and other staples that he could not economically produce himself. This lack of cash retarded the development of trade.

The Bank of Upper Canada was chartered in 1821,[24] but did absolutely nothing to alleviate the financial difficulties experienced by the majority. Typical of the time, the bank charter was granted to those members of the Family Compact who were at the apex of the social pyramid. The same could be said about a second bank established in Kingston. The banks, accordingly, became a ready target for the Reformers. Mackenzie, with some justification, labelled the banks "a dangerous engine of political power, improperly vested in the hands of a few families monopolizing the chief offices of the country."[25]

---

23 Gerald M. Craig, ed., LORD DURHAM'S REPORT, McClelland and Stewart Limited, Toronto, 1963. p. 118.
24 Act passed in 1819, proclaimed in force in 1821.
25 Dunham, p. 132.

The extent of the financial and monetary problems of the small landowner caused real problems for the local municipalities as they attempted to raise tax revenue. In Prescott, a lively debate ensued in town council concerning the collection of tax arrears.

Prescott had been incorporated following the Brockville model in 1834. The concerns of the Board of Police of the new town were the concerns of every town in Upper Canada – they wanted to improve the community. They wanted to clean up the mud and filth on the streets by installing paving stones on the sidewalks. They wanted to control disease. They wanted economic advancement for the town. All of these improvements cost money, and money was the one commodity that the ratepayers of Prescott lacked.

Alexander McMillan was the first tax collector for the Town of Prescott. Initially, the job was seen as something of a plum, but there was more to collecting taxes from the freeholders of Prescott than sending out assessment notices. By January 1835, McMillan reported to the Board of Police that many people were simply refusing to pay their assessments and others were ". . . utterly too poor to collect anything from."[26] McMillan tendered his resignation. The Board considered McMillan's report and, rather than accept his resignation, they requested that he ". . . go round once more and make his demands and report upon the same, and that they would then take the case of the poor into further consideration."[27]

As the recession wore on, the town searched for other means to secure local improvements. By April, the Board recognized its inability to pave the streets using its own funds and advised the landowners that if they were to flag the sidewalk in front of their property, the town would pay them half of the estimated cost.[28] By the next spring, the town offered to allow the poorer class of ratepayer the opportunity of working off their tax arrears by working to improve the streets.[29]

The specific grievances of the Reformers were constant and long-standing irritants. However, it was the change in the political climate, and the agitation of the radical reformers such as Mackenzie, that fanned these embers of discontent into a rebellious heat. The spirit of reform was blowing throughout the western world and the winds of change could be felt even in the political backwater of British North America.

26 Minutes of the Board of Police for the Town of Prescott, January 24, 1835.
27 Ibid.
28 Ibid., April 25, 1835.
29 Ibid., March 5, 1836.

In Britain, the Great Reform Bill had passed and the Whigs controlled parliament. The years of Tory rule under the prime ministership of the Iron Duke of Wellington had given way to the liberalism of Lord Grey. Indeed, so powerful were the forces of reform and liberalism, as Great Britain moved towards a new political enlightenment, that Grey's principal political problem came from the radical wing of his own party.

In the United States, the ideas of the federalist conservancy had given way to the fresh ideas of Jacksonian democracy and the extension of the franchise. It was time to put democracy to work for the people. America was proud of itself. The young republic began to consider its manifest destiny as the principal power in the new world. Davy Crockett and Jim Bowey would soon stand up to the entire Spanish Army at the Alamo wresting Texas out of colonial Mexico.

In Upper Canada, there were real grievances to be addressed, but none more compelling than the need to change the system of government itself. The new concepts of responsible government bandied about by Reformers and half understood by the people were garnished with an aura of British and American respectability. If British subjects in the mother country were to have the benefits of democracy inherent in the concept of responsible government, why not their counterparts in Upper Canada? And, if Americans were prepared to fight for their liberty in the badlands of Texas, why should Canadians not do the same?

Robert Gourlay, Scottish gadfly who became the first Upper Canadian political agitator, provided the first indication that all was not well in the political Garden of Eden crafted by Simcoe.

CHAPTER V
Introduction to Discord: Robert Gourlay

*T*HE FIRST INDICATION that all was not well in the political Garden of Eden crafted by Sir John Graves Simcoe came during the visit to Upper Canada of a tenacious Scottish gadfly by the name of Robert Gourlay. This upper-class Scot came from a long line of strong-willed forebears. He could trace his ancestry to the twelfth century and, by the time of his birth, the Gourlays, residing in their ancestral home of "Craigrothie," were the principal family in Fifeshire.

One ancestor, Norman Gourlay, who entered the Roman Catholic priesthood in 1515, subsequently met Martin Luther and embraced the tenets of the Protestant Reformation. The priest married and refused to recant the Protestant heresy, and leave his wife, when ordered to do so by his religious superior, Cardinal Beaton. The Cardinal had several illegitimate children and numerous mistresses of his own, but paid lip-service to the doctrine of a celibate clergy. He had Gourlay put to death as a heretic. Gourlay's body was burned on the Edinburgh road in a fire high enough to be visible to the heretic's clansmen across the firth. Years later, in 1599, the Gourlays had their revenge and put the torch to the Roman Catholic cathedral at St Andrews, the traditional seat of the Cardinal. The Gourlays, by that time, had whole-heartedly embraced Presbyterianism. "Enraged at idols, mass and beads," they had "Dang the cathedral doun."[1]

During his sojourn in the province of Upper Canada, Gourlay was alternately lionized, criticized, mocked, jailed and, finally, banished. It was alleged by many that he was insane, yet an analysis of

---

1 Lois Darroch Milani, ROBERT GOURLAY, GADFLY: THE BIOGRAPHY OF ROBERT (FLEMING) GOURLAY 1778 - 1863, FORERUNNER OF REBELLION IN UPPER CANADA, 1837, Ampersand Press, 1971, p. 2.

his positions on social issues and political reform reveals an amazing consistency. If he was mentally unbalanced, it was the insanity of a man who was so certain of his views that he refused to change or recant in spite of growing criticism and personal danger. Robert Gourlay had inherited the stubbornness of his clan.

Gourlay landed in Canada at the port of Quebec on May 31, 1817, with two purposes in mind. His wife had recently been willed 400 acres of land in the Niagara peninsula and, to add to the inheritance, Gourlay had purchased the adjoining 400 acres, sight unseen. He planned to develop those lands in order to provide a home in the new world for his family.

His secondary purpose was far more significant to the history of Upper Canada. Gourlay had witnessed the plight of the British masses dispossessed in a country ravaged by depression and the effects of the industrial revolution. Gourlay was a social activist and reformer who, during his travels through Scotland and England, had developed a plan to relocate the unfortunates of Britain to Upper Canada.

The industrial revolution made entire sections of society in Great Britain redundant. The Napoleonic Wars had temporarily mitigated the effects of dislocation as any surplus labour was quickly snapped up for cannon fodder. But, with Bonaparte's defeat at Waterloo, men were no longer needed for military service. Very quickly the working man fell from grace. After being praised as saviours of the nation, the troops were soon seen as a social problem. The poor were literally starving. Entire classes – in particular the handloom weavers of northern England, the Scottish cotters, and the agricultural workers of the south – were dispossessed. Children as young as seven went out to work in the mines and developing factories to help support their families.

The economic theory then in vogue was the unrestrained, laissez-faire economics of Adam Smith. Typical of the times, and perhaps typical of all times, the dominant attitude held that the poor were poor because they were lazy. Yet, when the landless poor begged for garden plots to grow food to feed their families, the request was denied on the basis that they could not be trusted to use the land wisely. The gentry placed mantraps on their hunting estates to prevent rabbit poaching and made the simple offence of trespass punishable by deportation for seven years.

Gourlay did not accept laissez-faire economics, and he was

prepared to voice his dissent loudly. As a result of his constant agitation, he soon found himself ostracized by polite society, disinherited by his father, and subjected to attacks by the Church. By the time of his emigration to Canada, Gourlay had challenged many tenets of the time. He attacked the Corn Laws, which provided price supports for grain to the detriment of the poor and of the obvious advantage of the gentry. He had argued for higher land taxes, which would adversely affect the economic position of the wealthy landowners, but assist the lower classes. He had attacked the Church of England for its imposition of the tithe, which took money from the poor who could ill afford it, to support the Church and the gentrified clergy.

The Church and the gentry were united in their opposition to Gourlay and the other reformers of the day. The tithe and the social order were ordained by God, they argued, and who were these upstarts, such as Gourlay, to agitate against the will of God.

As the post-Napoleonic War depression spread, agitation and discord grew. The government prepared the "Gagging Acts," authorizing any magistrate to order the end to any public gathering. Those who refused to disperse could be hanged. English and Scottish troops, fresh from their victory over Napoleon, were ordered to suppress bread riots and to execute any person who attempted to interfere.

In the midst of this social upheaval, Gourlay formulated the background for his proposal to transport Great Britain's surplus population to Upper Canada. His reasoning was simple: If there were too many people in England, yet not enough land, and Upper Canada enjoyed an abundance of land, but few people, then the obvious solution lay in transporting the starving masses of England to Upper Canada. It was this simple concept, coupled with Gourlay's arrogance and pride, which underlay all of Gourlay's actions during his Upper Canadian sojourn.

As Gourlay sailed through the Gulf of St Lawrence and up the St Lawrence River, he was awestruck by the enormity and potential of the remaining British possessions in North America. "You will not find . . . anything to compare . . . in point of grandeur to the waters of the St Lawrence,"[2] he wrote as his ship sailed onward from Quebec to Montreal.

In Montreal, he became intrigued at news of the successful military settlement of Perth, Upper Canada, a day's march inland from the St Lawrence River back from Brockville. This was just the

---

2 Ibid., p. 83.

sort of settlement in the virgin wilderness that he had envisioned. In order to meet the people and develop an appreciation of the country, he embarked on a walking tour from Montreal, through Cornwall and Morrisburg, onwards to Prescott and Brockville, and then northwards along the newly laid out track through the bush to Perth.[3] Gourlay was most impressed by what he saw in the new settlement. Here was a community of families from regiments disbanded following the wars against the French and Americans, prospering in the new world, who otherwise would have joined the destitute in Britain.

To popularize his findings, Gourlay wrote a statistical analysis, which was subsequently published in the *Salisbury Journal*, under the title: "Statistical Table Showing the Commencement and Progress of Improvement in Thirteen Months of Emigrant Settlement at Perth." This article represented the first occasion that Gourlay, or anyone else, had attempted a statistical analysis of any settlement in Upper Canada. To Gourlay, the result was of sufficient merit that he decided to undertake a similar analysis of the entire province.

On foot and by steamer, Gourlay made his way from Perth through the bush to Kingston and then around Lake Ontario to Niagara, where he introduced himself to his wife's relatives. He soon became acquainted with the wealthier landowners in the Niagara area, including Thomas Clark, Robert Hamilton, and William Dickson, three local members of the Legislative Assembly.

At dinner parties and around the inns and stores of the Niagara peninsula, he heard the same concerns that he had heard elsewhere in the province. The populace of the province of Upper Canada felt weighed down by the needless expense of the British colonial administration. Those with government positions were living high off the hog; the average settler lived in a hog's wallow. The province was underpopulated, but Sir Francis Gore, the lieutenant-governor at the time, did absolutely nothing to encourage British immigration and actively discouraged settlement by Americans. In the newer townships, the holdings of absentee landowners who had been granted large tracts of land by the government, together with land set aside for Crown and Clergy Reserves, constituted more than half of the total land available. In these townships, the land granting and reserve system severely impeded the development of roads and local trade.

---

3 Perth had been founded in 1816 as the centre for settlement for some of the disbanded troops of the Napoleonic Wars. The Brockville - Perth road had been laid out in the same year.

In an attempt to address this problem, the Legislative Assembly passed an Absentee Landowners Bill, which called for a tax on vacant land. This legislation was of supreme importance to the small farm owner as it encouraged development and lessened the incidence of land hoarding for speculative purposes. Nonetheless, the Legislative Council rejected the Bill on the basis that such legislation would be unfair to the interests of the large landowning members of the political elite.

The economic stagnation which Gourlay observed became even more apparent when he compared conditions in Upper Canada to those in the United States of America. Following his informal inspection of the Niagara frontier, Gourlay crossed the border and undertook a walking tour of the Genesee Valley of Ohio. This area had been opened up to settlement ten years after the original settlements of Upper Canada. However, it was apparent that the Americans were now at least ten years ahead. Everywhere Gourlay looked, he saw prosperous American farms, towns, and industries which, when juxtaposed with the current stagnation of Upper Canada, invited further study as to what was wrong with the system of government in the British province.

On his return to Niagara, Gourlay began his statistical analysis of the entire province. He drafted a questionnaire for circulation throughout Upper Canada on a township-by-township basis. In large part, the questionnaire dealt with concrete, practical, statistical information, such as: the date of first settlement; the number of taverns, churches, mills, and schools in the township; types of soil and availability of building stone and timber; wages paid to blacksmiths, carpenters and masons; and the amount of cleared land, crops grown, and livestock raised.

Additionally, Gourlay provided an opportunity for the residents in each township to express their growing discontent with the status quo by including a subjective question. This question, which became known simply as question 31, asked: "What, in your opinion, retards the improvement, of your Township in particular, or the province in general; and what would most contribute to the same."[4]

Gourlay also drafted a covering letter, which he called his "Address to the Resident Landowners of Upper Canada," to explain the questionnaire, which he also had published in every available

---

4 Milani, pp. 98-99, contains the text of the entire questionnaire taken from the Statistical Account I.

newspaper. In it he observed that the province was endowed with inherent wealth. He noted, however, that:

> When I speak in this sanguine manner of the capabilities of Canada, I take it for granted that certain political restraints to improvement will be speedily removed. The able resolutions brought forward at the close of your last Parliament and the opinion of every sensible man with whom I have conversed on the subject gives assurance of this.[5]

News of Gourlay's questionnaire and commentary at first caused shocked disbelief and then anger on the part of the governor and his principal advisors. It was naive in the extreme for Gourlay to think that his comments would be received calmly. The removal of the political restraints that he so cavalierly took for granted in his address would ultimately lead to the Rebellions of 1837 and 1838. The able resolutions of the Assembly which he so heartily endorsed had so enraged the lieutenant-governor that he had instantly dissolved that session of the Legislative Assembly and forbade the *Upper Canada Gazette* to publish the resolutions on penalty of prosecution for sedition. By any objective criteria, it should have been apparent to Gourlay that those sensible men to whom he referred were not in control of the power structure.

The political distance between the lieutenant-governor and the common folks in the townships was demonstrated by the difference in their responses to Gourlay's questionnaire. In the various townships to which the questionnaire was sent, the public responded enthusiastically. Meetings were organized to discuss the issues and to frame suitable responses. These returns provide a significant insight into the state of the province at the time. Word, however, quickly spread that the questionnaire did not have the sanction of the lieutenant-governor or of his advisors. The local Tories were advised that participation in Gourlay's questionnaire would be viewed as an act of recklessness contrary to the stability of the province.

In the village of Gananoque, for example, the questionnaire was originally received with some enthusiasm. A public meeting was held to discuss a response and the questionnaire was answered with the tacit approval of the Tory elite. Then, in the interval between the completion of the report and its return to Gourlay, Colonel Joel

---

5 Ibid.

Stone, the leading citizen of Gananoque and the surrounding townships, was alerted by his Tory friends at York of the inherent dangers of Gourlay's project. He saw to the interception of the town's report and refused to release the document.[6]

To the west, at the village of Adolphustown in the Counties of Lennox and Addington, John MacCauley, a highly placed Tory, had actually acted as the secretary of the township meeting held to respond to Gourlay's questionnaire. He was instructed by the meeting to return the completed document to Gourlay by post and readily agreed to do so. Shortly after posting the report he discovered, to his horror, that co-operation with Gourlay was politically unwise and could, in fact, result in the enmity of the lieutenant-governor. MacCauley immediately left for the main post office in Kingston. After some persuasion, he was able to retrieve the questionnaire and prevent its delivery to Gourlay.

The mystery of who was actively interfering with the return of Gourlay's questionnaires was solved when it was discovered that the Reverend John Strachan had toured through the eastern part of the province. It became obvious that during his tour he had taken the opportunity to speak with MacCauley, Stone, and others, to explain his position and that of the lieutenant-governor. It was apparent that the Archdeacon of York had taken the time to instruct the local Tories in the political realities of the time and that they had responded in a manner calculated to please those in power. Meanwhile, back at York, the lieutenant-governor's officials were making it clear to Gourlay that he had outworn his welcome in Upper Canada.

Gourlay had petitioned the lieutenant-governor for sufficient lands to begin his scheme to resettle Britain's poor in Upper Canada. The government refused to even consider his petition. "Sir," an official replied, "when you arrive in the Province with design to establish yourself in it as a settler, a location will be made in proportion to the opinion then formed of your means to become a useful settler."[7] Gourlay was aware of the land grants that others were receiving at the time. Only weeks before this curt refusal, he had met a shipboard acquaintance, a navy captain, who had just received a grant of 1,200 acres. He heard further that a mere clergyman, with whom he was also acquainted, had received a grant of 600 acres.[8] A new acquaintance, Charles Fothergill, reported that he had also

6 The Township report for the Township of Leeds, County of Leeds, which while not returned to Robert Gourlay, was preserved and is reproduced in total in THE HISTORY OF LEEDS AND GRENVILLE, by Thad. Leavitt.
7 Milani, p. 118.
8 Ibid., p. 102.

received 1,200 acres.[9] With these precedents, Gourlay had anticipated that his petition would be favourably received. He was about to receive a lesson in the practical politics of Upper Canada. Political action adverse to the interest of the established order would not be tolerated. The message in the government's refusal even to consider his petition was clear: He should submit to the control of the established order without complaint. If he did so, and rolled on his back like an old dog waiting for his master to rub his tummy, he might receive some scraps from the table. But, unlike the majority, Gourlay was not prepared to submit. He was outraged that his petition had been rejected out of hand without any articulated reason, while land in large quantities was granted to others. The battle lines between the feisty Scot and the lieutenant-governor and his Tory supporters had been drawn.

Girded for the battle, Gourlay drafted his Second Address To the Resident Landowners of Upper Canada. It was more pointed in its criticism than the first. In it, he declared that his intention in the first address had been one of absolute political neutrality. He explained that his sole object had been to gain objective information on the economic condition of the province which could then be used to inform and encourage potential British emigration. Since the questionnaire had been sent out, however, he had spent three months travelling the province, informing himself as to the state of the body politic. His investigation had convinced him that he must change his course of action. "This country, I am convinced, cannot be saved from ruin by temporizing measures, nor by the efforts and reasoning of any individual," he wrote. "If it is to be saved, reason and fact must speedily be urged before the throne of our Sovereign . . . a new leaf must be turned over in public conduct; and the people of Upper Canada must assume a character, without which all Parliaments naturally dwindle into contempt, and become mere tools, if not sport of executive power."[10] The gauntlet had been thrown down by the administration in refusing to consider Gourlay's proposal for land. It was clear that Gourlay, in his second address, had picked it up. The battle was joined.

In the interregnum between the departure of retired lieutenant-governor Sir Francis Gore and the arrival of his replacement, Sir Peregrine Maitland, Samuel Smith, the provincial administrator and

---

9 Ibid.
10 Ibid., p. 124.

career civil servant, acted as the interim head of state. He summonsed the Assembly for its annual session to commence on February 5, 1818.

The members of the Assembly were in an uproar over the manner in which the last session of the Assembly had been summarily prorogued by Smith as a result of his displeasure with the proposed Absentee Landowners Bill. They were now further incited by Gourlay's second address, which had been published on February 2, 1818. As a first order of business, the Assembly was moved to reintroduce legislation taxing land held by absentee owners and obliging absentee landowners to perform statute labour on roads in the same manner as the resident settler. They then moved to repeal the salary of the provincial agent in London, a position seen as an expensive and useless political plum. Finally, they refused to approve the civil list for salaries of the civil service, unless the Assembly was provided with an accounting of the expenditure of public funds provided to the administration in the previous two years.

All of these measures easily passed the Legislative Assembly only to be alternately rejected, ignored, or amended to such an extent that their original import was subverted by the Legislative Council. The bill to repeal the salary of the provincial agent in London was returned to the Assembly by the Legislative Council with amendments that would provide the agent with a salary for life. The balance of the legislative programme of the Assembly was simply allowed to die a natural death. The bills of the legislature would not receive the assent of the Legislative Council and would never become law. They were doomed to die on the legislative vine. The people of Upper Canada as represented in the Assembly, and the lieutenant-governor through his control of the Legislative Council, were stalemated.

Recognizing the stalemate, the members of the Legislative Assembly took what, for them, could only be considered precipitous action. If the will of the people as represented by their duly elected representatives in the Legislative Assembly was to be thwarted at every hand by the Legislative Council, the Executive Council, and by the lieutenant-governor himself, then, reasoned the members of the Assembly, they would appeal directly to the King for redress. A motion quickly passed the Assembly providing for a petition to the Prince Regent requesting that His Royal Highness ". . . remind the Legislative Council that it could not usurp the rights of His Royal Highness' faithful commons."[11] Rather than forward the petition to

---

11 Ibid.

the Prince Regent themselves, the Assembly added insult to injury by directing Administrator Smith to do it on their behalf. Then, as if amazed at their own temerity and recognizing the political danger inherent in their action, the members of the Legislative Assembly of Upper Canada high-tailed it out of town, like a bunch of school boys caught playing nicky-nicky-nine-doors on the headmaster's front door. The petition of the Assembly was duly delivered to Smith where it, like the stalled legislation of the Assembly, gathered dust. There would be no petitions forwarded to the Prince Regent by Smith expressing views contrary to his own. And Smith certainly did not agree with the contents of this petition.

When Gourlay heard of the Assembly's petition and of the administration's attitude towards it, he decided to intervene. It was clear to him that the administration was once more thwarting the will of the people by refusing to forward the Assembly's petition to His Highness. It was obvious to Gourlay that parliament was not functioning properly and that the only course of action open to the people was to bypass parliament and petition the Prince Regent directly. He retired to Niagara to draft his Third Address to the Resident Landowners of Upper Canada.

The new Address was published on April 9, 1818. Gourlay wrote:

> Gentlemen, Your Parliament is broken up! Good God, what is to be the end of all this . . . Surely British blood, when it has ebbed to its lowest mark, will learn to flow again . . . The constitution of this Province is in danger, and all the blessings of the social compact are running to waste . . . It is not the men it is the system which blasts every hope of good; and till the system is overturned, it is vain to expect any thing of value from change of Representatives, or Governors.[12]

Gourlay then referred to the ancient right of the British people to petition the monarch and directed the citizens of Upper Canada to do so directly. He called for public meetings in each township to elect a representative and a clerk. All eligible voters could attend their township meeting on payment of one dollar to defray expenses. The elected representative and clerk from the township meetings would attend a county or district meeting, which in turn would elect a delegation to attend a provincial convention at York. The provincial

---

12 Ibid., p. 138.

convention would then draft the petition to be forwarded to the Prince Regent and elect a panel of commissioners to see to its delivery in person.

From Niagara, four horsemen set out across the province, carrying the petitions and the call to action. The plan struck a responsive chord amongst the population. Gourlay himself chose to spread the news in the four eastern districts, including Johnstown. At the same time, he hoped to find out what had happened to the missing questionnaires from Adolphustown, Gananoque, and Prescott. Landing at Kingston on May 18, 1818, he soon learned of the earlier visits of his nemesis, Reverend Strachan. That solved the mysteries of what had happened to the Adolphustown and Gananoque questionnaires. He proceeded down river to Gananoque and Brockville, where he left a series of pamphlets calling for the township meetings. He then pressed on to Prescott, where he was expected, and where, in anticipation of his arrival, a meeting had been organized at Isaac Hurd's Inn for May 27, 1818.

Farmers and shopkeepers from Prescott and Augusta Township had packed Hurd's Inn when Gourlay arrived. The most outspoken of those assembled was not, however, a Gourlay supporter. Jonas Jones, the younger son of the old Loyalist, Ephraim Jones, was a young Tory on the rise who was prepared to make Gourlay fight for the township. Educated at Reverend Strachan's school and, by that time, a Brockville lawyer and Tory member of the Legislative Assembly, he had prepared both his argument and his supporters to oppose Gourlay. Gourlay entered the hall and assumed the podium to begin his bid to obtain endorsement for the Niagara petition and elect a representative from Augusta Township to attend the Grenville County meeting. But, before he could obtain control of the meeting, Jonas Jones took the floor and began a prolonged harangue against Gourlay, all reformers, and all other traitors.

The petition was wrong in both form and substance, argued Jones. Gourlay was attempting to usurp the function of the Assembly and of parliament as a whole. The whole procedure violated the constitution and the petition was not worthy of the support of the fair-minded electors of the Township of Augusta. Gourlay watched, powerless as his meeting spun out of control. He was unable to regain the floor and, recognizing that the day was lost to Jones and the Tory faction, Gourlay withdrew.

From Prescott, Gourlay proceeded in an easterly direction, down river through the eastern townships of the Johnstown District, through the counties of the Eastern District, Dundas, Stormont and Glengarry, then north and west up the Ottawa Valley to the villages of Hawkesbury and Vankleek Hill. As for Prescott, Gourlay was determined to revisit the village on his return voyage up the St Lawrence River to Lake Ontario, York, and Niagara.

Meetings took place throughout the eastern townships and districts as planned. In the County of Leeds, the backwoods Township of South Crosby held its meeting on June 6, 1818. On June 22, the Township of Kitley held its meeting, followed the next day by the Townships of Bastard and Lansdowne. The day after that, the Township of Yonge elected its delegates. A meeting is also said to have been held at Wiltsetown, at Dickson's Tavern, chaired by Captain Joseph. Finally, on June 26, 1818, at the residence of Abraham Dayton, the last township meeting in the County of Leeds was held, that being for the Township of Elizabethtown. As soon as the Elizabethtown delegates were selected, Dayton's door was thrown open and the delegates from the other townships in the county were invited in for the Leeds County meeting.[13]

The response to Gourlay's plan of action in the County of Leeds was typical of the province. There was a general feeling of dissatisfaction with the political structure. That feeling of malaise was evident in the general preparedness of a large segment of the population to participate in Gourlay's extra-parliamentary convention.

From the perspective of the Tory power structure, the enthusiastic response of the population to Gourlay's conventions was an example of democracy beginning to run amok. Things were getting out of hand and an analogy was drawn between the Gourlay meetings and the treasonous behaviour which had led to the American Revolution fifty years before. The situation could not be allowed to continue. As Gourlay, who was on his way back to Niagara, descended the gangplank from his steamer at Kingston, he was arrested on a charge of seditious libel. Bail was set at the horrendous sum of £1,000 sterling, an amount far beyond his ability to pay, and calculated to ensure his pre-trial detention and silence. Gourlay faced the prospect of waiting in gaol for his trial before the next Assizes

---

13 A list of the delegates from each of the various townships to the County meeting, and from the County of Leeds to the Provincial meeting, is contained in Leavitt's THE HISTORY OF LEEDS AND GRENVILLE, at p. 43, and is reproduced here as SCHEDULE C.

when, to his pleasant surprise, one of his wealthier Kingston supporters made bail on his behalf. Gourlay was free again. Free to prepare for his trial – free to continue his political agitation.

By June 25, 1818, Gourlay was once more in the Johnstown District overseeing the balance of the township meetings. The Prescott meeting had been rescheduled for that date and, on this occasion, Gourlay was at least able to speak. He had just concluded his three hour address and was confident that he would receive the meeting's endorsement. He was scheduled to speak later in the day at a meeting in New Johnstown,[14] but was delayed in his desire to get away promptly when Jonas Jones again intervened.

Jones presented his own petition to the meeting. In it he praised the current administration for its good work on behalf of the province and concluded that there were no legitimate grievances to address. Gourlay was pressed for time. He could not expect the New Johnstown meeting to wait for him indefinitely, and Jones could conceivably hold the floor in a filibuster for hours. Gourlay was again forced to withdraw. He left Prescott with a confident Jones still speaking, urging the meeting to adopt his petition and not Gourlay's.

Gourlay anticipated further difficulties at New Johnstown. On his previous visit to the area, the books and pamphlets that he had brought with him and left for distribution had been publicly burned. Stopping at an inn on the road to New Johnstown to water his horse, he was accosted by another traveller who produced a Gourlay pamphlet and demanded to know if he was its author. Gourlay acknowledged he was, whereupon he was attacked by a dozen Tories. In the ensuing melee, Indian Grant, from Brockville, came to his aid[15], and Gourlay and his supporters managed to battle the Tories to a draw.

As the hostilities wound down, Gourlay's rhetoric wound up. The Tories retreated and Gourlay found an attentive audience which had gathered to witness the fray. Gourlay seized the opportunity and began to speak passionately to the crowd, explaining the political ills of Upper Canada. From the confines of the inn, an old Tory, His Worship Richard Duncan Fraser, a Brockville justice of the peace, listened to Gourlay's diatribe against the administration in shocked disbelief. Finally, he could stand no more. Coming out of the inn, he demanded that Gourlay stop spreading sedition and, when he refused,

---

14 New Johnstown became Cornwall, Ontario.
15 Milani, p. 153.

Fraser rode off to Brockville to obtain a warrant for his arrest. Gourlay was still in the area when Fraser, accompanied by a fellow justice of the peace and the Member of the Legislature for Grenville County, John MacDonnell, returned with the warrant and arrested Gourlay on a charge of sedition. Placed in the custody of a constable, Gourlay was then sent off for the Brockville Gaol.

As the party passed through Prescott, the crowd from the earlier Prescott meeting, by that time on its way home, was confronted by the sight of Gourlay in irons. A collection was immediately taken and Gourlay's bail was negotiated on the spot. Free again, but with no time now to get to New Johnstown, Gourlay spent the night in Prescott. It had been a busy day in the cause of reform.

The following morning, Gourlay travelled to the residence of Abraham Dayton, north of Brockville, to attend the township meeting for the Township of Elizabethtown and the county meeting for the County of Leeds. As in Prescott, the meeting did not proceed without controversy. The opposition Tory forces on this occasion were led by Colonel Levius Peters Sherwood, another member of the local Tory elite. Sherwood, like Jonas Jones, was a Tory lawyer from Brockville. Also like Jones, he argued that only the Legislative Assembly had the lawful authority to petition the sovereign. When asked, however, he could offer no legal authority for the proposition. Unlike Jones, recognizing that his forces were outnumbered, he withdrew, and allowed the election of delegates to proceed. The County of Leeds would send a full delegation to the provincial meeting scheduled for York.

As delegates across the province prepared for the convention at York, Administrator Smith and his principal advisors, Attorney-General John Beverley Robinson, Reverend John Strachan, and Solicitor-General Henry John Boulton, huddled in the provincial capital. In Boulton's opinion, ". . . the petition to the Prince Regent is I conceive a most dangerous publication and . . . is punishable as a libel."[16] The Attorney-General was even more specific. He advised the administrator that, in his opinion, the township meetings were, ". . . dangerous to this country, chiefly from their example, as they point out the mode by which popular movements on pretences less specious than the present, can be effected, and as we have no adequate military

---

16 Public Archives of Canada, UPPER CANADA SUNDRIES, Vol. 39, correspondence from Boulton to Smith dated June 15, 1818.

force in this Province . . . to check the tumults excited by artful and discontented demagogues."[17]

While Gourlay's meetings were distasteful and even dangerous, Robinson's legal opinion was that the township meetings and the provincial convention were not illegal. Gourlay could be prosecuted for sedition if his specific statements warranted prosecution. Robinson pointed out that charges were pending against Gourlay at both Kingston and Brockville for statements made by him during his tour through the eastern districts. The process itself, however, could not be stopped by legal means under any current legislation. The meetings would take place.

Gourlay's provincial convention, which he called the "Convention of Friends to Enquiry," took place as scheduled at York on July 6, 1818. Gourlay participated in the debates, but since he was not an elected delegate from any of the participating townships he voluntarily refrained from voting. As expected, the convention adopted the petition to the Prince Regent. Out of courtesy to the newly arrived lieutenant-governor, Sir Peregrine Maitland, it was decided to present the petition to him first and then see to its delivery to His Royal Highness. The delegates also petitioned Sir Peregrine to dissolve the Legislative Assembly, which did not, in their view, reflect the will of the people, and issue a writ for fresh elections.

The convention closed without fanfare. The whole thing had been rather anticlimactic. However, to the consternation of the administration, various townships and districts continued to hold meetings. For example, a regional "Lower Branch" meeting was held at Kingston with representatives from the Midland, Johnstown and Newcastle Districts. Given a taste of town hall democracy, it seemed that the citizens of Upper Canada were not prepared to abandon their opportunity to vent their dissatisfaction. The new administration of Lieutenant Governor Maitland was incensed at the continued affront to its authority.

In the late summer of 1818, the trial of Robert Gourlay for seditious libel took place before a Frontenac County jury at the court house in Kingston. Gourlay lacked formal legal training, but demonstrated a sound understanding of the legal principles involved while acting in his own defence. Even more importantly, Gourlay demonstrated a sound understanding of the attitudes of the jury.

---

17 Public Archives of Canada, UPPER CANADA SUNDRIES, Vol. 40, correspondence John Beverley Robinson to Smith dated June 29, 1818.

His address to the jury was nothing less than brilliant, at times mocking, at others downright insulting, but at all times effective. "Gentlemen," he began with a sneer, "I have no patience with the whole of this stuff – it is all infamous. It is a disgrace to the British government to have such a thing as this acting as Solicitor General," referring to Henry John Boulton, who was acting as Crown Counsel at the trial. Then, turning his attention to the Attorney General, John Beverley Robinson, he told the jury:

> Gentlemen, the Attorney General of this Province is but a stripling – the foster child of a certain cleric and political school master (Reverend John Strachan); and we cannot suppose him yet weaned from the influence of early established authority, to say nothing of those still more powerful influences to which virtue is exposed in such a nest of inequity as the capital of Upper Canada. It is well known how active the school master has been in every quarter trying to thwart my projects; and how virulent his pupils have become, because their master has not been able to accomplish his ends.[18]

Having drawn into question the motivation of the Crown in laying the charge against him, Gourlay turned to the substantive portion of his defence. He established that at all times he had simply been acting as an agent of the original committee at Niagara by drafting and distributing its pamphlets. Finally and effectively, he argued that, as a British subject, he had every right to do what he had done. "I flatly deny the charge of bad intention . . ." he argued. "(What) is now contended for is not my honour and my right: it is the honour and right of thousands of your fellow subjects."[19]

The jury was out for only half an hour, not quite long enough to brew and drink a pot of tea, before it formally returned to the court room to acquit Mr Gourlay.

Acquitted in Kingston, Gourlay still faced charges in Brockville. Jonas Jones, whose acquaintance he had already made at the Augusta Township meeting at Prescott just prior to his arrest, appeared as co-prosecutor for the Crown. Solicitor-General Henry John Boulton, still smarting from his defeat at the Kingston trial, joined Jones at the counsel table.

---

18 Milani, p. 171.
19 Ibid.

METROPOLITAN TORONTO REFERENCE LIBRARY, J.ROSS ROBERTSON COLLECTION T-15016

John Beverley Robinson, Attorney General of Upper Canada.

The indictment charged Gourlay with "diffusing discontents and jealousies raising tumults" in certain passages contained in his Third Address to the Resident Landowners of Upper Canada. In particular, the indictment referred to three specific portions of the address. First, Gourlay had written that he ". . . had little hope of satisfaction from the sitting of parliament, after perusing the Administrator's speech from the throne; and this little was entirely extinguished with the disgusting reply made to that speech by your Representatives." Secondly, his address contained the comment that it had been his fate, ". . . to rest here nearly two months, viewing at a distance the scene of folly and confusion." And finally, that Gourlay had written, ". . . the blessings of a social compact are running to waste. For three years the laws have been thwarted, and set aside by executive power; for three sessions have your legislators sat in Assembly, and given sanction to the monstrous, the hideous abuse."[20]

During the trial, Gourlay appealed to the jury's sense of history and common sense. He described, first of all, his reasons for visiting the province. He then told them why he felt it necessary to draft the three addresses. The elected Members of Parliament were nothing more than the servants of the people, he argued. His criticism of their action, or lack of action, was calculated to do nothing more than hold the elected and non-elected Members of Parliament accountable and responsive to the wishes of the people. He reminded the jurors that honest criticism of a defective system could not be equated with sedition; it was the right of every British subject to do what he had done and what he had written was not significantly different from common electioneering in England. Once more the jury agreed and Gourlay was again acquitted. His supporters were jubilant. The streets of Brockville rang with shouts of "Gourlay and Freedom," while the post road to Kingston was festooned with signs proclaiming "Gourlay Forever."[21]

The acquittals at Kingston and Brockville merely strengthened the resolve of the administration to silence the troublesome Scot once and for all. It appeared that the Gourlay meetings were becoming more popular than parliament itself but, unlike the Legislative Assembly, they were not subject to any control. Gourlay himself continued to travel the province agitating for reform and, in view of his recent successes in court, he seemed virtually immune from effective prosecution. Lieutenant-Governor Maitland, following discussions with Reverend Strachan, John Beverley Robinson, and others, came to the conclusion that new legislation was required to control the situation. In the throne speech opening the next session of the Assembly, Maitland urged that new legislation be passed declaring township meetings illegal.

The Assembly was cowed. Its members were concerned about angering the administration. That could lead to their individual economic disaster. In addition, many members were beginning to resent Gourlay's growing popularity and his stinging criticism of their role in the Assembly. As the first order of business of the new session

---

20 Ibid., p. 177, citing Statistical Account II, pp. 581-582.
21 Ibid., p. 177.

of the Assembly, Jonas Jones, then the Member for Grenville County, proposed legislation ". . . to prevent certain meetings within the Province." The legislation was subsequently passed by a vote of 13:1. Only the member from Lennox and Addington, William Covey, objected.

Gourlay treated the new legislation with contempt. He simply advised his followers to refer to the gatherings as "purse string meetings," as opposed to "township meetings." The meetings continued to be called by interested residents to urge the members of the Legislative Assembly not to surrender in the ongoing fight to control the finances of the province. It was apparent that still stronger action was necessary to silence Gourlay.

The administration found its remedy by invoking the Seditious Alien Act of 1804. This legislation had never been used against a British subject and, in fact, the majority legal opinion was that it could not be made to apply to Gourlay. However, Gourlay had briefly absented himself from the province to go to New York in order to collect mail from his wife. The administration seized upon this temporary absence and declared him to be a seditious alien. Invoking the Act of 1804, they ordered him out of the province on penalty of death.

In referring to the legislation and the order of banishment, Gourlay wrote with typical disdain: "That sir is applicable only to aliens. I am a roman (British subject). . ."[22] He allowed the deadline for his departure, January 1, 1819, to pass and refused to leave. On this occasion, Gourlay had miscalculated the resolve of his enemies. Within days, he was arrested, jailed, and held without bail to await the summer assizes.

Six months in an Upper Canadian dungeon during the winter months had a remarkable effect on the legal victor of Kingston and Brockville. Gone was the spring in his step that had carried him across British North America and half of the United States. Gone was the good health, the sparkling eyes, the wit, and the intense attitude. Gone was the sparkling oratory which had carried the day in his previous trials. In any event, the charge did not lend itself to flights of rhetoric. The issues framed for the jury were simple: Had Gourlay been ordered to leave the province and had he failed to go? The jury saw no alternative but to answer both questions in the affirmative. They did their duty and Gourlay was convicted.

Not wanting to create a martyr, the government offered to commute the death penalty provided that Gourlay leave Upper

---

22 Ibid., p. 186.

Canada and give his word of honour that he would never return. Beaten and disillusioned, Gourlay made the only practical decision in his life. He crossed the border into the United States, never to return.

Gourlay's brief sojourn in Upper Canada provided demonstrative evidence of the level of discontent lying just under the surface of Upper Canadian society. It also demonstrated the lengths to which the administration would go to silence its critics. With Gourlay finally silenced, the province returned to its prior complacency and the controlling Tory faction was free to tighten its grip on the province. It would be a false victory. The systemic grievances of the people, which were the real reasons for Gourlay's meteoric rise to popularity, remained as glowing coals of discontent. They would be fanned to burn anew, this time into actual rebellion, by another Scott, William Lyon Mackenzie.

CHAPTER VI
Early Events of the 1830s

*F*ROM THE PASSAGE of the Constitutional Act up to the campaign of 1830, elections in the Johnstown District had been relatively sedate affairs. Considering the demographics of the district, this was hardly surprising. The area was almost entirely rural and the core of the dominant cultural and social group remained the disbanded remnants of Jessup's Corps of Loyalist troops and their descendants. The people knew one another. They agreed on the major issues. The subsequent American and British immigrants had come in limited numbers and had been quickly integrated into the dominant political culture. Particular candidates for election might stress different approaches on specific issues, but there was a general consensus on matters of principle. The leading families recognized that they shared a common heritage and interest. They treated one another with respect, as gentlemen. They intermarried. They formed business alliances and partnerships. They were bound together into local compacts with extended ties to their economic equals across the province. Rivalry between the leading families for positions of power and prestige, coupled with the ever present attempt to influence political decisions to favour the family and its members, was often of more significance than substantive issues.

The number of seats allotted to the Johnstown District in the Legislative Assembly increased from time-to-time in accordance with increases in population and municipal status. After 1831, when Brockville became entitled to its own member, the district elected five members: two in Leeds, two in Grenville, and one in Brockville. Typically, the candidates for elective office were selected from the ranks of the established Loyalist families. A review of the successful candidates reveals few surprises. The wealthy Loyalists who had settled the waterfront along the St Lawrence River occasionally exchanged duties as Members of the Assembly for Leeds, Grenville, or Brockville.[1] Of the politically active families, the Buells and the Howards in Leeds County and the Wells family in Grenville were generally perceived as favouring the cause of Reform. A clear majority of the upper-class established Loyalist families and, in particular, the Sherwoods and the various Jones families opposed all significant reform. They were Tory in all facets of their lives.

To be a member of the Assembly could be a time-consuming and not particularly lucrative position. During the session of 1805, Peter Howard, then the member for Leeds, was obliged to spend sixty days in attendance at the legislature. Remuneration was not fixed beforehand, rather it was debated after the fact and established by majority vote of the justices of the peace in quarter session in the riding represented. The justices of Leeds County determined that Howard's attendance on behalf of the constituency, together with his transportation and living expenses, ought to be rewarded by payment of £30 sterling.[2]

Ordinarily, a single candidate selection meeting sufficed to nominate all potential candidates for election. One candidate would be advanced to represent each of the marginally different views of the various factions. The custom of the time was for all interested electors, regardless of their political orientation, to gather at various central locations around the riding to vet the credentials of the various individuals who had shown some interest in standing for election. The practice allowed would-be candidates to test the waters for local support prior to formally declaring their candidacy. While the potential candidates might take opposite positions on the issues of the day, there was a sufficient respect and commonality of interest amongst potential candidates and their supporters that non-partisan meetings commonly took place without incident.

The actual nomination of candidates took place on the hustings at the opening of the poll. The various persons who had decided to contest the election would attend at the hustings on the opening of the poll, where they were openly nominated and seconded by two of their supporters. Each nominated candidate would then mount the

---

1 A list of elected members of the Assembly for the Johnstown District is contained in Schedule D.
2 Lyons, p. 60, citing Book A, Court of Quarter Sessions for the County of Leeds.

platform and publicly accept the nomination in a speech to the assembled crowd.[3] At the conclusion of the nominations, voting by the public declaration of each elector from the hustings would commence. The poll remained open for a period of several days, usually a week.

The election of 1830 ushered in a new era in the political history of Leeds County. George IV had died on June 26, and his brother William IV had ascended the throne. In keeping with British constitutional practice, the accession of the new king required elections in Great Britain and in all colonial possessions around the world.

In the old Assembly, Leeds had been represented by two nominal reformers, William Buell, the editor of the Brockville *Recorder*, and Matthew Howard, of Elizabethtown. Both Buell and Howard were prepared to face the people again and assumed they would have no difficulty in being re-elected. It was anticipated that their opponents would be Tories from the leading families of old-stock Loyalists, perhaps some combination of Sherwoods or Jones.

In the usual course, an open, non-partisan nomination meeting was scheduled for September 18, 1830, in Brockville. Those potential candidates who wished to be considered for nomination would be afforded the opportunity to speak and receive an indication of their support in the community. The organizers of the meeting were unaware of the significance of the introduction of Ogle Robert Gowan into their community. It soon became apparent that, with Gowan's presence, the polite politics of the past was impossible.

Gowan had stepped off the boat from Ireland only one year before. In that year, he had inaugurated the Grand Orange Lodge of British North America with himself at its head. By the summer of 1830, there were over 3,000 new Irish immigrants in the Johnstown District, 2,000 of them in Leeds County and 1,000 in Grenville.[4] These Irish were too numerous to be simply absorbed into the existing population as were earlier immigrants. They constituted a distinctive group within the larger community. They looked to Gowan as one of their own and they trusted him as their means of obtaining access to political power. Gowan, in turn, looked to his Irish countrymen for support in his quest for personal political power.

---

3 The tradition continued in Leeds and Grenville, in modified form, into the 1990s. It was expected that each candidate would attend at the Returning Office on the last day open for nominations where he or she would be formally nominated by his or her supporters and actually make a speech. In the rest of Canada, of course, candidates simply file their nomination papers, as per the Election Act.

4 MacPherson, p. 107.

As the Brockville meeting was called to order, the Buell and Howard supporters attempted to gain control of the nomination process. Matthew Howard himself took the floor and moved that the meeting approve a slate of seventy-five delegates suggested by Andrew Norton Buell, his running mate's brother. The chosen delegates would discuss the relative merits of potential candidates and agree on who should stand in the upcoming election. The Tory faction was outraged at the temerity of Buell and Howard. They knew exactly what the purpose of the seventy-five pre-chosen delegates was to be. If allowed to control the candidate selection process, the Tories would be frozen out.

Jonas Jones, now twelve years older than when he had matched wits with Robert Gourlay, voiced the concerns of the establishment Loyalist Tories and demanded an opportunity to discuss the motion. The meeting quickly split into two factions: the Reformers who supported Buell and Howard and the traditional Loyalist Tories who were opposed. Gowan briefly considered his options. He lacked sufficient supporters to stand alone. He needed an alliance with one faction or the other. The Reformers would welcome his support, but the Reform slate was obviously filled. Gowan's candidacy as a Reformer would displace either Buell or Howard and was effectively blocked. The Reformers would not allow him to replace either of the incumbents. His moment of refection over, Gowan quickly allied himself with the established Tory families. Gowan became a Tory.

His support was not universally welcomed amongst his new political allies. The Irish were political upstarts, crude, foul-mouthed, and poor. As new arrivals, many of them did not as yet have title to their land and, without a proper deed, they could not vote. In the opinion of many of the established Tories, Gowan was hardly doing them a favour by bringing this rabble into the Tory camp.

Despite the split in the meeting, it was hoped that the two factions would be able to caucus quickly amongst themselves and then reunite once more to endorse all potential candidates, as they had in the past. It was only a formality for the Reform group to confirm their support for Buell and Howard. However, with the addition of Gowan and the Irish, the Tories were no longer a homogenous group. They could not agree on anything except to meet again one week later on September 25, 1830, to continue their discussions on who they wanted as their standard bearer in the coming election.

Gowan used the week to hold hastily arranged meetings in the back country of Elizabethtown, Burgess, and Elmsley Townships. The Elizabethtown meeting was held at Lamb's Pond,[5] in the heart of the new Irish settlements. Gowan needed the endorsement of this and the other meetings to demonstrate the level of his personal support to the established Tories when they met again at the end of the week. Gowan had carefully orchestrated the meeting. First, those in attendance were led to observe that, ". . . at least one third of the county (were) European and mostly Irish by birth."[6] It stood to reason that one of the candidates ought to be of Irish extraction. The meeting then passed a resolution previously drafted by Gowan and calculated to demonstrate that the Irish wanted one of their own, namely him, as their Tory candidate.

> That we have heretofore supported Mr. Jones and Mr. Sherwood, with cordiality and almost with unanimity, also we hope that the members of both these respected families will upon the present occasion, yield their pretensions to the long cherished feelings and wishes of so large a portion of their warmest supporters whose unanimous desire is to support Mr. Gowan at this time.[7]

The remaining meetings organized by Gowan in the heavily Irish areas of north Leeds passed similar resolutions.[8] There would be no doubt when the Tories resumed their discussions about the merits of the potential candidates on September 25, 1830, that Gowan enjoyed the near unanimous support of the Irish.

When the Tories met again in Brockville, Gowan presented himself as an obvious candidate. The repercussions of refusing his candidacy were obvious. The Tories had lost to Buell and Howard in the last election and if they were to be successful in the coming election, they needed the support of the Irish. To get that support, they were prepared to accept Gowan's candidacy. The old established Loyalist Tories selected Gowan and one of their own, Henry Sherwood, as their candidates.

The nomination of Buell and Howard by the Reformers was never in doubt. The reform-minded met in a separate meeting,

---

5 Lamb's Pond, a settlement on the Sixth Concession of the Township of Elizabethtown, was soon to be renamed New Dublin, indicative of the new Irish-majority population in the area.
6 MacPherson, p. 110.
7 Ibid.
8 BROCKVILLE RECORDER, October 12, 1830.

styling themselves the Independent Electors of Leeds and, following the usual speeches, the incumbents, Buell and Howard, were duly endorsed. The election in Leeds would be contested by two nominal Reformers, one old-line Tory, and the new boy, Ogle Robert Gowan.

In the province as a whole, the election of 1830 produced a victory for the lieutenant-governor, the status quo, and Toryism.[9] Out of the fifty-four seats in the Assembly, the Tories were successful in thirty-seven. In Leeds, however, Buell and Howard had carried the day for the Reformers. The final vote tabulation was: Buell 613, Howard 567, Gowan 543, and Sherwood 507.

Buell and Howard had been able to counter the general provincial trend away from Reform. Their election indicated that a majority of electors in the county were prepared to support the cause of moderate reform when it was presented to them by respected and competent candidates. Gowan's results were, however, significant. Even though he had lost the election, the newcomer had polled ahead of his established Tory running mate, Henry Sherwood, and come within twenty-four votes of defeating the incumbent, Matthew Howard. It was a clear demonstration of his political potential and the growing political strength of his Irish supporters.

In the County of Grenville, the successful candidates were Richard D. Fraser and Edward Jessup. Both were Tories from old, established Loyalist families. Jessup was the son of Colonel Edward Jessup, the Loyalist commander of the Loyal Rangers and founder of Prescott. However, he died within the year, necessitating a by-election. Fraser was a justice of the peace and Tory activist. It was Fraser who had charged Robert Gourlay with sedition years before. Their election followed the provincial trend in favour of Tories. That trend was accentuated by the election in Brockville of another establishment Loyalist Tory, Henry Jones. Of the five-man delegation of elected members to the Legislative Assembly from the various ridings within the Johnstown District, three were Tories from the old established Loyalist families, while two were on the side of Reform.

Among the many issues facing the new session of the Legislative Assembly was the question of town status for Brockville. The newly elected members of the Legislative Assembly representing Leeds, Grenville, and Brockville joined in the debate over the terms under which Brockville might become a separated town.

Agitation within the community for town-status had

---

9 Dunham, pp. 120 & 136.

commenced in August of 1830. Meetings had been held and petitions forwarded to the lieutenant-governor urging that Brockville be separated out of the Township of Elizabethtown and given independent status. Both the Tory and Reform factions agreed that Brockville ought to be incorporated as a separate town. They differed, however, on matters of principle concerning the manner in which the new town ought to be governed.

Their positions on the issues involved in the town status debates reveal a great deal about the competing political philosophies of the time, and the close connection between matters of principle and matters of family self-interest. The two principal families, the Buells and the Jones, differed in political philosophy. They also were at loggerheads on the practical concern of which family would benefit financially through the sale and development of land in the new town.

All agreed that if Brockville was to grow as a town, it ought to have a designated market. Both the Buell and Jones families saw the opportunity and each suggested that the new town market ought to be developed either on land that they owned or at least on land close to their own. The Buells owned land on the west side of town. The Jones' land was on the east side. The family that sold the land to form a town market stood to make a tidy profit. In addition to the actual price of the lot, a major development such as a new town market would substantially increase the value of land adjacent to it.

In 1808, William Buell had been successful in having the district court house built on his land. The personal advantages to him were obvious. Aside from the marginal profit involved in the sale of the land,[10] the establishment of the Court House had provided a nucleus around which the town had grown. Unless the market was similarly located on Buell land, the town centre might shift and focus on the new market.

The Buell and Jones families also differed on the theoretical issue of how the new town ought to be governed. The debate centred on two issues: should the election be based on a ward system or a town-wide vote and, secondly, should all members of the town administration be elected or should the effects of democracy be modified by having some members appointed.

---

10 Records of the Court of Quarter Sessions make provision for payment to Buell for his land on the following terms: "It is hereby ordered that so soon as William Buell Esq. shall have perfected the title of the land on which the Court House and Gaol in Elizabethtown is built, by signing and executing etc., such memorial or other instruments in writing as L. P. Sherwood and Hamilton Walker Esq. shall advise, that the Treasurer of the District shall pay to the said William Buell the sum of £20 currency consideration money for the land aforesaid." Record of Proceedings, November 10, 1808, Court of Quarter Sessions, Book A, p. 226, as cited in Lyons, p. 71.

The Buells were in favour of a form of direct democracy, whereby all members of the Board of Police of the new town would be elected by the people. They favoured a town-wide vote, similar to the county-wide vote for the Assembly, in which all members of the governing body would be elected. They were confident that in a town-wide vote they could do very well. The Jones and the Sherwoods, on the other hand, favoured a ward system and put forward a ward division that would concentrate Buell support in one ward and thereby increase the chance of electoral success for themselves in the remaining ward.

The Tories also wanted to modify the effects of democracy. They favoured an indirect scheme whereby four members of the Board of Police would be elected by the people. These four elected members would, in turn, appoint a fifth member. The five would then select their chairman or president.

Typically, these issues were not decided by debate within the proposed Town of Brockville, but by legislation passed by the Assembly, amended, as usual, by the Legislative Council and ultimately proclaimed in force by the lieutenant-governor. On the practical issue of where the new market ought to be located, the Jones' proposal carried the day. This was undoubtedly influenced more by the results of the past election, than with any consideration of town planning. Even though Buell and Howard sat in the Assembly, the Tories controlled it, and the members for Leeds were identified Reformers. The Jones family were known and respected Tories who were entitled to support in matters that directly affected their pocketbooks.

On the issue of governing the new town, the Legislative Assembly favoured the plan advanced by Buell, with the support of the Reform minority. A bill proposing the election of all five members of the Board of Police passed the Assembly and went to the Legislative Council for approval. The Council, however, refused to approve the legislation as it was seen as being dangerously democratic.

The debate in the Assembly began anew, but with a clear indication as to what would be acceptable to the Council and lieutenant-governor. With that in mind, the Assembly opted for the plan proposed by Jones, which would provide for the election of four members of the Board of Police for the new town. The four elected members would then appoint a fifth member and the five would then select their president. The Legislative Council and the lieutenant-governor accepted this revised proposal. Late in 1831, Brockville was afforded town status, with provision for an independent internal adminstration conducted by a five-member Board of Police.[11] Upper Canada had its first incorporated town.

As the new session of the Assembly began, pressure for reform began to build across the entire province. William Lyon Mackenzie, the red-headed, firebrand orator, and leader of the radical voices of Reform in the Assembly, emerged as the most spirited and vocal, if not the most reasoned, voice of reform. Joining him in the Assembly, following the election of 1830, were other more articulate Reformers, such as Robert Baldwin and Marshal Spring Bidwell. Baldwin in particular was beginning to work through the intellectual problems associated with the concepts of responsible government and colonial status.

At the opposite end of the political spectrum, Ogle Robert Gowan continued to organize his Orange Lodge into a fighting force of reaction. His force was dedicated to ultra-loyalism and was prepared to use old-world Irish political tactics in British North America.

With the battle of town status for Brockville behind them, the people of the Johnstown District turned their political attention to Grenville County.

Edward Jessup had died shortly after his election to the Assembly in 1830. His death necessitated the Grenville County by-election of 1831. As the planning for the by-election began, each of the three principal factions – the established Loyalist Tories, the Reformers, and the Gowan Irish – pondered the possible strategies of the others.

The Reform group naively continued to consider the possibility of some form of alliance with Gowan and the growing Irish population. The Irish, after all, were, by and large, subsistence farmers from the back townships and concessions. Their economic interest lay with the traditional Reform platform and not with anything proposed by the Tories. In some areas of the province, Orangemen had adopted Reform issues as their own. Gowan, however, had not. He was one of those politicians who recognized that in the battle for political support, an appeal to the emotions was invariably more successful than an appeal to the intellect. Support for existing institutions was simply too strong among his Irishmen to be challenged. Rather than advocate reform, Gowan followed his natural Protestant Irish inclinations and

---

11 MacPherson, p. 104.

William Lyon Mackenzie, the red-headed, firebrand orator and leader of the radical voices of Reform in the Assembly.

became the ultra-Loyalist. He would question the loyalty of the reformers and anyone else who advocated change and, when expedient to do so, the loyalty of the established Loyalist families as well.

Gowan had considered seeking the nomination as a Tory candidate in the Grenville by-election. He correctly assessed the situation, however, and concluded that the election was simply not winnable. The concentration of Orange supporters in Grenville County was not nearly as significant as it was in Leeds. He recognized that his political future lay in Leeds County and any outside activity must concentrate on solidifying his support within his own constituency. Following this strategy, Gowan chose not to run. He would devote his time to supporting the Tory candidate, Jonas Jones, the Brockville lawyer and member of the old Loyalist Tory establishment, and thereby solidify his relationship with the old Tory political network.

News of the by-election brought William Lyon Mackenzie to the area. To welcome him, the Reformers organized a public meeting at the Court House in Brockville. The Court House at the time was seen as a public meeting place and was often used for partisan political events, including frequent Tory meetings and Gowan's inaugural meeting of the Orange Lodge. Nonetheless, when the sheriff, Adiel Sherwood, learned of the purpose of the meeting, he denied the Reformers access to the building. The Sheriff gave no reasons for the decision and showed no concern for his apparent political bias. There would be no political meeting held in his Court House in which opinions antagonistic to his own were expressed. The Reformers were forced to relocate their meeting across the Court House Green to the Methodist Church.

In keeping with the standard political strategy of the time, Mackenzie wanted to use the meeting as a demonstration of popular support for the Reform position on several current issues. Mackenzie had a predetermined agenda. He sought a resolution from the meeting endorsing his Reform platform, which he could present to the Assembly and to the lieutenant-governor as evidence of popular support in the district. In view of the recent electoral success of William Buell and Matthew Howard, and their support for his position, Mackenzie allowed himself to assume that the meeting would be receptive to his ideas. It was, of course, the Reformers who had organized the meeting. Two of their own, Truelove Butler and

Samuel Pennock, had been pre-selected as chairmen. With these thoughts in mind, Mackenzie entered the hall on the arm of Andrew Norton Buell, William Buell's brother and chief political advisor, expecting a warm and friendly reception. To his consternation, he was met by Ogle Robert Gowan and an antagonistic stone wall of Orangemen.

Gowan's opposition to Mackenzie should have come as a surprise to no one. He was already assuming the role of the ultra-Loyalist. When word reached the Johnstown District that the Irish in the York County area were supportive of Mackenzie and his Reform views, Gowan had replied publicly:

> Oh how the heart sickens and the blood recoils at the idea that even one Irishman could be found who, false to his country, his religion and his God, has veered about and united with the Yankee junto of hypocrites, traitors and knaves who hold their seditious meetings at York, and fulminate from thence their poison through the province.[12]

The chairmen, Butler and Pennock, called the meeting to order. They welcomed Mackenzie to the district and called upon him to speak. In his usual flamboyant style, Mackenzie spoke at some length on the current difficulties facing the province. At the conclusion of his speech, Mackenzie proposed his resolution to the meeting. It was then that Gowan intervened. He obtained the floor by asking permission to speak to Mackenzie's resolution. Once he had the floor, Gowan spoke effectively and powerfully against the resolution while his Orange Lodge brothers urged him on.

At the conclusion of his remarks, he proposed an amendment to Mackenzie's resolution. The amendment praised the good work of the lieutenant-governor and made a meaningless mockery of Mackenzie's original resolution. The Reformers quickly counted the hall. It became obvious that in addition to his oratorical skills, Gowan had also out-organized the Reformers. There were more than enough Gowan supporters in the hall to guarantee that no Mackenzie resolution would pass. In an attempt to avoid the ignominy of having the purpose of the meeting subverted, the Reform chairmen quickly adjourned the meeting. The Orangemen were furious and the proceedings soon degenerated into a mass fist fight, with the Reformers and the Orangemen squaring off against one another,

---

12 Akenson, p. 176, citing Brockville *Gazette* November 10, 1831.

intent on determining who had the best brawlers as well as the best debaters.[13]

In the end, as Gowan had suspected and despite his best efforts to the contrary, it was the Reformers who were successful in the Grenville by-election. Hiram Norton, a Prescott resident who operated a stage coach line between Montreal and Prescott during the summer and to Kingston during the winter, was elected. However, Gowan did achieve his goals. He had been seen as supportive of the Tory candidate, he had enhanced his credentials, and, most importantly, he now held favours that he could recall when necessary.

Hiram Norton continued to sit in the Legislative Assembly as a Member for Grenville, first with the Tory, R. D. Fraser, and subsequently with a fellow reformer, William Benjamin Wells. Following the armed rebellions at the end of the decade, and the resultant persecution and suspicion directed at Reformers, Norton abandoned Upper Canada for the United States. He finally settled in Illinois where he made his fortune.[14]

Over time, the direction of Gowan's rhetoric began to fall into predetermined patterns. His trump was the loyalty card, which he played whenever necessary. He would praise his Irish followers by reminding them of their illustrious history in preserving the English monarch and the constitution in the old country. Only they understood the true dimension of loyalty and he had been honoured by them as their chosen leader. At the same time as he was developing his image as the defender of the monarchy and the constitution, he would cast aspersions on the loyalty of his opponents. There were virtually no similarities between the opinions and tactics of William Lyon Mackenzie and either William Buell or Matthew Howard. Nonetheless, Gowan successfully tarred them with the same brush. Even more surprising, Buell and Howard, quite naively, allowed him to do so.

Gowan also attacked Buell and Howard for ignoring the Irish and other settlers in the back concessions. Harkening back to Mackenzie's visit to the area, Gowan pointed out that Mackenzie had been induced by the local Reformers to ignore the Irish and hold all of his meetings in the old, established areas of the district. In this manner, Gowan hoped to isolate the Buell and Howard Reformers from what should have been their natural constituency and to solidify

---

13 MacPherson, p. 140; see also Akenson, p. 176.
14 Leavitt, p. 128.

his own ties in the back country. He did not mention that if the Reformers ever had the temerity to hold a meeting in the back woods Irish neighbourhoods of Leeds County with William Lyon Mackenzie as their honoured guest, hordes of shillelagh-swinging Orangemen would have been there to meet them.

Gowan also portrayed the Reformers as favouring the urban interests of the well-to-do and suggested that they were town dominated and unresponsive to the needs of the ordinary settler. This flew in the face of the Reformers' platform as the town vote naturally favoured the Tories. By attacking the rural base of Reform, Gowan hoped to leave the Reformers with no political base of support at all.

As the decade wore on, Gowan and his phalanx of Orangemen became a standard fixture at all political meetings. If Gowan thought that he had enough supporters to carry the day democratically, then the meeting would remain relatively peaceful. Gowan would speak then call for a vote on any contentious issue, confident of the outcome. However, whenever Gowan calculated that he lacked sufficient supporters to carry the day democratically, then his Orange bully boys, properly armed with their traditional shillelaghs, would go into action and disrupt the meeting so that no vote at all could be taken.

In 1832, the lieutenant-governor, Sir John Colborne, called upon the various communities within Upper Canada to organize immigrant societies to assist the growing tide of immigrants to integrate into society. Reformers across Upper Canada embarked upon a strategy of using these officially sanctioned meetings as forums to pass resolutions critical of the administration. The strategy had worked in the Counties of Lennox and Addington, where the two Reform members of the Assembly, Marshal Spring Bidwell and Peter Perry, had been able to control the meeting and obtain resolutions endorsing Reform policies. The Leeds County Reformers, led by the Buells, were determined to employ the same strategy.

They arranged a public meeting in Brockville on March 7, 1832. Gowan arrived at the head of a party of his Orangemen and immediately attempted to take control. He moved that the meeting endorse the policies of the lieutenant-governor, forcing the Reformers immediately into a defensive position. Andrew Norton Buell attempted to regain control by putting forward his own resolution critical of the policy of the lieutenant-governor's immigrant policy. The Orangemen roared, hissed, and howled like enraged banshees.

Their uproar successfully prevented any discussion of Buell's motion. The Reformers were forced to retreat from their own meeting. Outside the hall, they quickly regrouped in the cold spring air and, for what it was worth, hurriedly passed Buell's resolution.[15]

The following year in the Rear of Yonge, some fifteen miles north and west of Brockville, the violence escalated. The actions of the Orange bully boys crossed the threshold of acceptability and resulted in criminal charges for assault. Buell and Howard had again organized a public meeting to be held at the village of Farmersville on March 9, 1833. On this occasion, the Reformers were seeking expressions of gratitude for the Colonial Secretary, Lord Goderich, who had sent dispatches to the lieutenant-governor urging reform. They also wanted demonstrations of public support for resolutions criticizing the position of the established church and the deplorable state of public education.

Hearing of the meeting, Gowan decided that the issues and the location of the meeting invited a serious response. He instructed his Orangemen to meet a short distance from Farmersville and approach the Reform meeting ". . . in a grand procession with music and good shillelaghs."[16] The Orangemen at first attempted to take over the meeting by declaring that Colonel Fraser, the old Tory war-horse, should act as chairman. The Reformers demurred but, rather than fight, they withdrew to a new location to conduct their meeting. They had just appointed David Fairbairn as their chairman when the Orangemen, led by Gowan, came marching down the road, chanting, "Down with all opposition." Fairbairn, who had urged his group to "Stand your ground," was pulled off the barrel, that he was using as a podium, amid shouts of "down with him," and "there will be no meeting here today." He was dragged into the street where Gowan's Irishmen, armed with their Irish shillelaghs, beat him to such an extent that they broke two of his ribs.[17]

The Orangemen had gone too far. The principal assailants were brought to trial and the jury took a brief fifteen minutes – hardly long enough to agree on a foreman to announce the verdict – to find them

---

15 Macpherson, p. 118.
16 MacPherson, p. 121, sets out that the words referred to are taken from the actual handbill prepared by Gowan for the event.
17 BROCKVILLE RECORDER, August 16, 1833, sets out the particulars of the evidence at the trial in the matter of The King v. Edward Moles, John Jelly, W. C. Crofton, John Moles, William Niblock, John Bolton, Archibald McGillis, Robert Hare, John Stewart, Francis Gray; charged by indictment with riot and assault against David Fairbairn.

guilty. In passing sentence, the presiding judge noted that it was lamentable that the peace and tranquillity of the country had been broken:

> When assembled for political purposes those assembled should be particularly careful to prevent breaches of the peace . . . In a land of liberty like this, all should be protected in their rights . . . In this country there is no need for strife.[18]

William Buell, in his capacity as the editor of the *Recorder*, recognized that those who had ended up in the prisoner's dock were merely bit players in a production orchestrated by Ogle Robert Gowan. "Since a wily and unprincipled individual came to reside amongst us," wrote Buell referring to Gowan, "that under the guise of loyalty (although in fact void of the most essential requisites of it) seemed to have impressed a certain party with the idea that they might be permitted to abuse and assault their fellow subjects with impunity."[19]

When Buell and Howard attempted to reschedule the meeting in Brockville for March 16, 1833, the president of the Board of Police, Daniel Jones, who had been appointed the previous year with Buell's consent and encouragement, showed that the political blood in Tory veins was thicker than the water of fairness. Hearing of the planned meeting, Jones wrote a polite note to Buell. "In consequence of the present highly exited state of the public mind . . ." Jones recommended, "the indefinite postponement of the county meeting advertised for next Saturday."[20]

While the President of Brockville's Board of Police was reluctant to allow a Reform meeting within the confines of Brockville, he had no qualms concerning a combined Tory and Orange rally held on the same day. Gowan and his Orangemen paraded to the Court House Green in front of the district court house with fife and drums where they were lauded in speaches by old line Tories – such as David Jones, his cousin Charles Jones, and Henry Sherwood. The meeting concluded with Gowan's response, whereupon the orators were carried around town on Orange shoulders in a lasting demonstration of the now firm Tory alliance.

Gowan and the Irish were clearly in the Tory camp. Gowan and his Orangemen, however, were Tories who marched to the beat of their own drum. That Orange drum brought a degree of violence and

---

18 BROCKVILLE RECORDER, August 23, 1833.
19 Ibid.
20 MacPherson, p. 122.

intimidation to the area that had previously been unheard of. The issue was not whether Gowan would support the Tory cause, but whether he could control the party. The Loyalist Tories from the old establishment assumed that these backwoods Irish immigrants would know their place and do what they were told. But all political alliances carry a price and, in the municipal election of 1833, the Loyalist Tories began to realize that the price of Orange support would be expensive indeed.

There had been sporadic outbursts of violence associated with municipal politics in the past. The violence invariably involved individuals closely associated with Ogle Robert Gowan and, in particular, James Gray, a Gowan henchman.

While the municipal election of 1831 was pending, Gray had assaulted W. H. Denaut in the streets of Brockville. Denault sued for damages and a civil jury found in his favour and awarded him £3 sterling.[21] Shortly after, during the summer of 1831, forty or fifty men led by James Gray, E. J. Hubbel, and Ormond Jones had attacked the residence of Billa Flint, a Brockville merchant, who at the time was exhibiting reformist tendencies. The attack again resulted in a successful civil suit and a jury award of £200 sterling against all three named defendants.[22]

Despite their general bully-boy tactics, Gowan and the Orangemen had never openly attacked a member of the old Tory establishment of Brockville. The elections for municipal office had been largely gentlemanly and relatively pedestrian in nature. In the Police Board elections of 1832, the east ward had predictably elected two Tories, Jonas Jones and Henry Sherwood. Equally predictable, the west ward had elected two Reformers, Samuel Pennock and John Murphy. The elected members of the board were then called upon to elect the fifth member and their president. In keeping with the Loyalist tradition of orderly compromise, the Tories and the Reformers settled their political differences and quietly agreed on an acceptable candidate.

Initially, Andrew Norton Buell, a well-known Reformer, had indicated a desire for the position. Similarly, Alexander Morris, an old-line Tory, had been quietly politicking among Tories for the presidency. In the end, however, Jones and Sherwood nominated Daniel Jones who may have been a Tory, but who was, at least at that

---

21 BROCKVILLE RECORDER, August 16, 1833.
22 BROCKVILLE RECORDER, August 23, 1833.

time, perceived as non-partisan and deserving of respect. The two Reformers accepted the nomination in a spirit of co-operation that they soon came to realize was misplaced.

Gowan entered the fray the following year. It was anticipated that the Reformers would run another strong campaign in the west ward of Brockville. It was also anticipated that if they were re-elected, they would never consent to another Tory being the fifth member and president of the Board of Police. Daniel Jones, the incumbent, had demonstrated during his term in office that a Tory could not be trusted. The Reformers had come reluctantly to that conclusion when they had wanted to reschedule the Farmersville meeting and Jones had frozen them out.

Gowan's strategy was to fight the Reformers at the ward level. If he could prevent them from electing police board members in the Buell-dominated west ward of Brockville, then they would be completely frozen out of local politics. Gowan, together with R. D. Fraser, attended upon the magistrates of Brockville and explained to the largely Tory law officers that violence was anticipated on the hustings in the upcoming election. The magistrates agreed with Gowan's suggestion of deputizing a group of Gowan-led Orangemen as special constables in order to maintain the peace.

As the voting commenced, Gowan's drunken Orangemen, cloaked with the authority of their appointments as special constables, surrounded the west-ward hustings. Ostensibly, their function was to intervene in the event of irregularities to restore order. In practice, they were the irregularity. Their real function was to impede voting by known Reform supporters. When Charles Jones, Jonas Jones' brother and a leading Tory in his own right, arrived to vote, he was shocked to find himself jostled by a bunch of drunken Irish Orangemen. The officially sanctioned hooliganism of the special constables so enraged Jones that he mounted the hustings and declared his support for the Reform incumbents, Pennock and Murphy. With that public pronouncement of Tory support, the Reformers were handily returned.

The Orangemen were outraged. They had been obliged to stand by and watch the two Reformers win the election. As the evening wore on and the whisky barrels emptied, Gowan's Irish Orangemen could no longer stand the insult. Their honour demanded action. That pompous ass Charles Jones had cost two honourable gentlemen

– friends of Ogle Robert Gowan – an election. Jones was supposed to be on their side. This was treason. In a drunken, window-smashing riot, they attacked the Brockville residence of Charles Jones and demonstrated that even the old Loyalist Tories from the best families were not immune from retaliation.

CHAPTER VII
From Political Confrontation to Mayhem

$\mathcal{U}$PPER CANADIAN REFORMERS prepared for the general election of 1834 with a sense of optimism. The Tories, who had dominated the House of Assembly since the election of 1830, had lost much of their popularity. Throughout the last term of parliament, William Lyon Mackenzie had cast himself as a Scottish thistle under the saddle of the Tory majority. He had advanced motion after motion in the Assembly demanding enquiries into various abuses while, at the same time, castigating the administration and its Tory supporters in his newspaper. The war of words had escalated, until the Tory-dominated Assembly determined that it would stand no more. The final straw came in December of 1831. Mackenzie, in an article in his *Colonial Advocate* had written, "Our representative body has degenerated into a sycophant office for registering the decrees of as mean and mercenary an executive as ever was given as a punishment for the sins of any part of North America."[1] On being presented with Mackenzie's latest insult, the Tory majority voted to expel him from the House of Assembly.

In the ensuing by-election, the electors of York returned Mackenzie to the Assembly with only one dissenting vote. He arrived back at the legislature in triumph. To celebrate his victory, his supporters formed a parade and carried Mackenzie to the Assembly on their shoulders. Over the next three years, the Tory-dominated Assembly voted to expel Mackenzie four more times, only to have him returned on each occasion by his loyal constituents in York.

The Reform cause benefited greatly from the publicity afforded to Mackenzie as a result of the actions of the Tories in the Assembly.

---

1 Dunham, p. 127.

The Brockville *Recorder*, along with many other reform-minded papers, copied Mackenzie's newspaper editorials and speeches verbatim. Across the province, his repeated expulsion from the House of Assembly was seen not just as an indignity against him, but as a blow to the constitutional rights of the electors of York, and of all the people of Upper Canada. As freeholders in a British colony, it was universally accepted that the people had an absolute right to elect the representative of their choice. By refusing to accept Mackenzie as that choice, the Tories were portrayed as the arrogant opponents of the will of the people. Mackenzie's expulsion became a symbol of Tory arrogance, which corresponded with the substance of all other Reform complaints.

By the time of the 1834 election, Reformers around the province had reason to hope that the next Assembly would see a marked increase in their numbers, and in the Johnstown District the prospects for the Reform cause appeared excellent.

In Grenville County, the 1830 election had resulted in a clear Tory victory with the return of Richard D. Fraser and Edward Jessup, but, in the by-election of 1831 following Jessup's death, the growing strength of Reform had become apparent with the election of Hiram Norton. He had campaigned openly as a Reform supporter and the electors of Grenville County had enthusiastically sent him off to the Assembly as their representative. It came as a jolting shock to his Reformer supporters two years later when Norton announced that he would not stand for re-election.

In early January of 1834, the Brockville *Recorder* noted, "Mr. Norton opened the way to a liberal representation of Grenville, which we trust will henceforth be travelled by none but the true friends of the people." The newspaper went on to express the fear that, "his declining to be a candidate . . . will undoubtedly give the tories an opportunity of re-action, which may prove fatal to reform."[2] In the end, Norton reconsidered his position and stood as a Reform candidate along with William B. Wells. The decision did not come easily and the path to the nomination was long and convoluted.

The Reformers in Grenville County held township meetings in much the same way as their counterparts in Leeds. The Reform movement in the county had been steadily growing in strength and, by 1833, Reform was sufficiently respectable that in some municipalities Reform supporters controlled the local council.

---

2 BROCKVILLE RECORDER, January 10, 1834.

In early January of 1834, the council for the Township of Augusta, the largest township in the county, passed an all-but-unanimous resolution – there was one dissident member who "gloried in being alone" – which found, ". . . highly reprobate the arbitrary and unconstitutional conduct of the majority of the present House of Assembly in their repeated expulsions of the member for York . . ."[3] They then appointed a township committee, to be headed by William B. Wells,[4] the young Prescott lawyer who had articled with Marshall Spring Bidwell, to nominate two fit persons as candidates in the upcoming election.

Wells scheduled a meeting with representatives of the other townships for the first Saturday in February at Theodorus Dety's Inn at Prescott. To prepare for the Dety's Inn meeting, Reformers in each of the townships held their own meetings. In the inns and taverns across Grenville County, they cheered for Reform and William Lyon Mackenzie, thanked Hiram Norton for his actions on their behalf, cursed the Tory majority in the Assembly, and elected their local committeemen. The Brockville *Recorder* was hopeful enough to declare, ". . . that from the committees chosen a death blow has been given to the representation of that county in the next parliament by ill-liberals."[5]

The Dety's Inn meeting of Saturday, February 8, 1834, was the first county-wide Reform meeting ever held in Grenville County. Following the usual spate of nominations and speeches, and a decision to join with the Leeds Reformers in a District-wide convention later in the month, the delegates voted to support Hiram Norton and Thomas Buck as the Reform candidates. Of the potential candidates, W. B. Wells tied Mahlon Beach with twenty supporters, while Buck had thirty-four and Norton sixty votes. It had been a fairly decisive victory.[6]

Buck's nomination, however, was not without controversy. He was accused of having Orange sympathies, and it was alleged that he had refused to hire Roman Catholics for work on the Rideau Canal. The accusations were of sufficient concern that Buck responded publicly, denying that he had ever been an Orangeman and pointing out that his chief foreman was a Roman Catholic.[7] His political popularity was never put to the test. Buck died unexpectedly in the

---

3 A report of the meeting is found in the BROCKVILLE RECORDER, January 10, 1834, under the heading, "Well Done Grenville."
4 Infra., p. 58, ff.
5 BROCKVILLE RECORDER, January, 1834.
6 GRENVILLE GAZETTE, February 11, 1834.
7 BROCKVILLE RECORDER, March 7, 1834.

late spring, and the Reformers of Grenville were once more without a candidate.

A second Reform nomination meeting was called for Prescott on September 19, 1834, to seek a replacement for Thomas Buck. By this time, the lieutenant-governor had dissolved the Assembly and issued the writ for the election. The Reformers had no time to waste. The meeting, however, began with more bad news. The chairman, John R. Christie, read a letter from Hiram Norton, who was acquiring a fresh set of cold feet. In his letter, Norton indicated that he would not be upset if he was relieved of his responsibility as a candidate. Norton was involved in various business enterprises and was concerned that he would not be able to represent the county, or the cause of Reform, in the manner that he felt it deserved. The meeting accepted his correspondence as notice of Norton's resignation. Norton's supporters were outraged. They had not interpreted the letter as notice of resignation. They bolted the meeting declaring that they would persuade Norton to run with or without the endorsement of the meeting. The meeting then proceeded to nominate two fresh candidates – William B. Wells and an entirely new candidate, Philemon Pennock.

When news of the results of the second meeting reached the shops, mills, and taverns of Grenville County, there was more dissention. Several townships declared that they had not been represented at the meeting and labelled the entire procedure as undemocratic. Another meeting was organized for September 19, 1834, at which time the candidacies of Wells and Alexander McMillan were endorsed. This group also demanded that the poll for the county be returned to Prescott from the village of Kemptville, where the lieutenant-governor had decreed the voting would take place.

With the polling to commence on October 6, 1834, time was running out on the Grenville reformers. The election was almost upon them and they still could not agree on two candidates to support. In yet another meeting, the Reformers of the northern townships met and demanded a candidate from the back country to represent their interests. This group decided to support Hiram Norton and Mahlon Beach.

When the poll opened in Kemptville, six candidates answered the returning officer's call for nominations. On the Reform side, Hiram Norton, William B. Wells, Alexander McMillan, and

Philemon Pennock were all duly nominated. Prior to the commencement of voting, Pennock resigned and urged all who would have voted for him to support Hiram Norton. The Reform vote might split, but now it would only be split in three. For the Tories, Richard Duncan Fraser and Ziba Phillips initially answered the call, but Fraser withdrew in favour of Phillips prior to the commencement of polling. Then, late in the day, Phillips withdrew in favour of McMillan. There was now no opposition to a Reform victory. The issue was which two of the three reform-minded candidates would represent the county in the Assembly.

In the end, Hiram Norton led the poll with 474 supporters. The young Prescott lawyer, William Benjamin Wells, was elected to join him in the Legislative Assembly, with 432 supporters. Alexander McMillan was a distant third with 250 votes.[8] It was a sweep of the county for the forces of Reform who were pledged to:

> . . . oppose all unnecessary taxes and advocate economy, retrenchment and prudence in the public expenditures, to seek for the legislature the control of all the public revenues of the province, to promote a system of general Education easy of access, and free from sectarian and party influence, to vote for the sale of the clergy reserves and application of the funds to the purpose of Education and internal improvements,to seek for equal civil and religious rights and privileges to all classes . . . (and) to support a law for voting by ballot.[9]

In the County of Leeds, the Reform candidates, Matthew Howard and William Buell, had the benefit of incumbency. The Tories and, in particular, Gowan had sniped at their record, alleging that they were "do nothing" Assemblymen who had neither accomplished anything of note for the county nor distinguished themselves in debate. They further argued that the two Reformers were Brockville-based to such an extent that they ignored completely the needs of the small farmers and settlers in the back country.[10] Despite this criticism, given the general political trend and their past electoral success, Buell and Howard were strongly favoured to carry the county for Reform once more. Gowan, the Orange Lodge, and the Tories were determined not to give them the chance.

---

8 BROCKVILLE RECORDER, October 10, 1834.
9 BROCKVILLE RECORDER, September 26, 1834.
10 MacPherson, p. 124.

Despite Gowan's alliance with the traditional Tories in the campaign of 1830, some of the Buell Reformers continued to consider the possibility of their own alliance with him and his Irish supporters. Each pronouncement by Gowan was analyzed for evidence that he was supportive of Reform. Andrew Norton Buell, always the none-too-practical political schemer, noted in his regular correspondence to his brother William:

> I see Gowan has condemned the Assembly for their conduct towards him (William Lyon Mackenzie). Gowan seems coming round to the liberal side and perhaps, with a little management, might be brought fully over. He has a letter in his last Antidote not unworthy of perusal. It professes to be written by a Canadian and is addressed to the Canadians of Leeds, but I suspect is written by himself. As usual Gowan is praised and is sure of being elected. What would you think of a union between the Canadians and Irish and allowing Gowan to go in at the next Election under strong pledges? Might it not allay the bitter feelings now existing between them and tend to draw them to support the cause of reform.[11]

Buell misread Gowan's intentions entirely. There was no prospect of his becoming a Reform supporter. Further, the concept of Gowan honouring any pledge given to Reformers was even more ludicrous. Finally, the correspondence shows that the Buells, or at least A. N. Buell, were prepared to abandon their oldest political friend and ally, Matthew P. Howard, for a transient political gain.

While Buell mused about the possibility of an alliance with him, Gowan strove to solidify his ties to the old Tory establishment. By 1832, Gowan was working closely with Charles Jones and other highly placed, traditional Tories. He and Jones were orchestrating public meetings in order to produce prearranged resolutions. In preparation of one such meeting, Gowan wrote to his new ally:

> When I last had the pleasure to meet yourself with Jonas Jones, we agreed to draw up some resolutions for the intended Public Meeting, in compliance with which I have hastily put my ideas on paper . . . You will perceive that I intend you should be called to the Chair, I have also taken the liberty to write across each resolution, some persons

---

11 Canadian Public Archives, WILLIAM BUELL PAPERS, MG24 B75, letter of Andrew Norton Buell to William Buell, dated December 12, 1833.

who might probably move them. The names of the committee I have written without much consideration, and they, no doubt, would require very considerable alteration.[12]

In the free-wheeling world of shifting political alliances, it was apparent that Gowan was solidly in the Tory camp.

Initially the Loyalist Tories, perhaps as a result of their arrogance, were confident that they would control the Irish. They naively thought that Gowan would know his place, do their bidding, and deliver the Irish vote when called upon to do so. Gowan had no intention of playing any subservient role. If there was to be an alliance, he was determined to control it. Gowan had worked assiduously in developing the Orange Lodge as his base of political support. He was the undisputed champion of the growing block of new Irish settlers with a well-deserved reputation for service and ability.

Obtaining a Crown patent for their land was a universal problem experienced by all owners of small farms in the district. Gowan put together an association of friends, cronies, and Orange associates, which he put at the disposal of the immigrant community, to work through the bureaucracy at York. This was no small feat and correspondence from Gowan to his brother, James, points out some of the difficulties involved:

> My object in writing to you at present is to ascertain from you if you could do for me the land business which otherwise might require my attendance in Toronto . . .

> There are many good loyal old country people in this part, who would support me, if they had their deeds, and a great many of them are entitled to their deeds, and only need some friend, who would take the trouble to produce them for them and I think it a pity to leave them without their titles . . .

> There is some trouble in procuring a deed. In the first place I will have to send the location tickets and settlement duties certificate; these you will have to take to Radenhurst (an official in the Surveyor General's office) who will file them and give you a description, which you can then take to the Attorney General's office, where you can obtain a fiat, which you take to Mr. Cameron's office (the Provincial

---

12 Public Archives of Canada, CHARLES JONES PAPERS, MG24-B7, letter from Ogle R. Gowan to Charles Jones dated July 28, 1832.

Secretary) where the deed is engrossed and the great seal affixed. If you mention to Mr. Cameron that the deed is for me, I think he will send it over to the government house and get his excellency's signature for you. Lastly you take it to the attorney general whose signature will complete the deed. There is no charge for all of this . . . and at any time you may want to make a search in the surveyor general's office, if you mention to Mr. Thornhill it is for me, he will do it for you, free of charge. Also, if you should have business at Mr. Baine's office (Secretary to the Clergy Corporation) if you tell Mr Baines it is for me, he will do anything in his power for you.[13]

Gowan's ability to obtain a Crown grant and other benefits from government increased his credibility with his constituency. The actual production of a valid Crown grant assisted not only the settler who received it, but Gowan as well, since land ownership was one of the criteria for the franchise. By obtaining a deed for his supporters, Gowan was ensuring their eligibility as voters.

Ogle Robert Gowan had arrived in Upper Canada in 1829 as a political neophyte. Beginning with no political support whatsoever, he had studiously developed a political base among his fellow Protestant Irishmen. In planning his first political campaign in 1830, Gowan had recognized the need for a traditional Loyalist Tory as a running mate – someone of local stature to add credibility to his own candidacy. In the intervening four years, his own organizational strength had matured to such an extent that he no longer needed to legitimize his candidacy by including anyone from the old Loyalist group. On the contrary, if he could develop a Tory campaign ticket in which he alone represented the local area, it would ensure his primacy in the county. The time had come, from Gowan's point of view, to elbow the old Loyalists aside. He devised a strategy that would, in one stroke, elevate his own status within the local community, diminish the power of the Tory establishment, and give him direct access to the government itself. Gowan wanted the newly appointed attorney-general, Robert S. Jameson, who had just been sent out to Upper Canada by the Colonial Office, as his running mate.

It is not clear when Gowan decided to court Jameson as his running mate. It is clear that it was always his intention to contest the

---

13 Akenson, p. 172, citing Archives of Ontario, GOWAN PAPERS, letter from Gowan to his brother, James Gowan, dated November 20, 1835. See also MacPherson, p. 125.

election of 1834, and by the spring of that year it was clear that he did not want a local Tory to share the campaign ticket with him. On March 14, 1834, one of many Tory-organized, but supposed public political meetings, was held at the village of Beverley. The purpose of the meeting was to determine who ought to be endorsed as candidates for the approaching election, but Gowan's friends had organized the meeting to ensure that he was endorsed as the popular choice.

To demonstrate the supposed non-partisan nature of the meeting, it was first moved that the meeting endorse the candidacies of William Buell and Matthew Howard. It came as no surprise that this motion was noisily defeated. Only Levi Soper, a notorious Reformer who attended the meeting as a mischief-maker, endorsed the resolution. It was then moved that Ogle Robert Gowan be endorsed as a candidate. The meeting heartily endorsed Gowan's candidacy, with Levi Soper again registering his dissent in a lonely but enthusiastic manner.

When it came to the nomination of the second candidate, Soper again intervened and seconded a motion put forward by a fellow Reformer, James Phillips, endorsing the candidacy of Gowan, but only as William Buell's running mate. Again the resolution was defeated. Daniel Jones and George Crawford, both well-known Tories, were then suggested as potential second candidates on the Tory slate, at which point Gowan intervened and suggested that it was premature to endorse a second candidate. He moved that the meeting adjourn leaving himself as the only endorsed candidate.[14]

Gowan's reason for not wanting a local running mate soon became apparent. At a further meeting of his supporters, who now called themselves the Constitutional Committee, held on April 12, 1834, Gowan obtained a resolution urging the attorney-general to stand for election with Gowan in the County of Leeds.[15] Armed with the resolution, Gowan travelled to York for a personal meeting with the young Mr Jameson. Following a series of personal meetings, he obtained an undertaking from Robert Jameson to stand for election in Leeds County. Jameson, obviously flattered by the attention, wrote to Gowan's chief organizer, Joseph K. Hartwell, who had chaired the meeting of the Constitutional Committee, which had urged him to stand.

---

14 BROCKVILLE RECORDER, March 14, 1834.
15 Public Archives of Canada, CHARLES JONES PAPERS, MG24 B7, letter from Robert S. Jameson to Joseph K. Hartwell, dated April 23, 1834.

METROPOLITAN TORONTO REFERENCE LIBRARY

Robert Jameson, the newly appointed Attorney General for Upper Canada, was persuaded to join Gowan as a Tory candidate in Leeds County.

It has been my earnest wish, if possible, to confine myself to the function of my office only: but though this feeling might restrain me from offering myself as a representative of the people, I should ill discharge my duty to the country I am bound to serve, if any selfish views to my own private peace should deter me from devoting myself with all my heart to the service of that country and its constituents when invited to do so by so highly respectable a portion of the community as the Constitutional Committee of the County of Leeds,[16]

he wrote shortly after Gowan left him.

At the Tory nomination meeting, the old Loyalist faction could do nothing but acquiesce in the inevitable victory of Gowan and Jameson. Daniel Jones, the only other potential candidate, withdrew, leaving Ogle Robert Gowan and Robert S. Jameson as the acclaimed Tory candidates for the coming election. The old Loyalist elite had been frozen out of their own party.

Gowan had the running mate of his choice to attack the incumbents, Buell and Howard. His attention now shifted to tactical considerations of how the election itself ought to be fought. The lieutenant-governor had absolute discretion in selecting the number and location of polls in each riding. On being advised by his Attorney-General of the situation in Leeds, His Excellency, Sir John Colborne, decreed that the entire county would vote at a single poll to be located in the village of Beverley.

The poll site was a hotbed of Orangism – Gowan's supporters – and the bailiwick of Gowan's Orange Lodge Lieutenant for north Leeds, Justice of the Peace, Joseph K. Hartwell. Buell and Howard's support was in Brockville and along the front concessions. It would be a long walk or wagon ride to the Beverley hustings for any Reform supporter who wanted to vote. To compound the advantage to Gowan and Jameson, the lieutenant-governor appointed the sheriff for the district, that arch Tory from an old Loyalist family, Adiel Sherwood, as the Returning Officer. At every turn, the administration had tipped the scales in favour of the Tory candidates. The pieces of the puzzle were coming together quite nicely for Gowan.

There was never any serious doubt that William Buell and Matthew Howard would again be called upon to represent the

---

16 Ibid. In addition, the complete exchange of correspondence was published in the BROCKVILLE RECORDER.

NATIONAL ARCHIVES OF CANADA, C-3506

Travelling to the Beverley poll in style.

Reformers of Leeds County. A group of reform supporters calling themselves the Friends of Reform and Liberal Measures organized a meeting for each township, all to be held on January 25, 1834. With only a few local variations, each township meeting passed a series of identical resolutions. As a first order of business, the Reformers in each township approved ". . . of the political course pursued by our worthy representatives, William Buell and Matthew M. Howard, and the minority of the present House of Assembly."[17] Many townships then condemned the Tory majority in the House of Assembly for its repeated actions against William Lyon Mackenzie. Only the Township of Kitley was remotely critical of Mackenzie. The Kitley Reformers resolved ". . . that some of the policy, and much of the spirit and language of William Lyon Mackenzie, is unbecoming, and merits reprehension, yet the conduct of the majority of the present parliament in relation to him is vindictive and illegal."[18] All of the township meetings resolved that a delegation of their members ought to attend the convention being organized for the county.

These committees provide a preview of some of those who got swept up in the winds of rebellion. James Phillips, who was killed with a gun in his hands at the Battle of the Windmill in 1839, was elected as a delegate for the Township of Bastard and Rear of Young. So was

17 BROCKVILLE RECORDER, January 31, 1834, contains a report on the meeting held in the Township of Elmsley.
18 Ibid., Report on the meeting held in the Township of Kitley.

Levi Chipman, who was taken prisoner along with his brother at the same battle.

Buell was obviously content with the campaign organization as in an editorial in the Brockville *Recorder*, he wrote, "The committeemen chosen we believe are, with a few exceptions, liberals of the rightstamp . . ."[19]

The Leeds County convention of the Friends of Reform and Liberal Measures met as scheduled in Brockville at the residence of David Mair on February 5, 1834. The numbers attending required a larger hall and the meeting actually convened in the large frame building of Billa Flint, nearby. The meeting began with a prayer for racial harmony. The Reformers then offered their assurances to the Irish community that the cause of Reform would welcome its participation, before moving to the nomination of Reform candidates in the upcoming election. A total of eight people were suggested as potential candidates. A few, including Jonas Jones, were obvious Tories and not even present, but their nomination as potential candidates allowed the meeting to appear non-partisan. Their rejection also provided Buell with the opportunity to point out in his newspaper that the meeting considered them unacceptable. To no one's surprise, in the end, William Buell and Matthew Howard were overwhelmingly endorsed as the Reform candidates.[20]

The tone of the actual election in Leeds County was set early. The hustings had been erected in the village of Beverley and the week-long election commenced on October 6, 1834. At the opening of the poll, the returning officer, Adiel Sherwood, called for the nomination of candidates. Buell, Howard, Jameson, Gowan, and Richard Gray were all duly nominated. They were then invited onto the hustings to accept their nominations and speak to the electors.

In accepting the nominations, Buell and Howard spoke first. Jameson spoke next. Mounting the hustings, he told the crowd that he had always been a Reformer. He then reminded the crowd that as the Attorney-General, he had a great deal of influence with the government. He implied that his influence could be employed either for the benefit or detriment of the area. He contrasted his capacity to assist the county with Buell and Howard's apparent lack of activity as the incumbent representatives of the area. He castigated the Reformers for their lack of effort in obtaining funds for the

19 Ibid. The quote is from Buell's editorial.
20 BROCKVILLE RECORDER, February 21, 1834.

improvement of the Gananoque River system. In his view, this was unfortunate since development of the Gananoque River as a canal would open a means of transport to the hinterland of the county.[21]

Ogle Robert Gowan was next. In typical fashion, his acceptance speech focused on the emotions of his supporters, and he successfully excited the passions of the Irish against all of their traditional enemies.

On a point of order, at the conclusion of the speeches, Buell was afforded the right of reply to the allegations that had been made against him in Jameson's speech. He attempted to speak, but Gowan's rhetoric had wound up the crowd to such an extent that they would have none of it. The Tory-dominated crowd, gathered around the base of the hustings, shouted Buell down each time he attempted to speak.

As Buell ceded the floor of the hustings, the poll was declared open for voting and Gowan's Orangemen set to work in earnest. As suspected Reform supporters approached the hustings, the Tory scrutineers blocked the entrance and began to harass and intimidate them with exhaustive questioning as to their eligibility. When it became apparent that this harassment would not dissuade Reform voters, Gowan's men increased the pressure. Buell and Howard supporters, intent on voting, were surrounded, crowded up against the hustings, punched, poked, and occasionally stabbed with penknives and hatpins. In a final, humiliating manoeuvre, Orangemen would encircle the suspected Reform voter, grab his underwear and hoist the poor man's pantaloons up to his shoulders, all the while laughing uproariously.[22]

At the conclusion of the first day of voting, the Reformers led. A total of fifty voters had run the Tory gauntlet, mounted the hustings, and declared their choice of candidate. Seventeen of those voters had declared support for William Buell. Howard was second with fifteen, while Gowan had nine and Jameson had only eight supporters. At least two voters had split their votes between the Tory and Reform slates. Someone had chosen to support only one candidate. Despite the heavy-handed tactics of the Tory goon squad, Gowan and Jameson were trailing the incumbent Reformers. The situation called for drastic measurers.

---

21 In the debates surrounding the planning of what became the Rideau Canal, the local population had favoured a route up the Rideau River from Bytown, and then up Irish Creek to Plum Hollow, through the Beverley Lakes into the Gananoque River system, and down the Gananoque River to Gananoque. This route, rejected on military grounds, would have benefited the local economy.

22 MacPherson, p. 127, citing the BROCKVILLE REPORTER, of October 10, 13, 17, and November 28, 1834.

On day two, the Tories increased their pressure tactics. Gowan's Orangemen made it virtually impossible for the Reformers to continue. Buell and Howard complained to the returning officer about the conduct of the Gowan and Jameson supporters. Adiel Sherwood listened to their complaint and haughtily told them that he had no authority to control the conduct of the electorate anywhere but on the platform of the hustings itself.[23] If they had concerns about the conduct of people in the village then, he advised them, they should direct those concerns to the proper authorities. The Reformers knew that there was little point in looking to the local justices of the peace to enforce the law or maintain order. His Worship, Joseph K. Hartwell, the Justice for Beverley, was a savage Orangeman and confirmed Tory. It was Hartwell who had chaired the meeting convened by Gowan to obtain the resolution encouraging Jameson to stand for election in Leeds and who had been the first to welcome Jameson to Beverley.[24] The balance of the justices were scarcely better than Hartwell. All were well-known Gowan supporters who, prior to the election, had openly opposed Buell and Howard.[25] Nonetheless, the formal complaint was made to the magistrates who agreed to hear submissions during the evening.

Gowan and Jameson, who feigned shock and dismay at the disruptions that had occurred, attended before the justices along with Buell and Howard. At the end of the meeting, having heard the arguments of the candidates, the justices of the peace issued a meaningless request that each candidate "exert all influence possible for a peaceful election."[26] They would do nothing more. The following day of polling saw more atrocities. Reformers were beaten up and chased from the poll, while Tory voters were carried from the hustings as conquering heroes on the shoulders of Gowan's Orangemen.

During the third day of polling, Levi Soper came to vote. The old militia Captain and ardent Reform supporter was not prepared to be intimidated by the Tory hoards who controlled the entrance to the hustings. In a discussion with the Reform candidates, he was heard to mutter that he should attend with his militia company and clear the village. Officialdom and Orangemen needed no further excuse. Sherwood ordered the poll closed until the threat of attack by Soper's

23 Ibid., p. 128.
24 Ibid., p. 126.
25 The justices of the peace were J. K. Hartwell, P. Schofield, G. Breakenridge, W. Atkins, J. Goff, and T. Huffield.
26 MacPherson, p. 128.

militia unit ceased. There had been no suggestion that voting ought to be suspended until the actions of the Orangemen were brought under control, but at the first suggestion of some action in retaliation by a Reform supporter, he closed the poll. Meanwhile, the Orangemen attacked and beat Soper severely. The poll was reopened shortly thereafter for the rest of the day. When the poll finally closed at the end of the third day of voting, only 293 people out of a total of 1,200 to 1,500 electors had been able to vote.

The Reformers demanded a further meeting with the returning officer and the local magistrates. They demanded that action be taken to restore some semblance of order to the poll. It was apparent that both Sherwood and the magistrates thought that the election was proceeding in an appropriate fashion and they were not prepared to interfere in any way. Neither the returning officer nor the magistrates refused to do their duty. They simply suggested that it was the other's responsibility. Sherwood declared that he had no authority except on the hustings proper, a legal position in which the Tory candidate, Robert Jameson, in his capacity as the Attorney-General of the province concurred. The justices of the peace declared that they had no authority during the polling by reason of the superior authority of the returning officer. It was apparent that Tory officialdom would take no action.

By the morning of the fourth day, the Reformers realized that to continue was futile. What they might have won on the hustings, they had lost in the fisticuffs surrounding the poll. They withdrew under formal protest. Even though the result was no longer in doubt, Sherwood could not simply close the poll. Richard Gray was a nominated fifth candidate. The voting would continue in the absence of the two Reform candidates and their supporters. Ogle Robert Gowan and Robert Jameson were elected to represent the County of Leeds in the next Legislative Assembly of the Province of Upper Canada.[27]

Across the province, Reform candidates had done well and the cause of Reform in the Assembly would benefit from the oratorical skills of William Lyon Mackenzie, the calm reason of Marshal Spring Bidwell and Peter Perry, and the theoretical depth of Robert Baldwin. Mackenzie was now free to embark on fresh enquiries into inequities of the defeated Tories with a clear majority of the Assembly behind him. He relished the opportunity. Buell and Howard pressed their official protest which would be heard in due course by the newly

---

27 BROCKVILLE RECORDER, October 17, 1834.

elected, Reform-dominated Legislative Assembly. When the new Assembly turned their attention to the election scandals in Leeds County and the Buell and Howard protest, they were obviously receptive. At the conclusion of the hearing,they declared the election in Leeds a nullity and the seats for the County of Leeds vacant. This verdict was supported informally at the local level.

Mr S. C. Frey had held a wager for £50 between Messrs McLean and Richards on the outcome of the election. Prior to the Assembly's decision, Frey had reached the same conclusion:

> An Election for members of Parliament consists in the free choice of such members, by persons qualified to vote, and altho (sic) the returning officer has made a return in favour of the Attorney General, yet from the best evidence I have been able to collect no such free choice has been made, and the return is false and not true in fact. I say therefore under all the circumstances, that neither party has won the wager and I therefore return to each one his £50.[28]

The Assembly, in accordance with their power under the constitution, scheduled a by-election for March 1835, but it remained the prerogative of the lieutenant-governor to select the number and the location of the poll or polls and to appoint the returning officer. The lieutenant-governor was obviously content with the results of the last election, so he saw no need for change. He decreed that the by-election would again be conducted from the single poll at Beverley. Even more significantly, the returning officer selected to conduct the by-election would be none other than Gowan's close friend and confidant, Joseph K. Hartwell, the leader of the Orange Lodge at Beverley and the chairman of the original meeting that had urged the attorney-general to run. Adiel Sherwood had been neutral in comparison.

It came as a surprise to no one that the by-election was a repeat of the election of 1834. On the second day of voting, Buell and Howard were again forced to withdraw under protest. Gowan and Jameson were once more declared the members for Leeds. In describing the election to her brother, W. B. Wells, then the member for Grenville County, Sally Malloch wrote:

> You will have heard of our elections ere this and I am sure will be disgusted . . . There are various reports in circulation respecting the disturbance some say there was no rioting

---

28 Public Archives of Canada, CHARLES JONES PAPERS, MG24 B7, Memorandum of S. C. Frey, dated October 20, 1834.

others that a more dreadful time has not been known. John Shipman was a good deal hurt in rescuing J. Jones who was some hurt. I was in great alarm you may be sure. Malloch (her husband) was all prepared to go the news came – this was the 2 day – that the Election was over.[29]

Tempers were frayed and patience non-existent as Reform and Tory supporters left the village of Beverley to begin their trek home. As Buell and Howard harnessed their horses for the return to Brockville, a group of their supporters headed north a few miles to the inn of a fellow Reformer, James Phillips, where they planned to drown the defeat in whisky. On leaving Phillips' Inn, and feeling much better with the glow of whisky clouding vision and sense, they chanced upon a group of Gowan and Jameson supporters heading up the same trail to their homes in the Smiths Falls area. The Tories were drunk and exuberant, still sporting their campaign ribbons, and noisily mouthing Tory cheers and Orange sentiments. The resulting clash was inevitable. The Tories were outnumbered. The Reformers stripped them of their Tory campaign ribbons and forced them to retreat down the trail to Beverley while they returned to Phillips' Inn to celebrate the only Reform victory in the past several days.

At the Tory campaign headquarters at Beverley, the victory party was gathering strength and the bruised and battered Tories had no trouble recruiting reinforcements. Within minutes they were heading north once more, prepared to show the Reform rabble that they controlled Leeds County. This time it was the Reformers who were forced to retreat. The Tory hordes swept into Phillips' Inn where they showed no mercy and gave no quarter to anyone they found, including the owner, James Phillips. He was forced to abandon his inn and flee with the others as the Tories began to tear the establishment apart. The Reformers gathered in a gully to watch the rampage unseen, until Phillips could stand no more. Out of the gully and across the field he led the charge to save what was left of his home and tavern. As a man possessed, he entered the inn swinging his stick like a claymore of old until, finally, the last of the Tories retreated. When the dust settled, it was plain that one Tory would not go home. Amid the wreckage of Phillips' Inn, young Edward Tusic lay dead with a broken skull and Phillips stood charged with his murder.

---

29   Queen's University Archives, THE WELLS FAMILY PAPERS, letter from Sally Malloch to her brother, W. B. Wells, dated March 11, 1835.

His trial took place at the next Criminal Assizes for the District of Johnstown at the Court House in Brockville. Robert Jameson, the Attorney-General for the Province of Upper Canada, and the new member of the Legislative Assembly for the County of Leeds, personally presented the case for the Crown. Evidence and argument consumed some three days and, in the end, the twelve men on the jury refused to convict Phillips.

The violence at the Beverley poll during the general election of 1834 had become notorious throughout Upper Canada during the Assembly debates surrounding Buell's challenge to the election of Gowan and Jameson and the motion to void the result and declare the seat vacant. The entire province was focused on the Leeds County by-election and was shocked at the news that Buell and Howard had been again forced to withdraw under protest as a result of further Tory and Orange atrocities. The further graphic accounts of political gang warfare at Phillips' Inn and the murder of Edward Tusic only compounded the matter.

The resulting trial and acquittal of Phillips at the Criminal Assizes confirmed the belief that the Tories were the instigators and that Phillips had merely been defending himself and his property. The population of the province overwhelmingly identified the Orangemen as the cause of the difficulties and the general perception was that they had gone too far.

Buell and Howard proceeded with their challenge once more. The Assembly remained firmly reformist in attitude, and it was quickly agreed that the electoral results in the Leeds County by-election could not stand. Once more, the Assembly declared the election null and void, and another election was called for March 2, 1836.

In an attempt to limit the ability of Gowan and his Orangemen to pervert democracy yet again, and to prevent future violence in the next Leeds County by-election, the Assembly considered special legislation. Andrew Norton Buell, William Buell's brother, campaign manager, and legal advisor drafted legislation that provided for the erection of hustings at four poll locations spread across the county. Robert Baldwin and William Lyon Mackenzie, the acknowledged leaders of the Reform members, presented the Leeds Election Bill to the Assembly on Buell's behalf, where it easily passed. Given the public outrage concerning the situation in Leeds, the Legislative Counsel endorsed the bill when it came up for approval. The lieutenant-governor, the newly appointed Sir Francis Bond Head, similarly felt obliged to sign the legislation into law.

When the electors of Leeds trooped to the polls in March of 1836 to attempt once more to exercise their franchise, they did so at four locations around the riding. Those from the northern part of the county voted at either Smiths Falls or Beverley. Along the front of the county, the hustings were erected at Gananoque and Coleman's Corners.

There had been no doubt that both William Buell and Matthew Howard would again stand for election as Reformers. On the Tory side, Robert Jameson had determined not to stand again. The adverse publicity associated with the elections, Tusic's murder, and the acquittal of James Phillips combined to convince the attorney-general that he should withdraw from the electoral politics of Leeds County. He opted to dedicate his time to the administration of justice in Upper Canada. Someone else could play the political games of mayhem in the Johnstown District.

Jameson's refusal to let his name stand for election necessitated a further Tory nomination battle. Jonas Jones had indicated that he was prepared to stand and, under the unwritten rules that had governed Tory politics in the past, it appeared that he would be given the opportunity to do so. The rules, however, had changed. Gowan's position within the party was now so strong that his personal choice for a running mate, R. D. Fraser, received the nomination over Jones, who in the absence of Gowan's influence would have handily won the right to represent the Tory cause.

The by-election itself was anticlimactic. The past conduct of Gowan and his Orangemen had become an election issue. Given the opportunity to exercise the franchise without interference from the Orange Lodge, the electors of Leeds followed the provincial trend and elected Buell and Howard by large margins.[30]

To celebrate the victory, the Reformers held a feast at Lusher's Hotel in Brockville. Dinner was served amid congratulatory speeches and toasts, while volunteers carved a roasted ox, which they distributed among the poor of the town as a Reform offering.[31] The warmth of the April sunshine seemed to symbolize the true birth of meaningful reform in the Johnstown District.

---

30 The final results were Buell 700, Howard 691, Gowan 547, and Fraser 513.
31 BROCKVILLE RECORDER, April 15, 1834.

CHAPTER VIII
Bond Head and the Campaign of 1836

*I*N JANUARY OF 1836, Sir Francis Bond Head, the newly appointed lieutenant-governor of the province of Upper Canada, arrived in Toronto to assume his duties. Sir John Colborne, whom he had replaced, was transferred to Quebec to assume military command of all British regular and militia forces in Canada.

Bond Head was an enigma, his appointment peculiar. The new King's representative had neither the military nor political credentials that Upper Canadians had come to expect in their lieutenant-governors. He had seen military service during the Napoleonic Wars, but with the Royal Engineers as opposed to a combat regiment. Outside of his limited military service, his sole connection with government administration had been a stint as the Assistant Poor Law Commissioner in Kent.[1] He had shown no interest in politics. He even noted on one occasion that he had never in his life, prior to his assumption of the duties of the lieutenant-governor, bothered to vote. To compound the potential problems associated with this lack of experience, his standing instructions from Lord Glenelg, the Colonial Secretary, were vague and offered the neophyte lieutenant-governor no clear guidance on how he was to deal with the growing discontent in the province.

Shortly before embarking for Upper Canada, Bond Head had been given a copy of Mackenzie's Seventh Report On Grievances. The report was the culmination of William Lyon Mackenzie's enquiries into the body politic of Upper Canada condensed into 533 pages of angry prose. The new lieutenant-governor tucked his copy of the report into his luggage as reading material for the long sea voyage to Canada. "With Mr. Mackenzie's heavy book of lamentations in my

---

1 Dunham, p. 165.

NATIONAL ARCHIVES OF CANADA, C-18789

Sir Francis Bond Head led the forces of reaction through the election of 1836 and into the rebellions that followed.

portmanteau, and with my remedial instructions in my writing case, I considered myself as a political physician . . ."[2] he noted in his memoirs. In response to the grievances, Bond Head was instructed ". . . to reform all `real grievances' and to treat the Assembly with `the most studious attention and courtesy.'"[3] It remained, however, within the sole purview of Sir Francis Bond Head to determine what, if any, grievances were real and what reforms, if any, were appropriate.

By the time of Bond Head's arrival in Upper Canada, the political situation was approaching a crisis. The Reform majority in the Assembly was growing increasingly restive and had identified multiple issues in which government policy was contrary to the wishes of the people that it represented. The Assembly had, over the past two years, enacted bill after bill to address the problems experienced by its constituents, only to have the legislative program stalled in the Legislative Council. Each piece of legislation that they passed had been turned back by the Upper House as unacceptable, all with the support and encouragement of the lieutenant-governor, Sir John Colborne. With growing frustration, the members of the Assembly had come to the realization that they had no effective control over the public administration of the province.

As if to underscore the impotence of the Assembly, in the dying days of his governorship, Sir John Colborne had endowed fifty-seven rectories of the Church of England in Upper Canada with 27,000 acres of clergy reserve land.[4] The Assembly was apoplectic and the general population shared the sense of outrage. The Assembly had received no intimation that the endowment was even under consideration. The lieutenant-governor was fully cognizant of the opposition in the Assembly, and among the people, to the established church and the existing system of clergy reserves, but had chosen to ignore it. Rather than attempt to address the concerns of the Assembly, the lieutenant-governor had exacerbated the problem by this further act of blatant religious favouritism. Sir John's actions made it very clear that fundamental, systemic change was necessary if the electorate was to have any effective control over the affairs of the province.

---

2 William Kilbourn, THE FIREBRAND, WILLIAM LYON MACKENZIE AND THE REBELLION IN UPPER CANADA, Clarke, Irwin & Company Limited, 1964, p. 131.
3 Ibid., p. 165.
4 Dunham, p. 100, citing C.O. 42/431 Head to Glenelg December 17, 1836; Report of the Committee of Assembly on the Clergy Reserve Sale Bill; C.O. 42/439 Head to Glenelg October 18, 1836.

The Reform coalition in Upper Canada had looked on the arrival of Sir Francis Bond Head with a sense of expectation and optimism. Bond Head, after all, was a Whig appointment and, therefore, it was assumed, he must be an advocate of reform. His entrance along King Street into the frozen capital of Toronto was turned into a triumphal procession amid placards and banners proclaiming him to be a "TRIED AND TRUE REFORMER."[5]

Initially, the new lieutenant-governor appeared to live up to his advance reputation. On assessing the qualities of the members of his Executive Council, he correctly noted that the councillors exercised their power and influence for their personal gain and for the gain of their families and friends. Bond Head, therefore, had them dismissed. He then persuaded Robert Baldwin and John Rolph, both leading moderate reformers, and John Henry Dunn to join the Council. Baldwin and Rolph did so in the belief that Head was interested in reform and would afford the Executive Council real power. They were sadly mistaken.

Robert Baldwin was the leading political thinker of the time. He advanced the theory of responsible government that ultimately permitted Upper Canada, and the balance of British North America, to achieve a system of working democracy within the structure of the British Empire.

From his new position as an executive councillor, Baldwin persuaded his fellow members on the Executive Council that the lieutenant-governor ought to be obliged to seek their opinions on each piece of legislation and on all matters of public administration. Sir Francis demurred. Baldwin then suggested that the members of the Executive Council ought to enjoy the support of the majority in the Legislative Assembly. The idea that the executive branch of government, represented in Upper Canada by the lieutenant-governor, ought to be responsible to and enjoy the support of the elected Assembly was anathema to the lieutenant-governor himself, and to the Tories who supported him. In the opinion of Sir Francis Bond Head, parliament ought to be responsible to him;[6] not the other way round. The proper role of the Assembly, in Bond Head's conception, was advisory only. The Assembly should provide information as to the views of the populace on specific issues, information and advice which he might accept or reject in the exercise of his discretion as the sovereign's chief administrator in the colony.

---

5 Kilbourn, p. 131. See also Dunham, p. 166.
6 Dunham, p. 168.

The battle lines between these two competing conceptions were very clearly drawn. All six members of the Executive Council presented Head with written notices that unless he accepted their view of the role of the Council they would be forced to resign. Sir Francis was not prepared to engage in a debate with his hirelings on the issue. He accepted their resignations.

Mackenzie and the Reform majority in the Assembly were furious over the dismissal of Baldwin, Rolph, and the balance of the Executive Council. By a margin of 42:7, the Legislative Assembly passed a resolution demanding full information concerning the dismissal. In another resolution, they advised Sir Francis Bond Head that they shared Baldwin's conception of responsible government. They resolved that the lieutenant-governor ought to be obliged to listen to the advice of the Executive Council and that the Council ought, in turn, be answerable to the majority in the Assembly. When Bond Head refused even to discuss these demands, the Assembly passed a motion of want of confidence in the lieutenant-governor. Then, in a final, desperate attempt to exert some power and influence over the lieutenant-governor, on April 16, 1836, the Assembly voted to refuse supply to the administration of Sir Francis Bond Head.

The withholding of supply to the executive branch of government had been the remedy of British parliaments against recalcitrant kings and queens of England for generations. It had never before been seriously attempted in Upper Canada, because of the other sources of revenue available to the executive free of the control of the Assembly.[7] The Assembly, however, had no other remedy. Verbal attacks and legislative action had been tried in the past to no effect. The withholding of supply might prove to be ineffective, but it was the strongest possible action that the Assembly could take.

Sir Francis Bond Head could have continued the operations of the government with only minor readjustments. The funds that the Assembly had resolved to withhold from the lieutenant-governor amounted to some £7,000, an insignificant fraction of the revenues of the government, which amounted to a total of £162,000 sterling. The argument was not over the ability of the administration to continue to govern, it was over who ought to be in control of the province. Should His Majesty's chosen representative be allowed to govern in accordance with his instructions from the Colonial Office, or ought the people, through their Assembly, be responsible for their own affairs. By

---

7 Infra., p. 22.

withholding supply, the Assembly had handed the lieutenant-governor an issue on which he could fight the larger battle. It was an issue that the lieutenant-governor knew he could turn to his advantage.

Bond Head chose to call the Assembly's bluff and retaliated in kind. He ceased all government activity. He immediately stopped all public works in the province, refused to provide funds for contingencies, and reserved all money bills. The lieutenant-governor explained that the Assembly had stopped the supply of funds to the government and that he, accordingly, had no funds with which to function.[8] While the impasse continued, there would be no money for roads, services, or schools in any county or district in the province. If the people of Upper Canada accepted Sir Francis Bond Head's explanation, the lack of schools, roads, bridges and other public facilities was the result of the actions of the irresponsible, power-hungry, treasonous Reform majority in the Legislative Assembly.

News of the political crises over supply divided the population of the Johnstown District, just as it was splitting the entire province. The Reformers, fresh from their recent victories in both counties, anticipated overwhelming public support for the position taken by the Assembly.

Alexander McCrea, a well-known Reform supporter from northern Grenville County, quickly organized a meeting in the village of Merrickville to obtain public endorsement of a petition that William Lyon Mackenzie had forwarded to him. The petition urged the provincial parliament to stand firm in its position of refusing to vote supply for the administration and dismiss immediately the Executive Council that Bond Head had appointed to replace Baldwin, Rolph, and the others.

To McCrea's consternation, it soon became apparent that the meeting would take the opposite position. A contrary motion declaring that those assembled from the Townships of Wolford, Montague, and Oxford ". . . view with distrust the proceedings of some of the inhabitants of Toronto at a meeting held in that city where William Lyon Mackenzie acted as secretary, and that we look upon resolutions passed at that meeting as being vain and unconstitutional, and fraught with calumny, ill-will, vindictive, arbitrary, and in every respect uncalled for," passed easily.[9]

McRea then urged the meeting to endorse Mackenzie's Reform

---

7 Infra., p. 22.8 Dunham, p. 172.
9 BROCKVILLE RECORDER, April 22, 1836.

rhetoric damning Sir Francis Bond Head. Instead, they declared, ". . . we shall never be wanting in due respect to the authorities derived from our Sovereign, and we now express our gratitude to his Excellency."[10] McCrea scrambled to salvage the meeting and attempted to reopen the issue on the basis that some late arrivals had not been able to vote. His motion to reconsider was soundly defeated. Then, to add a stinging impact to their resolutions, it was moved, seconded, and carried that a petition endorsing Sir Francis Bond Head be drafted and that the petition, together with the resolutions of the meeting, be given to William B. Wells and Hiram Norton as the elected representatives of the county with instructions that they present them to the lieutenant-governor personally.

Bond Head had the political acumen to recognize a winning political issue when he saw it. As the debate developed, he was able to redirect the refusal of the Assembly to pass the supply motion into an issue that portrayed the Reformers in the Assembly as arrogant and irresponsible. The population accepted his argument. They accepted as fact his assertion that he had been effectively barred from governing because of the Assembly's action.

From time to time, some Reformers tried to suggest that Bond Head could govern without the Assembly voting supply. William Buell, in an editorial, pointed out that the administration was not dependent upon funds over which the Assembly exercised control.[11] The argument, however, fell on deaf ears. The Reformers, after all, had stated repeatedly that they were withholding supply to prevent Bond Head from governing. It was, therefore, impossible for them to argue later that their motion to withhold supply had no effect.

Like a modern politician ahead in the polls and with his winning issue in hand, Sir Francis Bond Head decided to go to the people in a general election. The man who hitherto had never even bothered to vote was prepared to become an active political campaigner in what became the first modern, province-wide election in the history of Upper Canada. The lieutenant-governor of the province toured and spoke to the people, exhorting them to assist him in the smooth administration of the province by returning Tory candidates to the Assembly. "I have made up my mind to stand against the enemies of reform, but I have been unexpectedly disconcerted by its professed friends," he wrote to Lord Glenelg, as he prepared for the election.

---

10 Ibid.
11 BROCKVILLE RECORDER, June 12, 1836.

"No liberal mind can deny that I have been unnecessarily embarrassed – no one can deny that I have been unduly accused – no one can deny that I have evinced an anxiety to remedy all real grievances – that I have protected the constitution of the province – and that I, by refusing to surrender at discretion the patronage of the crown to irresponsible individuals, I have conferred a service on the backwoodsman and on every noble-minded Englishman, Irishman, Scotchman, and United Empire Loyalist."[12]

The election was held in late June of 1836. In Leeds, the announcement that the county would revert to a single poll, which would once more be located at the village of Beverley, set the tone of the coming campaign. Bond Head further decreed that His Worship, Joseph K. Hartwell, JP, would act as the returning officer. Gone was the brief experiment with four polls spread throughout the county. Gone also was the flirtation with neutral returning officers, who might attempt to provide some degree of equity between the various candidates and peace at the polls. It was apparent that the electoral process would again be perverted by Orange bully-boy tactics in a single poll that the Tories could control.

To prepare for the election, the Friends of Reform and Liberal Measures in the County of Leeds met at a nomination meeting held on June 11, 1836. Once more, the Reformers nominated William Buell and Matthew Howard. The Reformers also staked out the fundamental issue for the coming campaign. In a unanimous resolution the meeting declared:

> That it is an essential and inalienable feature of the British Constitution that the King shall be assisted in all affairs of government by the advice of known and responsible councillors and officers who possess the confidence of the people and of a majority of their representatives.[13]

The concept of responsible government, poorly understood even by the intellectual elite short years before, had found its way to the main stage of rough and tumble Leeds County politics. It now found expression in a meeting of shopkeepers and farmers and would form their rallying cry in the coming campaign.

The Reformers were too practical to be interested only in declarations of political philosophy. There was an election to be

---

12 Dunham, p. 172, citing C.O. 42/429 Head to Glenelg, April 20, 1836.
13 BROCKVILLE RECORDER, June 17, 1836.

fought. To prepare for the hustings at the Beverley Poll, they not only activated Committees of Vigilance and Management in each township, but actually appointed a special committee whose job it was to fight the Orangemen. The committee consisted of well-known Reform supporters: James Phillips, Joseph Wiltse, William Howard, John Booth, Arthur Fox, Levi Soper, James Simpson, Philip Wing, and George McKelvey. They were to meet each morning at the opening of the poll prepared to take whatever measures were necessary to protect Reform voters.[14] Phillips and his men were to be the Reform infantry to fend off Gowan's Orange storm troopers.

The Tories, now firmly controlled by Ogle Robert Gowan, nominated Jonas Jones and, of course, Gowan himself as the Tory candidates. Buell attempted to make much of the fact that Jonas Jones, a man from an upstanding Loyalist family, would stoop so low as to stand for election on a Gowan ticket. "That Mr. Jones would allow himself to be brought forward with a man of Mr. Gowan's known character is . . . astonishing: as it involved a sacrifice of moral principle which we were not disposed to look for in Mr. Jones."[15]

While Buell may have been astonished to see Jones running with Ogle Robert Gowan, he was not surprised to see Jones as a Tory candidate. The old concept of inter-family respect was quickly dying and Buell recognized Jones as an enemy of Reform. The enmity he felt for the enemies of Reform now far outweighed any lingering respect he may have felt for men of substance from the old Loyalist families. Jones had been, ". . . an advocate for the unconstitutional and tyrannical measures lately adopted by Sir Francis B. Head."[16] He was ceasing to be a friend.

Gowan prepared for the election in his typically thorough manner. Nothing was left to chance. He recognized the reluctance of some of the old-family Tories to support him and moved quickly to ensure their votes. He jotted off a hasty strategy letter to his new ally, Charles Jones, mixing lies, cajolery, threats, and promises in order to ensure that Jonas Jones and his supporters would sing from the Gowan hymn book once the campaigning started.

> The Radicals here in Bastard and Crosby, are putting up a union! The ostensible object of which is to support Howard

---

14 BROCKVILLE RECORDER, June 17, 1836.
15 BROCKVILLE RECORDER, June 10, 1836.
16 Ibid.

& Gowan! I understand that James Phillips, all the Hollidays, Dr. Schofield, Stephens, Merriman and Major Soper are at the head of it. They are to wait on me with it in a day or two. How superlatively absurd are those Radicals . . .[17]

he wrote, subtly sending out the big lie.

Jonas Jones as lawyer, politician, and judge opposed any suggestion of reform. METROPOLITAN TORONTO REFERENCE LIBRARY, T-16853

There was no such plan. There was no possibility that James Phillips, Levi Soper, or the others would ever support Gowan. Phillips had just been acquitted of the murder of one of Gowan's men. Soper, during the by-election of 1834, had threatened to use his militia unit to clear the village of Beverley in the cause of Reform. Both were also active members of the special fisticuffs committee of the Friends of Reform and Liberal Measures. The thought that they would now support Gowan was absurd. Gowan's intention, therefore, was to have Jones believe that he needed Gowan more than Gowan needed him. The threat was clear; if Jones did not heartily endorse his candidacy, then Gowan could turn to the Reformers and still win the election.

> I am happy to say, and I am sure you will be equally happy to hear, that since I got home I have seen Messrs. Stafford, Kendrick, P. Johnson and others who were hostile to your brother. I have got them to cast their prejudices to the winds and consent to go – in Yankee phraseology – `the whole hog.' But in order to render this feeling universal and perfect, it will be requisite that a few of your brothers' immediate friends such for example as Messrs. H. & S. Jones, Dr. Hubble should attend and vote the first day, which will have the happiest effect and induce all my friends to step forward and give their cordial support instead of lying back in a wary and guarded manner.[18]

Gowan was using his cajolery to show Jones the degree to which he was already helping the Jonas Jones campaign. Finally, Gowan placed the hook. Gowan was making it clear that Jones was to have his leading supporters publicly declare their support by voting for Gowan at the earliest opportunity. If Jones did not comply with that request, then he could not count on any support from Gowan.

Gowan was aware of the Reformers' plans to have their own squad of muscle-men at the hustings and, in the same correspondence to Charles Jones, he made it clear that he would have the situation well in hand:

> It is confidently reported and believed that the Radicals have resolved to erect a sort of temporary encampment at or near the Hustings in which their friends are to remain over night so as to be ready to assemble round the entrance

---

17 Canadian Public Archives, CHARLES JONES PAPERS, MG24 B7, letter from Ogle R. Gowan to Charles Jones, dated June 16, 1836.
18 Ibid.

to the poll every morning. Effectual measures must be taken to prevent an improper blocking of the poll. This can be done by the Returning Officer and Magistrates.[19]

Finally, Gowan planned the logistics of feeding his supporters and keeping them ready for action during the polling:

> It will be necessary to get some pork and bread for persons coming from a distance but the use of spirituous liquors we must strictly prohibit as if our friends get it we shall lose all control over them and cannot tell what consequences would follow. In the whole I think our prospects are brightening.[20]

Not only Gowan was involved in election preparations. The Jones approach was more direct. In Brockville, Francis Hacket, an employee of Jonas Jones who was at the time part of a steamboat building crew, was asked repeatedly how he proposed to vote. Hacket refused to tell explaining that every man should go to the poll free to vote for whomever he pleased. Jones recognized a traitor when he saw one. Hacket was fired on the spot.[21]

The election itself followed an all too familiar pattern. The hustings at the village of Beverley was again the scene of fisticuffs and Orange bully-boy tactics. Buell and Howard were once more compelled to withdraw under protest. Phillips and his special squad of Reformers charged with protecting Reform voters were outnumbered and outmuscled by Gowan's Orangemen. In the end, the returning officer, His Worship Joseph K. Hartwell, JP, declared Ogle Robert Gowan and Jonas Jones elected.

In Grenville County, the cause of moderate reform was sustained by the re-election of the incumbent Reformers, Hiram Norton and William B. Wells. In their victory, Norton and Wells were the anomaly. There were very few identified Reform candidates anywhere in Upper Canada who withstood the Tory onslaught led by Sir Francis Bond Head. But unlike the peaceful polling of 1834, violence marred the Grenville County election of 1836.

The entire county voted at a single poll located in the village of Merrickville. The voting took place during a full five day period from Monday to Friday and tension built as it became apparent that the incumbents would be re-elected. As the poll closed, a riot broke out;

---

19 Ibid.
20 Ibid.
21 BROCKVILLE RECORDER, June 24, 1836.

The lads talk politics on the main street in Merrickville.

the poll clerk was mobbed and the poll book was torn from his hands. The original voting records were destroyed as the poll clerk attempted to make his way onto the hustings and announce the results of the voting. After the riot had subsided, the poll clerk's deputy, the check clerk, surfaced with a duplicate book, which was verified as it had been compared to the original moments before the latter's destruction. The returning officer then declared Norton and Wells the victors by a margin of sixty-five votes.[22]

The two Tory candidates were divided on an appropriate course of action. Stephen Burritt expressed his opinion that the election had been conducted fairly and that the Reformers had been properly returned. His counterpart, Alpheus Jones, however, whose brother Jonas had just been returned as the member for Leeds, immediately announced his intention to challenge the result. He blamed the Reformers for the riot. He claimed that the vote had not been calculated properly and that without the poll book it was impossible to verify the tally. Nothing of significance ever came of Jones' protest. The Legislative Assembly discussed the charges from time-to-time in the early days of the session but, despite the Tory majority in the new Assembly, no concrete action to set aside the result was taken.

Nothing ever came of the Leeds protest, initiated by Buell and Howard, either. Supporters of the Grenville Tories in the Assembly found themselves in a stand-off as a result of the challenge filed by the Reform candidates from Leeds. The Tory majority in the Assembly would take no action to void the Leeds election as the former Reform-dominated Assembly had done in 1834 and 1835. However, due to the obvious electoral fraud in Leeds, they were not in any position to deal with the trumped-up charges of Alpheus Jones.

In Leeds, Jonas Jones and Ogle Robert Gowan had been declared returned, subject to the Buell and Howard protest. In Grenville, William B. Wells and Hiram Norton had been returned, subject to the protest of Alpheus Jones. If the Tories pressed the Jones' challenge to the limit, it could well prove embarrassing for Jonas Jones since it was universally acknowledged that the violence in Leeds far exceeded that in Grenville.

Elsewhere in the province, Reform candidates went down to defeat like dead trees in a November gale. Mackenzie was defeated in his riding of York where previously the electorate had been rock solid in its support of him. Throughout the 1830s, the yeomen of York had

---

22 BROCKVILLE RECORDER, July 8, 1836.

returned Mackenzie to the Legislative Assembly each time the Tory majority had expelled him but, in 1836, they followed the advice of Sir Francis Bond Head and turfed him out. In Lennox and Addington, Marshall Spring Bidwell and his running mate, Peter Perry, found themselves at the foot of the poll after holding the seats for twelve years. The strong body of Reformers who had dominated the previous Assembly was reduced to a dispirited rump. Tory success was near universal. The Reformers had been routed.

In riding after riding, the Tories had been successful in raising doubts in the minds of the electorate as to the loyalty and integrity of previously popular Reformers. With the assistance of Sir Francis Bond Head, the Tories had been successful in equating reform and Reformers with treason to the Crown and the constitution. The people of Upper Canada responded. The movement towards democratic reform was crushed. The Reform majority had been swept aside in a Tory tide of reaction led by the lieutenant-governor. Buell, Howard, and many of the other moderate reformers simply withdrew from active politics. Others, thwarted in their efforts at peaceful, democratic reform, moved inexorably closer to open, armed rebellion.

CHAPTER IX
The Troubles Begin

ORD OF THE ENORMITY of the Reform defeat spread quickly across the province. The electoral returns from each riding poured into Toronto.[1] From the capital, the news spread outward again to the very corners of Upper Canada. In the eastern districts, such as Johnstown, the news came first to the towns fronting the St Lawrence River – Gananoque, Brockville, and Prescott – since they were connected by steamship lines to the major centres of the province. From there the knowledge spread north by word of mouth, concession by concession, into the inns, taverns, mills, farmyards, and kitchens of the back country. Only later would the news be confirmed by shared newspapers or in correspondence from friends along the front.

Once the enormity of the defeat had sunk in, William Buell and Matthew Howard recognized that their protest concerning the election in Leeds County was futile. The violence around the hustings at the Beverley poll had been at least as bad as in the previous elections where the result had been set aside, but now there was a Tory majority in the Assembly. Their prior, successful protests had been argued before an Assembly dominated by Reformers. As they assessed the situation, Buell and Howard quickly realized that Gowan and Jones would easily survive any challenge. Recognizing the futility of further complaint, they abandoned their formal protest. The electoral return of Ogle Robert Gowan and Jonas Jones would stand.

William Buell and Matthew Howard had carried the banner of Reform all throughout the tumultuous 1830s and now chose to retire from the field. They realized that quiet reason, discussion, and debate

---

1 The town of York had become the city of Toronto in 1834.

to advance the cause of moderate reform within the province was no longer viable. At the same time, they were not prepared to resort to non-constitutional means, even though they realized that it was the constitution itself, as presently structured and interpreted, that was the cause of the current malaise. These two men were intent on continuing to live, do business, and raise their families in Brockville and Leeds County. It was time for them to withdraw from politics, lick their wounds, mend fences, and put the cause of reform on hold for the foreseeable future.

Elsewhere in the province, defeated Reformers were not as prepared as Buell and Howard to concede defeat. Two of the leading defeated Reformers, Robert Baldwin and Dr Charles Duncombe, travelled to England to argue the unjustness of the election before the British House of Commons and the colonial secretary. While there, Baldwin learned the extent of the calamity.

Sir Francis Bond Head had Baldwin's father summarily dismissed from his position as a District and Surrogate Court Judge. Dr William Warren Baldwin was a highly regarded and dedicated jurist. He was also a long-standing supporter of political reform and, following the election of 1836, Bond Head was not prepared to have justice in Upper Canada dispensed by traitors sympathetic to reform.

In the Home District, Mackenzie's angry rhetoric became increasingly strident. Far from humbling the fiery Scot, his electoral defeat in York County had merely strengthened his resolve. "Tories! Pensioners! Placemen! Profligates! Orangemen! Churchmen! Brokers! Gamblers! Parasites! allow me to congratulate you. Your feet at last are on the people's necks,"[2] he raged in his new newspaper, *The Constitution*.

Even after the election, Sir Francis Bond Head continued to stump the province. On September 5, 1836, he landed at Prescott and, after a brief stay, travelled overland to Brockville. The victorious Tories gathered at the county court house to meet the lieutenant-governor where "flaming addresses" were given by Charles Jones, Joseph K. Hartwell and Gowan himself. When his turn to speak came, Sir Francis exhorted ". . . his hearers to lay aside party spirit and act together for the general good . . ."[3] To honour the occasion the town fathers of Brockville fired off a cannon but, in their exuberance, they overloaded the artillery with powder and the blast shattered the

2 Kilbourn, p. 144.
3 BROCKVILLE RECORDER, September 9, 1836.

windows of Lusher's Hotel where Head was staying, ". . . . a circumstance of no small annoyance to Sir Francis."[4]

The new Tory Assembly met in November and immediately voted supply to the administration. Bond Head had been able to administer the province from the June election until November without difficulty, confirming the Reform claim that the supply crises had been manufactured by Head for popular consumption during the election campaign. The refusal of the Reformers in the Assembly to vote supply had not impeded the actual functioning of the government.

Next, as if unable to believe that they might ever be re-elected and reluctant to face the people again, the Tories in the Assembly passed legislation declaring that the current parliament would not dissolve, as tradition dictated, on the impending death of the sovereign, but would continue for a full term.

Then, as if to confirm that Buell and Howard had been right in withdrawing their protest concerning the election in Leeds, the Assembly proceeded to give two other defeated Reformers, Dr. John Rolph and Mackenzie himself, short shrift regarding their protests. The Tory majority in the Assembly had just been through an election where they had successfully characterized all Reformers as traitors. Following the election they were not about to agree that any Reform candidate had been unfairly treated. Those traitors got exactly what they deserved!

Some of the Tories in the Assembly wanted to go much further. They agitated for intervention in those ridings where the Tory candidates had been unsuccessful. Ogle Robert Gowan and Jonas Jones, the members for Leeds, were not prepared to let the loss of neighbouring Grenville County to the Reformers pass without protest. One of the defeated Tory candidates, after all, was the brother of Jonas Jones. In late November, Gowan introduced a motion in the Assembly to establish a committee to deal with the Grenville election. The returning officer, in reporting the return of Wells and Norton as the elected representatives, had noted the protests of Ephraim Jones, Dr Hubble, Ziba Phillips, and David Mair – three leading Tory supporters. The protest centred on the riot that had occurred at the conclusion of polling and the loss of the original poll book.

To Gowan, a strong attack was always the best defence. There had been considerable controversy surrounding the role played by his

---

4 Ibid.

Orangemen in the election of 1836. The violence that had become commonplace in Leeds County had spread to other areas of the province where the Orange Lodge had taken root. From the security of his power base in Brockville and his seat in the Assembly, Gowan orchestrated the protest on behalf of the defeated Tory candidates in Grenville. The protest may have concerned the election in Grenville County, but those who supported it and provided the evidence to carry the protest forward were Gowan's friends from Leeds. In reviewing the affidavit material filed, Buell noted in the Brockville *Recorder*:

> . . . we should rather suppose it got up in this town, than in the County of Grenville . . . (only) three of the nineteen actually voted at Merrickville, – one was on the limits here and could not go – one was in Toronto at the time – one was in the United States – one is an American thrashing machine peddler – five are known not to be voters in that County.[5]

It became increasingly apparent that the evidence would not support the claim of interference by the Reform faction. On the contrary, it became evident that it was Gowan's Orangemen who had caused the disruptions at the poll in Merrickville and, when they recognized that the election was lost, it was they who had destroyed the poll book.[6]

Throughout this period, Wells was in Europe. He had left shortly after the election and arrived in Liverpool, England, on September 31, 1836, after an arduous thirty-six day voyage. Once he had secured his lodging, he wrote to his father:

> The people of Liverpool are, a majority of them – Reformers. (They) send two Reformers to Parliament and elect their Mayor and Council from the Reformers. There is some talk of a dissolution of Parliament when it is supposed the Radicals will increase their numbers. Liberal opinions are all the rage of the day here. I wish we could say as much for Canada.[7]

While the politics and scenery of England were interesting, thoughts of Upper Canada were not far from his mind. He knew of the election protest launched by Alpheus Jones and was concerned enough to mention to his father, "I hope my good friends will not let

5 BROCKVILLE RECORDER, December 9, 1836.
6 BROCKVILLE RECORDER, November 25, 1836, contains copies of the affidavits filed by the complainants.
7. Queen's University Archives, WELLS FAMILY PAPERS, letter from William B. Wells to his father, dated October 1, 1836, at Liverpool, England.

Jones have all his own way in the House but will send witnesses up."[8] If Gowan and Jones were to press their challenge, Wells wanted Reform witnesses at the hearing.

The defeat of his motion to establish a committee of inquiry into the Grenville County election was only a minor setback for Gowan. He listened to the rhetoric of Mackenzie and the rest of the defeated Reformers and knew intuitively that the time had come to press home the advantage won in the last election. Now was the time to rid the province of Reformers and all talk of reform.

Gowan introduced into the Assembly a motion to revise the Militia Act. It may be that Gowan foresaw the coming rebellion and sought to increase the military preparedness of Upper Canada. His Militia Bill, however, dealt with far more than military matters. The proposed legislation was intended to silence the voice of reform. Gowan's Militia Bill continued the existing practice of conscripting all men between the ages of sixteen and sixty into the militia. In addition, one hundred men in each regiment would be recruited as an elite corps to provide fourteen days of military service in addition to the traditional one day in June. All men would be liable to contribute one dollar towards the wages of the elite corps. It then provided that, in time of war or any other "state of emergency," the lieutenant-governor could call out the militia for up to six months at a time and press horses and carriages into military service.

The most contentious parts of Gowan's Militia Bill had nothing to do with military matters. Gowan proposed to make it a crime for anyone to speak disrespectfully or utter words "tending to the hurt or dishonour" of the royal family or of the lieutenant-governor. This was too much even for the new Tory Assembly. The proposed legislation would have disavowed several hundred years of the British tradition of free speech and made a mockery of the rights of British subjects as free men. "These are the days of lip loyalty – Orange flags – Endowment priestcraft – and servile Legislation," wrote Buell in an editorial concerning the bill. He characterized the Militia Bill as one of the most tyrannical ever introduced.[9] Gowan's fellow Tories in the Assembly recognized that he had gone too far and refused to pass the legislation.

By spring, the unsettled political situation in Upper Canada was compounded by a serious downturn in the economy. As the trilliums poked through the sodden leaves of spring, the province entered a

---

8 Ibid.
9 BROCKVILLE RECORDER, December 23, 1836.

state of real unrest. As the crops ripened, the political and economic situation progressively worsened.

Sir Francis returned to the Johnstown District in August. By that time, he was unpopular even among Tories and was effectively snubbed by Brockville society. The lieutenant-governor arrived by steamer from Toronto and met briefly, without fanfare, with Mr Justice Jonas Jones, whom he had recently appointed to the Court of King's Bench, and with a few others before taking his leave overland to Prescott and places east. The Brockville *Recorder* was pleased to report, "No notice of a flattering nature whatever was taken of his Excellency."[10]

As the situation worsened, a faction of the Reform group under the leadership of Mackenzie grew increasingly radical. The talk amongst the radical Reformers turned inexorably to armed rebellion.

The Upper Canadians were spurred on by the actions of their French Canadian counterparts. In Lower Canada, the overriding issues of race and ethnicity exacerbated the political and economic difficulties. Les Patriotes, under the leadership of Louis-Joseph Papineau, had majority control in the Assembly but, just as in Upper Canada, control of the Assembly was irrelevant. All power was vested in the Executive, represented by the Governor.

The last session of the Assembly of Lower Canada was held in August of 1837 and, copying the unsuccessful tactics of the Upper Canadian Reformers, the members refused to vote supply. Mass demonstrations began. The governor called out the militia. The captains of militia refused to read the proclamations of the governor to the troops. The situation was spiralling out of control.

In the fall, the actual fighting began. On October 23, 1837, a meeting of Patriotes declared themselves to be the lawful and legitimate assembly of the province and began to lay plans to form a provisional government. A month later at St-Denis, British troops marching to arrest a few identified Patriotes were fired upon. The rebellion in Lower Canada had begun.

By July of 1837, Mackenzie was organizing Committees of Vigilance in the various communities of the County of York and throughout the Home District. He had come to the conclusion that rebellion was the only realistic option for Reformers.

In the outlying districts such as Johnstown, Reformers had, at the urging of the radical Reform leadership, established marginally less-militant organizations referred to as political unions. Mackenzie,

10 BROCKVILLE RECORDER, August 10, 1837.

in his newspaper, had called for the creation of these political unions ". . . through out every township in the province where reformers, however few, are to be found."[11] These were political activist organizations composed of men who had come to recognize that democracy in Upper Canada was non-existent. Their discussions focused on tactics to effect substantive change.

The essential feature of these groups was secrecy, which cloaked their talk of sedition and preparations for military activity. The authorities were aware of their existence, but were alarmed by the furtiveness that hid their activities. They had no idea of the nature of the matters under discussion nor of who was involved. They had no way of determining whether the political unions were composed of a few local crackpots or whether they constituted a real threat to the security of the colony. Their lack of knowledge compounded the difficulties occasioned by the rebellions. At first, the secret groups were discounted completely, and the degree of unrest across the province was seriously underestimated. Then, in the paranoia following the first outbreak of rebellion at Toronto, the presence of secret societies throughout the province caused the authorities to seriously overreact and provided the local Tories and their Orange friends with an excuse to engage in wholesale repression.

Spurred on by the events in Lower Canada, Mackenzie managed to persuade enough radical Reformers to follow him into rebellion. To the consternation of many, as soon as the actual fighting began, it became apparent that Mackenzie's skill lay in rhetoric and not in organization or military leadership. Mackenzie's rebels from the farms and villages surrounding Toronto, armed with an ill-will towards Tories and little else, gathered at Montgomery's Tavern just north of Toronto. There was confusion as to the date they were to assemble. There was dithering and further delay while Mackenzie wondered whether more men would rally to the cause, allowing the authorities to make at least rudimentary preparations for the attack. Finally, as the ragtag rebels marched south towards the centre of Toronto, intent on capturing Bond Head and seizing the government, they were crushed in a brief show of force. The entire engagement could be described as a farce, but for the loss of life. Too many good men, on both sides, died in the cold Canadian air to make Mackenzie's sad rebellion the comic opera that it is so often described.

---

11 BROCKVILLE RECORDER, January 6, 1837, reprinting an article originally published in the Toronto CORRESPONDENT AND ADVOCATE.

Illustration by C.W. Jeffreys of the commencement of hostilities and the death of Colonel Moodie.

Mackenzie made good his escape across country to the Niagara frontier where he crossed into the United States. There, he continued his harangue against the established order from the relative security of the land of liberty. Elsewhere, in the western portion of the province, the radical Reformer from London, Charles Duncombe, led the rebellion there to the same end.

Reformers who had not taken part in the rebellion immediately recognized the potential for personal disaster. During the election of 1836, they had been labelled as disloyal. Following their defeat at the polls in 1836, they had been subjected to the concerted actions of the Tories and the lieutenant-governor to discredit and remove them from any position of influence. All Reformers recognized that the abortive rebellions, perpetrated by people with whom they were associated, would result in severe repercussions. They waited for the whirlwind.

One of the first to feel the effects of the abortive rebellion was the former Speaker of the Assembly, Marshall Spring Bidwell. There was no evidence to connect Bidwell to the rebellion, but he was an identified leader of the Reform movement and closely linked to Mackenzie. Sir Francis Bond Head would not allow his continued residence in the province. On the morning of December 8, 1837, Sir Francis met with Bidwell and provided him with two options: leave the province forthwith and promise never to return, or be prosecuted for sedition and treason.

Bidwell opted for exile. He left instantly, leaving his wife and son behind, barely taking time to pack a bag and write a few notes to his friends and former compatriots. To Robert Baldwin he wrote:

> I am obliged to leave without having an opportunity to see you. I wish you to understand that I have been as ignorant of this lamentable affair as yourself . . . This is not a time when any body, however innocent, could successfully contend against the expressed wish of the Lieutenant Governor. A Flag was found at Montgomery's (sic) with the words `BIDWELL AND THE GLORIOUS MINORITY OF 1837.' This of course would be conclusive evidence of my guilt, with many I should be Arrested.[12]

---

12 Public Archives of Canada, CORRESPONDENCE OF THE PROVINCIAL SECRETARY'S OFFICE, Vol. 9, File 1212, correspondence from M. S. Bidwell to Robert Baldwin, dated December 9, 1837.

METROPOLITAN TORONTO REFERENCE LIBRARY, T-15345

Marshall Spring Bidwell, former Speaker of the Assembly and member of the Glorious Minority of reformers who survived the election of 1836, was banished from Upper Canada.

To his friend Cassidy of Kingston, who was to look after all of his business interests in Canada, he dashed off an explanation and some hurried instructions:

> I am leaving at the request of the Lieutenant Governor, suddenly and forever. I am apprehensive that he suspects me of participation in the revolt, but I am entirely innocent . . . whatever . . . I think it would be best without hesitation to comply.[13]

Once safely across the border, he wrote at length to Bond Head:

> I deeply regret, that your Excellency should think my former political life and opinions, the garbled extracts of a hasty and carelessly written letter . . . the finding of a flag at Montgomery's Tavern inscribed Bidwell and the Glorious minority which I suppose had been a banner prepared for some election or public meeting, but certainly not for such a purpose as a revolt, and never used by the insurgents, sufficient reasons for signifying to me your wish that I should suddenly and forever leave my home and country.[14]

For his part, the lieutenant-governor explained his informal banishment order in correspondence to Bidwell dated March 23, 1837:

> You know better than I do what has been your line of political conduct in this Province. You know better than I do what use you have applied your acknowledged talents, and you know as well as I do what have been the lamentable results of the policy which has been pursued by the party which considered you as their leader. I must say that as long as I remained the Lieutenant Governor of this Province I should have considered it my duty to Upper Canada not to have annulled the agreement you made never to return here.[15]

Head wished him well as he established himself in his successful legal career in the United States and reminded him:

> You were here constantly obstructed by a conscientious predilection in favour of elective institutions which you must be quite aware are subversive of Monarchical Government.[16]

---

13 Public Archives of Canada, MG24 B123, letter from Bidwell to Cassidy, December 9, 1837, Kingston.
14 Ibid., letter from Bidwell to Sir Francis Bond Head, dated December 11, 1837, Lewiston.
15 Ibid., letter from Sir F. B. Head to Bidwell dated March 23, 1837.
16 Ibid., letter from Sir F. B. Head to Bidwell dated March 23, 1837.

Bidwell's twenty-six year career as a lawyer and politician in Upper Canada was over.

News of the insurrections reached William Buell in his editorial office in Brockville the day before it became general knowledge. Buell immediately recognized the potential for disaster to himself, his family, and to all who had been associated with him in the cause of moderate reform. The next edition of the *Recorder* provided the details of the insurrection together with the proclamation of Sir Francis Bond Head:

> In a time of profound peace, while every one was quietly following his occupations, feeling secure under the protection of our laws, a band of Rebels, instigated by a few malignant and disloyal men, has had the wickedness and audacity to assemble with arms and to attack and murder the Queen's subjects on the Highway. To burn and destroy their property – to rob the pubic Mails – and to threaten to plunder the Banks – and to fire the city of Toronto.[17]

The actions of the Mackenzie rebels had placed Buell in an untenable position. In an unusually long editorial, he disassociated himself from their actions while reiterating his own position of incremental and peaceful reform:

> On Friday evening last (8 December 1836) we were put in possession of Toronto papers, one day in anticipation of the regular mails. They contained the important intelligence of an outbreak in the Home District (York) . . . It is well known . . . that we have looked upon the administration of his Excellency (Sir Francis Bond Head) as unwise and impolitic . . . Such being our views in relation to our colonial administration we have from time to time expressed our opinions freely in opposition to the course pursued, as well by his Excellency as by the Provincial parliament, which under the circumstances of their election, we have never looked upon as a body calculated to express the true feelings of the people whom they ostensibly represent. Our aim has, therefore, been to show the impropriety of the acts of the Assembly on many important questions (but more particularly the conduct of those styled the representatives of Leeds) . . . with the design of producing an ultimate and beneficial change. But we have never entertained the desire

---

17 BROCKVILLE RECORDER, December 14, 1837.

or inculcated the sentiment, that a resort to arms should be had for the accomplishment of the several objects of reform . . . we would rather suffer the evils under which we labour, than plunge the country into others we know not of . . . We are an advocate of reform so far as is consistent with the true principles of the British Constitution. We go no further. In the present state of things there is but one course, that which we have ever endeavoured to pursue, namely, to discharge our duty to the Government, at the same time that we use all lawful and proper means for the removal of such abuses as are known to exist.[18]

Buell obviously wanted it to be clear that while he despised Gowan and had worked towards many principles of reform, he was not a party to any insurrection. He would not and could not be seen to condone rebellion. His timely protestations of loyalty, coupled with the status of his family, isolated William Buell from many of the Orange recriminations that quickly swept the province.

In the Johnstown District, the reaction to the news of the rebellions was typical of the province. This was just the sort of apprehended insurrection that Gowan, his Orangemen, and all local Tories had been waiting for. It provided them with the opportunity to prove their loyalty and to consolidate their positions of power.

The first requirement was the stabilization of the military situation. The lieutenant-governor who, prior to Mackenzie's rising had discounted the potential for armed insurrection, now recognized the potential threat posed by radical Reformers across the province and ordered the mobilization of the militia. The reaction against all who could be suspected of rebellious sympathies was swift, determined, and crushing. Arrest was made of anyone who had in the past exhibited overt radical sentiments. Restrictions were placed on travel between Upper Canada and the United States. The door of repression was closing.

The grass on the cross-country trail down which Mackenzie had fled on his way to the border did not have time to straighten before the Tory elite of the Johnstown District had organized a meeting of local militia officers at the court house in Brockville. The regiment commanders resolved to muster their various militia regiments immediately. They agreed to exert all possible influence over their troops to convince as many as possible to volunteer for active service.

---

18 Ibid.

The volunteers for active duty from all the regiments in Leeds County would assemble and drill at Brockville, those from Grenville would assemble at Prescott.

The military agenda of the meeting was concluded, but it made no sense for those assembled to allow their preparations on behalf of Her Majesty to go unheralded. There was no point in going to this expense and trouble unless it was drawn to the attention of the authorities that much was being done by the loyal subjects of the Queen at Brockville. What better way to do that than in a humble resolution of thanks. The assembled militia officers unanimously expressed their appreciation to Colonel Corbitt, Major Fitzgerald, Major Bonnycastle the senior commissary clerk, and the other officers at Kingston, "for the promptness with which they had forwarded arms and other military stores, to this District."[19] Charles Jones forwarded a copy of the resolutions together with a personal note to John Joseph, secretary to the lieutenant-governor. Later in the same day, Jones wrote a further note to Joseph advising that it was his personal intention ". . . to raise without delay thirty men for the purpose of composing a guard to be permanently kept up until otherwise ordered." He asked only that the government make all of the necessary provisions and "defray the expenses of this force."[20]

Following the meeting of the militia officers at Brockville, the mobilization orders went out calling the members of the militia to assemble in every village and hamlet. From Yonge Mills, Lieutenant D.B.O. Ford ordered Sgt Robert Kincaid to make a roll of every male from the age of sixteen to sixty and to note anything that might excuse any potential militia member from active service.[21] Colonel Hugh Munro called out the division of his regiment that resided in Prescott, and 300 men appeared on parade in answer to the call.[22] Daniel Jones, the officer commanding the Fifth Regiment of the Leeds Light Infantry, ordered his men to assemble on December 23, 1837, at the village of Frankville in northern Leeds County. He warned his troops that any man between the age of sixteen and sixty, within the boundaries of the regiment, who failed to appear would be prosecuted.[23]

---

19 Public Archives of Canada, CHARLES JONES PAPERS, MG24 B7, Minutes of the Meeting of the Militia Officers at the Court House at Brockville, December 9, 1838.
20 Ibid., letter from Charles Jones to John Joseph, Secretary to the Lieutenant Governor, dated December 11, 1837.
21 Ibid., copy of order dated, December 9, 1837.
22 Public Archives of Canada, ADJUTANT GENERAL'S OFFICE CORRESPONDENCE, Vol. 22, GRENVILLE, letter from Munro to Col N. Coffin, dated December 11, 1837, at Prescott.
23 BROCKVILLE RECORDER, December 21, 1837.

LOYALISTS TO YOUR DUTY.

Queens Royal Borderers.

COMMANDED BY LIEUT. COLONEL GOWAN.

Wanted 100 Loyal Volunteers, for the above Corps, for six months service only.

Each man will get 8 dollars bounty, a new suit of clothes, and a great Coat & pair of Boots, also a free *Gift* of seven *days* pay when *discharged at the end of the six months. Their pay will be one Shilling* Sterling Money, per DAY, *and* free *Rations.*

Let no Man pretending *to* LOYALTY HANG BACK, *at* this time. FORWARD *LADS,* FORWARD.

APPLY TO LIEUTENANT COLONEL GOWAN, AT BROCKVILLE.

GOD SAVE THE QUEEN.

Ogle R. Gowan calls for volunteers.

Ogle Robert Gowan had formed his own company of militia in 1836 and, not surprisingly, Gowan's Brockville Invincibles were entirely Irish and Orange in composition. Gowan was the recognized leader of the Irish community, and his militia company was a further manifestation of his control. It was a position that he insisted be recognized by those in control of the general community. In correspondence to Charles Jones, the overall commander of the local militia, Gowan advised, "Should you determine on having another Company of Volunteers, I would respectfully suggest the propriety of letting the Captain be a Canadian as I am apprehensive the Irish would all wish to volunteer under me . . ."[24]

The message could not be clearer; the Irish would serve under Gowan and no one else. He had volunteered his men for service in Lower Canada and the thought of subduing the French Catholic population of Lower Canada by force of arms was something that had a universal appeal to Gowan's men. Unfortunately, events in Upper Canada had intervened. With the outbreak of rebellion at Toronto, it became apparent that Gowan's troops might be needed at home.

The organization and motivation of militia members were never very far removed from political considerations. The formal order of Colonel Charles Jones calling the Second Regiment of the Leeds Militia to turn out at Beverley on December 19, 1837, read more like a Tory political tract from the last election than a military command:

> The traitor Mackenzie has recently verified beyond contradiction, what were his ulterior views when he professed only simple Reform; he has recently presented himself at the head of Six or Eight Hundred armed Rebels and already commenced the work of Murder and Burning.

> Already are the Courts of Law suspended, and Her Majesty's Loyal Judges in the field at the head of brave volunteers defending our glorious Constitution.

> Martial Law has already been declared in the Sister Province and in all probability must soon be the Law of this Province.

> This Meeting of the Second Regiment, will afford to all within its limits an opportunity of manifesting their Loyalty to their Gracious Queen. Those who have

---

24 Public Archives of Canada, CHARLES JONES PAPERS, MG24 B7, Letter dated Monday 1/2 past 2 o'clock, December 11, 1837, from Ogle R. Gowan to Charles Jones.

heretofore advocated Reform will now have the opportunity by their future conduct to manifest their sincerity; it will now be seen whether their real object was simple Reform or Revolution.[25]

Calling out the militia when the men would ordinarily have been preparing for Christmas with their families was only the first step in protecting the province from rebellion. In Brockville, arms and ammunition were seized from those under suspicion and warrants for the arrest of radical sympathizers were issued. Extraordinary powers were given to local officials to control travel between Upper Canada and the United States. In Prescott, citizens wishing to cross to the American shore needed the consent of Alpheus Jones, the local collector of customs.[26]

The physical arrest of suspected rebels began on December 13, 1837, with a most unlikely accused. Reverend Wilson, a Methodist Episcopal preacher, was ". . . brought in and lodged in jail charged with some matters connected with his refusal to do military duty."[27] Several other persons were picked up with Wilson, only to be released when the authorities realized that while there was ample rumour and suspicion against those arrested, there was no evidence to link them to rebellion. None of those arrested were ever brought to trial.

Members of the Methodist Church had traditionally been suspect. The Mackenzie uprising renewed all the old suspicions about a religion more common in the United States than in England. Sylvester Skinner, another leading local Methodist, soon joined Wilson in a gaol cell. Skinner had spoken publicly and harshly as a representative of the quarterly meeting of the Brockville Station of Methodists in its dispute with the Canadian Conference of Wesleyan Methodists. The Brockville Station of Methodists had castigated the Wesleyans for their acceptance of clergy reserve revenue funding from the government. To Skinner, the acceptance of state funding was morally bankrupt, "unjust and unconscionable."[28] To the Tories and the funded religious leaders of the province, he was a dangerous fanatic.

Those who were arrested cut across class lines. William Buell escaped arrest, but his brother-in-law, Stephen Richards, and his nephew, William Buell Richards, the future Chief Justice of Canada,

25 Ibid., Order of Colonel Charles Jones, December 9, 1837, Brockville.
26 Public Archives of Canada, ALPHEUS JONES PAPERS, MG24 B98, letter from Alfred Hooker to Alpheus Jones, dated December 19, 1838.
27 BROCKVILLE RECORDER, December 14, 1837.
28 Ibid., January 12, 1838, contains Skinner's letter to the editor on the subject, and the entire exchange of correspondence between him and the Wesleyan Methodists.

became fugitives for a time when warrants were issued for their arrest. A close friend and confidant of Buell in the Reform movement, S.C. Frey,[29] a Brockville jeweller who had been the stakeholder in the wager of 1834, joined those arrested. Those in gaol were soon joined by Gideon Shepherd, two of the Bellamy brothers of north Leeds, William Pike, John Thomas, Jamie Malone, William Parrot, and Philip Wing of Farmersville, the clerk for the Township of Yonge.[30] Of the lot, William Sherman, a shoemaker, was held in custody longer than any of the others, but in the end he too was released without having to stand trial.[31]

On December 21, 1837, Buell reported in the *Recorder*, ". . . there is no one at present imprisoned on any such charge (political) except an individual named Sherman, from Kitley (Township), who has been committed for utterances of Seditious language." Buell, never missing the opportunity to reiterate the position that he had taken in his earlier editorial added, "In fact, although there are many Reformers in this District, they are not revolutionists, nor are they disposed to countenance an armed rebellion."[32]

All of those arrested were discharged prior to trial. There was, quite simply, no evidence upon which they could be tried for any offence against the state.

The arrest of the politically suspect was not limited to major centres such as Brockville. Arrests were also made in the outlying villages such as Merrickville, with the same feelings of hysteria, paranoia, and vengefulness. The local magistrates saw to the arrest of the obvious and noisy Reformers. In most cases, these were men who chose to talk of revolution, but who lacked any serious commitment.

John Graff and Robert Nicholson had each, from time-to-time, got quite drunk and made intemperate speeches in favour of rebellion. Graff had been in the village of Merrickville in mid November of 1837, and while drinking he declared himself to be a ". . . full blooded Papanau (sic) man."[33] The magistrates were aware that his general reputation in the community was that of a radical

---

29 KINGSTON CHRONICAL AND GAZETTE, December 27, 1837.
30 BROCKVILLE RECORDER, January 11, 1837, contains a list of all public salaries paid in the Johnstown District at the time.
31 Leavitt, p. 44, provides eight names, together with the date of their arrest, disposition, and the date of their release.
32 BROCKVILLE RECORDER, December 21, 1837.
33 Read and Stagg, ed., THE REBELLION OF 1837, Toronto, 1985, p. 269: citing Public Archives of Canada, Upper Canada Sundries, vol. 181, pp 99882-6: Justices of the Peace at Merrickville December 20, 1837, in the matter of The Queen v. John Graff.

Reformer with a vocal commitment to Reform politics. Worse, it was believed that he had attended some secret meetings of the political union operating in the area. That evidence was sufficient to warrant his arrest.

Robert Nicholson had, like Graff, exhibited Reform tendencies in the past. In addition, at the time of Mackenzie's rebellion in the Home District, Nicholson had sent his wife, children, and assets south for safekeeping in the United States.[34] He, like Graff, was charged with sedition and treason, and was bound over for trial. Graff was released on a cash bond of £50 pending his trial, when two well-known Reformers, Walter and Alexander McCrea, agreed to act as sureties.

There were people more important than Graff and Nicholson in the Merrickville area that the Tory magistrates wanted behind bars. Principal amongst them were Graff's sureties, Alexander McCrea, the leading Reformer in the north Grenville townships, and his son Walter. The younger McCrea exhibited the hot-headed and boastful nature of youth and was soon arrested. The evidence against him included an allegation that, two years previously, he had expressed dissatisfaction with the government. He had become increasingly vocal as the political situation in Upper Canada worsened and, by the time of the rising north of Toronto, it was reported that he had told a neighbour that he supported Mackenzie and the cause of reform and, if necessary, would die in his country's cause.[35]

The justices expressed consternation that they could not obtain any evidence against Walter's father, Alexander McCrea. In their opinion, the father presented a far greater danger to the security of the community than did the son. He was one of William Lyon Mackenzie's warmest friends. Whenever Mackenzie had visited the area, he had stayed at McCrea's home. McCrea had become Mackenzie's local emissary prior to the rebellion. The magistrates could find, however, no evidence to link him to the alleged conspiracy, and no charge could be laid.[36]

Of equal concern to the magistrates was the conduct of their colleague, Dr Basil R. Church, a Merrickville doctor who, since 1833, had served as a fellow magistrate in Wolford Township. Dr Church had been licensed to practise medicine since 1828. He had married a

---

34 Ibid., p. 272, citing Public Archives of Canada, Upper Canada Sundries, vol. 181, pp 99880-1, correspondence from Terrence Smith of Merrickville to Christopher Hagerman, dated December 26, 1837.
35 Public Archives of Canada, UPPER CANADA SUNDRIES, Vol. 181, pp 99890-1.
36 Ibid., pp 9980-1, correspondence from Terrence Smith to Christopher Hagerman, December 26, 1837, Merrickville.

Universalist and became a Universalist himself. To the dismay of his fellow magistrates, he became a steadfast supporter of the Reform cause and had campaigned actively on behalf of Norton and Wells. Church was a thorn in the side of his fellow magistrates. He could never be trusted to keep someone in gaol, nor to authorize the arrest of someone of questionable politics. The time had come to silence Dr Church. In his absence, the balance of the local magistrates from the Merrickville area reported that Church showed an excess of sympathy towards the prisoners just arrested for treason and pursued a ". . . course altogether at variance with the true Character of a Justice of the Peace." There was no evidence upon which charges could be brought against him, but they suggested that an opportune moment had arrived for his dismissal.[37]

William B. Wells, the near-radical Member of the Legislative Assembly for Grenville, was the most influential of those against whom a warrant was issued. In both political philosophy and tactics, Wells was far more radical in his approach to reform than his counterparts in Leeds had ever been. His newspaper was seen as an organ of radical reform opinion. As such, Wells had attracted the enmity of the Tories and, in particular, Ogle Robert Gowan. Gowan had failed in his earlier attempt to have the electoral returns of Wells and Norton set aside by the Tory majority in the Assembly. Undaunted, Gowan had continued his attack with relentless determination, and the Mackenzie rebellion provided him with another opportunity.

From the perspective of the Tories following the Mackenzie rising, Wells had been preaching sedition for years. A warrant was issued for his arrest. A group of magistrates and constables was dispatched to execute the warrant, but was unsuccessful in finding the member for Grenville County. They did find his brother, however and, as indicated in their report:

> . . . H.C. Wells appears to have been implicated by harbouring and entertaining him (William), we considered it necessary to arrest H.C. Wells and search his house which I attended with 2 other Magistrates – nothing suspicious occurred and he voluntarily took the oath of allegiance. We therefore released him from custody.[38]

---

37 Read and Stagg, ed., p. 273, citing Public Archives of Canada, UPPER CANADA SUNDRIES, Vol. 181, pp 99961-3.
38 Public Archives of Canada, CHARLES JONES PAPERS, MG24 B7, letter from George Baker to Charles Jones, December 16, 1837, Bytown.

Further investigation revealed that there was no evidence linking William B. Wells to the Mackenzie rebellion, nor to any similar conspiracy. In the absence of any evidence, the warrant against Wells had to be rescinded. Ogle Robert Gowan, however, was not prepared to allow an absence of evidence to deter him from his crusade against Wells. On February 8, 1838, he took another tack. Rising in the Assembly, he reported that W.B. Wells had absconded to the United States during the rebellion leaving the County of Grenville without representation. The subjects of Her Majesty in the County of Grenville deserved representation, Gowan argued. In light of Wells' failure to provide that representation in a time of crisis, Gowan moved that he be expelled from the House and that a by-election be held. The motion was defeated. Not even the Tory majority was prepared to accept Gowan's argument. The Assembly, perhaps remembering the difficulties associated with the expulsion of Mackenzie, recognized that there was insufficient evidence to establish that Wells had absconded.[39]

The loss of the motion did not end the matter. In early March, 1838, when a group of Patriot adventurists under Rensellaer Van Rensellaer and Bill Johnston, invaded Hickory Island in the St Lawrence River across from Gananoque, Gowan was provided with a fresh opportunity. An official delegation from Upper Canada had crossed the river to discuss the situation with the Americans. Soon after their return, reports began to circulate that William B. Wells had been seen in the American village of French Creek consorting with the enemy. Wells responded with a letter to the Brockville *Recorder*:

> I understand from a friend that a person by the name Wilkinson has circulated through the Canadian papers, that he saw me on a bed at French Creek in a state approaching to intoxication on the eve of the 22nd ult . . . The report is a base and infamous calumny, for which I will hold the author to a just accountability.[40]

Undeterred, Wilkinson responded with details of his allegations.[41] The protestations of the member from Grenville fell on ears deafened by the sound of rebellion. Politically, Wells could not

---

39 Proceedings of House of Assembly Upper Canada for February 8, 1837. The proceedings are reported as well in the BROCKVILLE RECORDER, February 12, 1837.
40 BROCKVILLE RECORDER, March 22, 1838, contains the letter from Wells dated March 5, 1838.
41 Ibid., March 15, 1838.

survive. This time, the Assembly voted to expel him and declare the Grenville seat vacant. The people of Grenville County began once more to erect the hustings in the village of Merrickville for a by-election, while in Brockville. a fresh warrant was issued for the arrest of William Wells.

The by-election was held in Merrickville on April 2, 1838, amidst a new political climate. In 1836, local political leaders had rallied to the standard of Reform and fought for the privilege of the nomination. Now, only Samuel Crane, a traditional Reformer, gave notice of his intention to stand. Bordering on the apologetic, Crane declared ". . . it has been said that the term reformer has been expunged from our political vocabulary, and that the only distinctions now are Tory and Rebel."[42] Crane repeatedly advertised his intention to stand for the election in the local press but, on reflection, he ultimately chose not to do so. He gave as his reason the refusal of the lieutenant-governor to move the poll from Merrickville. The last election in Merrickville, after all, had ended in a riot and controversy. Crane argued that the poll ought to be located at Prescott, the major town in the county, and if not, then in some centrally located village. In the end, Henry Burritt, a Tory, was declared elected unopposed. Two other Tories, Dr H.D. Jessup and Dr Phillips, were nominated on the hustings, but withdrew during their acceptance speeches in favour of Burritt.[43]

Even though the Reform faction had not contested the by-election, emotions ran high. Thomas D. McCormack, a young Tory gentleman ". . . of very respectable parentage and extensively connected," had the honour of helping to escort the new Tory member of the Assembly back to his home from the hustings at Merrickville. On his return to Merrickville, flush with the sense of victory, he met a fellow young Tory on the trail. There had been rude things said at the Merrickville poll by a group of disrespectful Reformers. The two young Tories set off to a local inn intent on finding the most outspoken and impudent of the Reformers, one Burke. They found Burke and quickly decided to teach him some manners. Burke proved a reluctant pupil and a fight broke out in the barroom of the inn. McCormack and Burke squared off and fought their way into the kitchen where McCormack stabbed Burke several times in the belly with his penknife and left him to die on the kitchen floor.

---

42 Ibid., contains Crane's announcement dated March 10, 1838.
43 PRESCOTT SENTINEL, April 5, 1838.

McCormack fled the inn leaving a seriously wounded Reformer behind. Burke's friends, recognizing a Tory murder, called for the constables and Dr Church, the reform-minded justice of the peace. A charge was soon sworn for assault with intent to murder and a band of constables was dispatched to effect McCormack's arrest. McCormack fled to the shop of his father-in-law where he refused to surrender to the gathering Reform mob. By that time, night had fallen and Dr Church and the constables had settled in for an all-night seige. Huddling together in the April night, they warmed themselves by yelling out to the young Tory what they would do to him when they had him in custody.

In the morning, Stephen Merrick, a younger member of the founding Merrick family of Merrickville and an acquaintance of McCormack, arrived and successfully negotiated McCormack's surrender. Merrick, Dr Church, and some of the constables entered the shop to take him into custody. On seeing the group, McCormack panicked, changed his mind, and fled upstairs grabbing another knife on his way. Up the stairs charged the posse meeting McCormack, who had the knife in one hand and a lead post in the other, at the head of the stairs. Merrick grabbed the accused around the waist, but was thrown to the floor in the melee. In a final act of desperation, McCormack stabbed him, cutting the shirt and just grazing his skin. McCormack, by then subdued, was transported to the Brockville Gaol where he was held without bail until Burke was out of danger. At his trial, McCormack was acquitted by a jury on the charge of assaulting Burke, but convicted on the subsequent assault occasioned during his arrest.[44]

While local officialdom proceeded with the political liquidation of Reform leaders wherever possible, the Tory majority in the Legislative Assembly moved quickly to enact enabling legislation legitimizing the repression. Unlike the political reforms suggested by the previous Reform Assembly, the Tory reforms were quickly proclaimed in force. The ancient right of habeas corpus, the right of an accused to have the lawfulness of his arrest questioned by an independent judiciary, was suspended indefinitely.[45] All meetings for the purpose of military training and drilling were declared unlawful[46], and anything that could be used as a weapon, which was kept for a

---

44 Public Archives of Canada, The Queen v. Thomas D. McCormack, Report on the Indictment for assault with intent to murder one Stephen Merrick, RG1 E3, Vol. 54; Reel C-1197, Vol. 54, pp 21-26.
45 Upper Canada Gazette, Toronto, January 18, 1838.
46 AN ACT TO PREVENT UNLAWFUL TRAINING, Upper Canada Gazette, March 15, 1838.

purpose dangerous to the public peace, could be seized by a justice of the peace.[47] Anyone suspected of keeping a potential weapon for a purpose dangerous to the public peace was also subject to arrest. The legislation was broad enough to cover not only firearms, but such usual farm implements as pitchforks and peeve pikes. In effect, any farmer could be arrested on the information of anyone that he was dangerous to the established order. Finally, legislation was passed to protect and save harmless from any lawsuit any loyal citizen who, in assisting the authorities in putting down the insurrection, might have acted illegally.[48]

With the militia mobilized and his new legislation in place, Sir Francis Bond Head declared Tuesday, February 6, 1838, a day of public thanksgiving.[49] Then the lieutenant-governor and his advisors in Upper Canada unleashed the Tory hoards of Orangemen and set them to attacking anyone suspected of harbouring sympathies for reform.

---

47 Ibid., s. 4.
48 "AN ACT FOR INDEMNIFYING PERSONS WHO SINCE DECEMBER 2, 1837, HAVE ACTED IN APPREHENDING, IMPRISONING, OR DETAINING IN CUSTODY, PERSONS SUSPECTED OF HIGH TREASON OR TREASONABLE PRACTICES." Upper Canada Gazette, March 15, 1838.
49 Ibid., January 25, 1838.

CHAPTER X
Preparations for War

_F_OR REASONS THAT social psychologists have long studied but little understood, men through the ages have been prepared to fight for ideals they only partially understand, but passionately believe in. For those passionate reasons, neither the electoral defeat of 1836, nor the military defeat of Mackenzie's rebels on Yonge Street, nor the political repression that followed, could eradicate the desire for radical reform in some of the people of Upper Canada. Those people were the minority. The majority had been drawn, seductively, toward the candle flame of democracy then, recognizing the danger, they had drawn back. Only a few continued on the path to rebellion. They were undeterred by what had happened to their French Canadian allies in Lower Canada at St-Denis, St-Eustache, and Napierville. Unlike the majority, they did not cheer when the English and Scottish militia units from Upper Canada marched home, victorious, putting the torch to every French Canadian house and outbuilding in their path.

In Upper Canada, the combined voices of Sir Francis Bond Head, the Orange Lodge, and the Tories had succeeded in making the Reformer's call of freedom and liberty sound more like treason and treachery. Bond Head and his political allies had raised the louder and more compelling cry of loyalty. Nonetheless, a minority of men remained prepared to die in the cause of freedom. Most of this radical minority left Upper Canada for the more fertile fields of the United States of America, where that same cry of liberty was instantly recognized and appreciated.

The apparent plight of Canadians provided Americans with an opportunity to act out the mythology of their fathers and grandfathers. Those now in their prime had grown up on the tales of their grandfathers' victories in the War of Independence and of their fathers' in the War of 1812. They listened with rapt attention to the exploits of their fellow Americans in the deserts of the south west, where Davy Crockett, Jim Bowie, and Sam Houston were wrestling the new state of Texas from Spanish despots. To these American border men in the north east, it was plain that the British Red Coats were another force of tyranny subjugating their brothers and sisters in Canada. By assisting Canadians, and finally driving the British out of North America, they would be fulfilling not only their national manifest destiny, but that of democracy itself. American men were ready to die to assist in the liberation of Canada. It was the right thing to do.

While the cause of liberty in Canada enjoyed the popular support of the American people, the enthusiasm for renewed conflict with Britain was not shared by the American government. The official position of the American government was one of strict neutrality enforced by the provisions of the Neutrality Act, which President Van Buren had proclaimed in force on January 5, 1838. The individual American states shared the desire of their federal government for peace. Along the Canadian frontier, the states of New York and Vermont followed the federal initiative and enacted their own neutrality acts. As the tensions along the border increased, the American government took increasing pains to convey the sincerity of its desire for peace to the British.

Lord Durham, sent to the Canadas following the outbreak of rebellion in 1837 and charged with finding a solution to the political crisis, was understandably concerned about the American position should rebellion break out anew. Durham dispatched Lieutenant Colonel Grey from his personal staff to Washington in June of 1838 for discussions. President Van Buren and his Secretary of State, John Forsyth, repeatedly assured Grey that the Americans had no desire to involve themselves in the internal affairs of Canada. Satisfied with the assurance, Grey advised his superior, "The President also desires me to assure Lord Durham in the strongest manner of his desire to do all in his power to keep up a good understanding between the two countries."[1] As if to confirm Grey's findings, the Americans dispatched two steamers to the Canadian border area during the early

---

1 William Ormsby, ed., CRISIS IN THE CANADAS: 1838 - 1839, THE GREY JOURNALS AND LETTERS, MacMillan of Canada, Toronto, 1964, p. 37, Diary of Charles Grey, Friday, June 15, 1838.

summer of 1838, one to patrol Lake Erie, the other Lake Ontario and the upper St Lawrence.[2] Each steamer was manned with fifty troops. Their purpose was not to protect the United States from the British in Canada, but to prevent incursions by American nationals into Upper Canada.

The prospect of formal hostilities between the United States of America and the British colonies diminished. The established Tory families of the Johnstown District of Upper Canada who had openly anticipated war relaxed somewhat. Alpheus Jones, Prescott's leading Tory, who the winter before had bet his hat that there would be war, was, by May of 1838, being called upon to make good on the wager and produce the hat.

> I presume that you will by this time be fully satisfied that there will be no war between the States and Britain growing out of the border difficulties and sympathetic movements; if so, I shall thank you to send me the value of a hat,[3]

wrote James Holmes from Montreal concerning his bet made at Gananoque the winter before.

The Neutrality Laws were declaratory in nature. No law could detract from the popular support shown by the American people to the exiled Canadians. In a free country such as the United States, it was virtually impossible to prevent the populace from meeting with the Canadian radicals, encouraging them and ultimately joining with them in the grand plan for the liberation of Canada.

In American towns along the border, Canadian radicals, who by then referred to themselves as Patriots, joined with their American sympathizers to form Hunters' Lodges. The Lodges were paramilitary organizations dedicated to securing Canadian freedom by force of arms. Originally, the Hunters' Lodges were the creation of the exiled Patriotes of Lower Canada. Robert Nelson, Dr Cote, and the rest of Papineau's exiles had called their loosely organized bands of banished rebels Les Freres Chasseur. The organization quickly spread into northern New York, Illinois, and Ohio where the name was anglicised, first to The Brotherhood of Hunters and, finally, to Hunters' Lodges.

By the fall of 1838, it was estimated that 200,000 men were

---

2 Ibid., p. 37, Diary of Charles Grey, Friday, June 15, 1838.
3 Public Archives of Canada, ALPHEUS JONES PAPERS, MG24 B98 Vol.1, letter from James Holmes to Alpheus Jones dated May 11, 1838,

involved in the Hunters' Lodges, spread out along the Canadian border from Maine to Michigan.[4] There were as many as 1,174 individual Lodges, each with its own internal command. Along the St Lawrence frontier, there were twenty-one separate lodges, including those at Salina, Watertown, Sackets Harbor, Cape Vincent, Alexandria Bay and Ogdensburg. The Lodge at Watertown, organized in May of 1838, soon boasted 1,900 members.[5]

The secret societies directly challenged the American government on the Canadian issue. To the Canadian authorities, they posed a vocal and substantial danger, and in both Upper and Lower Canada, rumours reverberated, not only of the activities of the Hunters' Lodges south of the border, but of secret subversive meetings within the province itself.

In September of 1838, the Hunters met in a general convention at Cleveland, Ohio, and voted to establish a provisional republican government of Canada. Border attacks began. At Windsor and Niagara, the Hunters made relatively ineffectual incursions into Upper Canada and were quickly repulsed. These attacks were mere preludes to the attack on the Eastern Townships of Lower Canada. On November 3, 1838, Robert Nelson led his Hunters, Les Freres Chasseurs, up the ancient warriors' route over Lake Champlain and across the border to Napierville where he proclaimed himself president of the new Republic of Lower Canada. Hindenlang, a French soldier of fortune who had accompanied the ragtag army of liberation, was promoted to the rank of brigadier general and assumed command of the fledgling army of the new republic.

At the high point of the invasion, Brigadier Hindenlang had amassed a force of 3,000 men to carry the battle forward. Unfortunately, his army consisted of militarily unskilled French Canadian habitants, the majority of whom were armed with nothing more than clubs and pikes. Like Mackenzie's farmers at Montgomery's Tavern, and Papineau's Patriotes at St-Eustache, they were no match for the loyal, armed militia backed by British regulars who quickly encircled the Napierville encampment and severed the supply lines to the United States. The habitant soldiers of

4 Thomas H. Raddall, THE PATH TO DESTINY, CANADA FROM THE BRITISH CONQUEST TO HOME RULE: 1763 - 1850, Doubleday Canada Limited, Toronto, 1957, p. 399.
5 Richard A. Pierce, NILS VON SHOULTZ - THE MAN THEY HAD TO HANG, in a paper to the Kingston Historical Society published in Historic Kingston (Number 19), Kingston Historical Society, February, 1971.

Hindenlang's army assessed their position and, one-by-one, they quietly faded away into the forest and returned to their farms. The self-proclaimed president recognized that his invasion was doomed. If his Patriotes were to fight again, he needed to lead the remnants of his army in a strategic retreat to the security of the United States. Nelson moved his men to the south, intent on fighting his way through the British lines to the border.

On November 9, 1838, at the village of Oddletown, the retreating Patriotes met the British forces moving into position to cut off their escape. The militia units, which made up the bulk of the British forces, lacked the training and discipline of the British regulars, but they were more than a match for this cold and hungry rabble. As Brigadier Hindenlang ordered his men to attack, many of his habitant soldiers sank to their knees in the snow and began to recite their rosaries. Others made a valiant but futile assault on the British position before fleeing for their lives back up the road to Napierville. In the excitement of the battle, Robert Nelson slipped away. He crossed the border into the United States alone, leaving his army to its fate. Hindenlang remained with his troops and was captured. Following due process of law, the British hanged him along with an even dozen of the leaders of his army. The Patriote invasion of Lower Canada had been an unmitigated disaster.

While Les Patriotes marched up the Champlain Valley, their English-speaking counterparts plotted the liberation of Upper Canada. Some of the radical Reformers of the Johnstown District had crossed the St Lawrence River by the fall of 1838. Some had done so of their own volition, while some had been driven out by the Tory repression following the Mackenzie rising at Toronto. They made contact with the Hunters' Lodges in the border villages and towns in northern New York; Ogdensburg, Sackets Harbor, French Creek, Oswego, and Salina[6] were all centres of agitation and Hunters' Lodge organization.

One of the Canadian Patriots in the United States was the acquitted murderer from Bastard Township in Leeds County, James Phillips. Phillips may have been acquitted by a jury of his peers for the murder of Edward Tusic following the election riots at Beverley in 1835, but Tusic had been an Orangeman and a strong supporter of the Tories, who after the election of 1836 were in complete control of the county and the province. Phillips had been active in the Reform campaigns to elect Buell and Howard and, following the Tory victory

---

6 Salina is now the city of Syracuse, while French Creek is now the town of Clayton.

of 1836, both economics and politics had dictated that he leave Upper Canada. By 1837, it is clear that he had done so.[7]

Phillips was not alone. The Chipman brothers, Levi and Truman, two more members of the rebellious minority of Bastard Township, had also crossed the river and were living in northern New York. They too were prepared to fight for the freedom of Upper Canada.[8] Levi was forty years old, while his older brother Truman was forty-four in 1838.[9] They were the sons of Ami Chipman an American immigrant who had arrived in the Johnstown District from the state of Vermont with his brother, Barnabas, in 1795, and had settled Lot 13 in Concession 6 of Bastard prior to 1820.[10] Two of his other brothers had served with the American army during the Revolution. The Chipman family was amongst those American immigrants to Upper Canada that Lieutenant-Governor Simcoe had openly encouraged to move north into the British colonies. In 1837, Ami Chipman, a freshly converted Mormon, together with his wife, two of his children, and several of his neighbours left Bastard Township, crossed into the United States, and travelled west intent on joining Brigham Young in the fledgling Mormon settlements.[11] They would be gone for over a year and, by the time they returned, an armed insurrection had shattered the peace of the Johnstown District and their sons, Levi and Truman, were in custody at Fort Henry charged with treason.

These Canadian men from the back country of Leeds County had crossed into the United States, joined the Patriot forces, and were ready to return to liberate Upper Canada by force of arms. They had given up on the idea of incremental reform and had concluded that the country required a republican form of government. It was an idea shared by James Cummings, a native of Grenville County, Ezra Brockway, of South Gower Township,[12] and one of the Laraby men[13] from the Prescott area. All of these men had left Upper Canada by 1838. They resided in northern New York State as voluntary political

---

7 Public Archives of Canada, RG5 B41, Vol. 17-20, Reel C-1569. MILITIA GENERAL COURTS MARTIAL, evidence of Levi Chipman, November 1838, Fort Henry.
8 Ibid.
9 Ibid., p. 124.
10 Leavitt, p. 121.
11 Leavitt, p. 125.
12 Leavitt, p. 77.
13 Public Archives of Canada, Reel 15691. MILITIA GENERAL COURTS MARTIAL, Trial of Howth, Price, Garrison, Delino et. al., November 1838, Fort Henry.

exiles and were prepared to fight for the republican ideal. Numerous French Canadians who had left Lower Canada and who now happened to be in the area shared their opinion. All that they required to set them on the path to rebellion was leadership and opportunity.

Along the St Lawrence frontier, armed hostilities began in March of 1838, with a limited incursion onto Upper Canadian soil. The Patriots were led by an American, General Rensellaer Van Rensellaer, but guided by Bill Johnston, a river rat who knew the Thousand Islands area of the St Lawrence River better than most farmers knew their barnyards. The Patriots had long discussed the capture of the village of Gananoque. From there, it was thought they could launch an assault on Kingston and on Fort Henry itself.

In late February, the Patriots began to put these plans into operation by seizing Hickory Island, an insignificant island uninhabited except for a single widow, lying in the St Lawrence River between French Creek, New York, and Gananoque. The Patriots under Rensellaer Van Rensellaer took the island, held it for a time, and then retreated to the American shore before the British moved to expel them by force. Nothing of substance had been accomplished.

The original purpose had been to use the island as a staging area for a full-scale attack on Upper Canada, but when Van Rensellaer called the roll to assemble his volunteers for the assault on the Canadian mainland, only eighty-three men responded. Fearing a mistake, the roll was called a second time at which time only seventy-one volunteers responded. When the roll was taken a third time, the potential assault force had declined to thirty-five stalwarts. There had been no mistake. The task of an actual assault against the fortified mainland of Upper Canada was a far more daunting prospect from their new perspective in the middle of the St Lawrence River than it had appeared from the security of the inns and bar rooms along the American shore. The assault never took place. The incursion was described as a failure attributed to ". . . the stupidity, cowardice, drunkenness, or some other trait in Van Rensellaer."[14] The American press noted that ". . . if the Canadian patriots expect to accomplish anything favourable to their hopes they must select another leader."[15]

On their return to the American shore, American troops arrested the raiders, and Bill Johnston was held to bail in the sum of $5,000 on a charge of violating the Neutrality Acts. His subsequent trial before

---

14 WATERTOWN JEFFERSONIAN, March 1, 1838.
15 Ibid.

a Jefferson County, New York, jury exemplified the practical difficulties with the Neutrality Act. To the typical American, Bill Johnston and all of the Patriots were heroes. There was no lack of evidence that Johnston had been instrumental in leading the Hunters into Canada, but the jury refused to convict. New York juries would not convict local heros for acting heroically.

Shortly after the Hickory Island incursion, Colonel Phillpotts, the Assistant Quartermaster General of the British regular army, crossed the river on the thick spring ice to demand of the Americans ". . . what steps have been taken to punish the lawless band of Brigands and rebels, who lately presumed to invade this province by crossing over to Hickory Island on their route from French Creek to Gananoque."[16] He brought with him John MacDonald, Gananoque's leading citizen, and an escort of twelve soldiers. The Canadian contingent was met midway across the St Lawrence River by a party of American infantrymen. They were welcomed by the Americans who treated them with all due dignity and escorted them to the American shore. Following visits to the border villages, they were transported to the county seat at Watertown from where, following discussions with the area commander, they retired to the Canadian shore satisfied that the American government was doing its best to control its nationals. It was during this sojourn to the American shore that the person alleged to be William Benjamin Wells was observed by a member of the Canadian party in a compromising position, drunk, and in the company of some wanton American woman.

The British authorities remained confident that the prospect of all-out war with the United States was virtually non-existent. At the same time, the local authorities in Upper Canada anticipated continued trouble from the Americans who, in turn, thought that they were simply assisting the popular will of Canadian people. Regardless of the various perspectives, residents along both sides of the St Lawrence River remained anxious as border incidents became commonplace.

In April, approximately nine miles down river from Prescott, Aikins' Inn was invaded by an American "gang of desperadoes."[17] One of the Americans involved in the incursion was Captain John Lytle, a man whom the American press described as ". . . a distinguished officer in the last war, and more latterly by his connection with the Patriots at Hickory Island."[18] He had crossed the

---

16 BROCKVILLE RECORDER, March 27, 1838.
17 PRESCOTT SENTINEL, April 12, 1838.
18 WATERTOWN REPUBLICAN, April 12, 1838.

river at the invitation of a Canadian who had sold him a horse and who instructed him to attend at Aikins' Inn to take delivery. Having crossed the river, and announced his presence, he was rudely ordered out by Mr. Aikins who would have no truck with Americans. The American and his friends refused to leave. They stood a round of drinks for the revellers at the inn and bragged about their involvement at Hickory Island. Aikins threatened to raise the party of British Dragoons asleep in the upstairs bedroom and was dared to do so by Lytle, who taunted ". . . you were a Tory in the last war and probably there has been no alteration for the better since."[19]

The British Dragoons came down as the fight broke out. Lytle and the Americans fought their way out of the inn and down to the river, but before leaving Aikins' Inn, they took time to steal Aikins' crossed swords from their place of honour on his wall as a memento of the night. The American press praised Lytle for his gallantry. The Canadians were outraged. The residence of a respected member of the community had been invaded, two swords had been stolen from the wall of his drawing room, and he had suffered a beating at the hands of the American "ruffians."[20]

When the ice finally melted, the winter's interference with navigation on the river was replaced by Bill Johnston and his band of pirates. Operating from their home base at French Creek, and using St Lawrence River boats manned by up-to-a-dozen oarsmen, the pirates became a perpetual curse to British shipping on the river.

Bill Johnston was an expatriated Upper Canadian. Before the War of 1812, he had operated a store at Kingston and had been called out to serve with the Frontenac Militia for the duration of hostilities. Johnston arranged for his brother to serve on his behalf, so that he might return to mind his store. When his brother deserted, Johnston was ordered to resume his post with the militia. He refused, found himself charged with desertion, and was finally jailed. With his business ruined and the war over, Johnston settled on the American shore of the St Lawrence River and turned his talents to smuggling. He harboured an obvious resentment against the British and enthusiastically supported William Lyon Mackenzie and all others who sought to end British rule in Upper Canada. If a profit could be made at the same time, so much the better.

---

19 Ibid.
20 PRESCOTT SENTINEL, April 12, 1838.

NATIONAL ARCHIVES OF CANADA, C-329

Bill Johnston, river rat, pirate, and ultimately the Admiral of the Patriot Navy.

In the late spring of 1838, Johnston and his band of river rats, by then numbering forty or fifty men, embarked on their most audacious raid. On May 29, 1838, the Canadian steamer, *Sir Robert Peel*, set into Wells Island for wood on her journey up river to Lake Ontario. When the crew turned in for the night, the pirates struck. Dressed as Indians, they captured the steamer and forced the crew and passengers to take to the water and swim for their lives. The steamer was looted, towed into the channel, and burned to the waterline.[21]

---

21 Public Archives of Canada, ALPHEUS JONES PAPERS, Affidavit of Roderick McSween, MG24 B98, vol. 1; see as well William Ormsby, CRISIS IN THE CANADAS 1838 - 1839, THE GREY JOURNALS AND LETTERS, Toronto, 1964, p. 22.

NATIONAL ARCHIVES OF CANADA, C-1029

Action at close quarters among the Thousand Islands.

The British doubled and redoubled their efforts at bringing the pirates to justice, but they were hopelessly outmanoeuvred by Johnston and his men who seemed to roam the Thousand Islands with impunity, immune from capture. Cognizant of the diplomatic need to stabilize the border, the American government ordered Major General Alexander Macomb into the area. His orders were clear enough:

> Desirous of adopting every measure in the power of the Government to maintain the treaty stipulations existing between the United States and Great Britain, and to restrain our own citizens, and others within our jurisdiction from committing outrages upon the persons and property of the subjects of Her Britannic majesty, The President has instructed me to direct you to proceed, without unnecessary delay, to the frontier of Canada, and to take the command there.[22]

He was advised:

> that a gang of desperate men have assembled in that part of the river St. Lawrence called the Thousand Islands and within the territory of the United States, with the intention of committing hostilities upon that of a friendly power, you will proceed immediately to scour those Islands . . .[23]

Finally, he was instructed to seize all arms found and "arrest all persons engaged in hostile expeditions" against Upper Canada. The order was easier to give than to carry out. The skill and knowledge of the river possessed by Johnston and his renegades, combined with the topography of the Thousand Island area, made the pirates more than a match for either the British or American authorities.

As tensions grew along the border, the wheels of military justice were slowly but inexorably disposing of the Mackenzie rebels who had been captured following the Montgomery Tavern rising. News of the trials and hangings in Upper Canada served to incite further the members of the Hunters' Lodges in the United States.

On April 12, 1838, the Upper Canadian government publicly executed two of Mackenzie's officers, Colonel Lount and Captain Matthews, in a back-to-back hanging. The Canadian authorities intended to make the executions a public spectacle that would provide general deterrence to any other potential insurrectionists. The effect,

---

22 Ormsby, ed., p. 46, letter dated June 12, 1838, from Department of War to Maj. Gen. Macomb.
23 Ibid.

however, was quite the opposite. The executions served only to elevate two ordinary and decent men to martyrdom.

Lount and Matthews were both family men, known and respected in the Home District. Following their trials and before their executions, a petition had been circulated which attracted more than 30,000 signatures imploring Sir George Arthur, Bond Head's successor as lieutenant-governor, to commute their sentences. He refused convinced that a demonstration of mercy would be interpreted as a sign of weakness.

The report of the executions themselves was graphic and bloody; just the sort of incident that creates martyrs and incites violence under the guise of revenge. As to whether or not the gory reports bore any resemblance to reality is of little consequence. The Patriots believed in their accuracy. Captain Matthews, they heard, had died slowly, twisting and kicking at the end of the rope, while the drop for Colonel Lount was too long, resulting in his head being nearly severed from his body by the rope. Lount's corpse was covered in blood, but the assembled crowd of Orangemen merely cheered all the louder and, in a final outrage, they grabbed the hangman's rope still attached to Lount's body and proceeded to drag his bloody corpse through the crowd.[24]

The leaders of the Hunters' Lodges were quite independent of William Lyon Mackenzie and the rest of the Upper Canadian radical reformers. They shared, however, Mackenzie's dominant strength and weakness. Like Mackenzie, they were strong on rhetoric, but woefully inadequate in matters of general organization and military logistics. At the Cleveland convention of September 16, 1838, the Patriot Hunters elected General J.V. Bierce as Commander-in-Chief of all Patriot troops in Upper Canada – but a military command based on popular election by the troops is rarely effective.

Dealing entirely with volunteers and with no way of enforcing discipline, neither Bierce nor his subordinates could enforce a central command. In northern New York, matters were progressing with neither the knowledge nor approbation of Bierce or his generals. Unbeknownst to General Bierce, Mr Birge of Cazenovia, calling himself Commander-in-Chief of the Eastern Division New York, was raising his own force of Patriots to liberate Canada. In that capacity he contacted Nils Szolteocky Von Schoultz, a thirty-one year old self-

---

24 D. McLeod, A BRIEF REVIEW OF THE SETTLEMENT OF UPPER
CANADA, (reprinted) Mika Publishing Co., 1972, p. 238; but see the report of the
execution in the BROCKVILLE RECORDER, which describes the executions as
uneventful.

styled Polish exile who had emigrated to the United States in 1836 and taken up residence in Salina, New York.

Nils Gustaf Von Schoultz was born in Finland on October 7, 1807, into an upper-class family. His grandfather had been a successful Finnish army officer, while his father had been a circuit court judge, chief administrator of the town in which the family resided, and member of the Royal Swedish Musical Academy of Stockholm. The pleasant life of the Von Schoultz family was shattered forever by the wars then sweeping Europe. In 1808, Russia invaded Finland and the judge was compelled to turn his talents to the unsuccessful defence of his country. The Russian victory forced the

Nils Gustaf Von Schoultz, European adventurer caught up in the winds of war.. ONTARIO ARCHIVES, S-785

family into exile in Sweden, where the young Von Schoultz grew up. His father died when he was nine.

In keeping with his station in life, Nils Gustaf Von Schoultz received his education in a military academy before entering the Swedish army. Discharged in 1830, Von Schoultz fancied himself as a soldier of fortune. The student and cadet uprisings at Warsaw, Poland, appealed to his spirit of adventure and, until his capture by the Russian army, he fought valiantly alongside the Polish freedom fighters in another losing cause. Escaping from eastern Europe, Von Schoultz travelled to France, joined the French Foreign Legion and saw service in Algeria. In the spring of 1834, he married Ann Campbell, a Scottish girl he met while in Italy. They had one child early in 1834, whereupon Von Schoultz left Europe for America.

Arriving in the United States in August of 1836, Von Schoultz settled in Salina, New York, where he perfected a refinement on the process of extracting salt from the salt springs in the Salina area. All seemed serene. Von Schoultz was at the threshold of prosperity. He would soon be able to ask his wife and daughter to join him in the new world and put the seemingly endless ethnic battles of Europe behind him. But something in the Von Schoultz character made that impossible. The call of adventure proved irresistible. Talk of the Canadian political situation was endemic in the Salina area and Von Schoultz got caught up in the plans for military action.

For a time, he operated a recruiting office in New York City attempting to win military recruits to the Patriot cause. He also began to stress his Polish connection and changed his name to variations of Nils Szolteocky Von Schoultz, a bastardization of Czultzecky, a family name that was connected, distantly, to his own. In addition, he began to represent to the world that he was Polish and that his father had been a Polish, as opposed to a Finnish, officer.[25]

Von Schoultz had previously contacted General Bierce to offer his services to the central command of the Patriot forces but, on being contacted by Birge, he cancelled his plans to join Bierce's group and threw in his lot with the Eastern Division. Many others, coming from all walks of life, religions, and ages, were also volunteering. John (Jean) Baptiste Raza had been born at Montreal, Quebec, but had emigrated to the United States and now lived in northern New York

---

25 Ella Pipping, SOLDIER OF FORTUNE, THE STORY OF A NINETEENTH CENTURY ADVENTURER, Gambit Incorporated, Boston, 1971.

State.[26] He was prepared to join in the adventure to free Canada. So, too, was Laurent Melhuit, a fourteen year old native of Boucherville, Quebec, who had left Lower Canada three years before and taken up residence at Rossie, New York.[27] The recruits also included men from the Counties of Leeds and Grenville who had abandoned hope of peaceful reform in Upper Canada.

Most of the Patriot volunteers were American nationals. Austen Samuel, a seventeen year old Methodist from Jefferson County, New York, was prepared to invade Upper Canada. So was Allen Charles, a twenty-four year old Presbyterian from Onondaga County, New York, Anderson Duncan from Livingston County, New York, and Allen David, a thirty-seven year old Baptist from Massachusetts.[28] They shared a fervent belief in the democratic principles enunciated in the American revolution and the misapprehension that Upper Canadians would join the revolution and throw off British rule if given the opportunity to do so.

They congregated in the American villages along the eastern end of Lake Ontario and the south western shore of the St Lawrence. They rallied, almost daily, listening to speeches of British atrocities in Canada and assurances that the Canadian people were anxiously awaiting the start of hostilities so that they could join their American liberators and throw off the yoke of tyranny. They also listened to promises of free land for the members of the volunteer army once the British were driven out. The men of Oswego, Miller's Bay, French Creek, Sackets Harbor, Salina and of the country all around had joined with the few Canadian refugees for the Patriot invasion of Canada. They were ready for war.

---

26 Public Archives of Canada, MILITIA GENERAL COURTS MARTIAL, Trial of Nils von Shoultz, evidence of Jean Baptiste Raza, RG5, B40, Reel C 1560. See also, Trial of Martin Woodruff, RG5 B41, Reel C 15691.
27 Ibid.
28 Public Archives of Canada, MILITIA GENERAL COURTS MARTIAL, November,1838, RG5 B41 vol. 1.

CHAPTER XI
$\mathcal{C}$annons at $\mathcal{W}$indmill $\mathcal{P}$oint

*O*N SUNDAY, NOVEMBER 11, 1838, the steamer *United States* was scheduled to sail from Oswego, New York, on a regular run up the eastern shore of Lake Ontario and down the St Lawrence River to Cape Vincent, French Creek, Alexandria Bay, Morristown, Ogdensburg, and American ports to the east. At the last moment, 150 Patriot Hunters came on board disguised as regular deck passengers. When the steamer put in at Sackets Harbor, they were joined by another group of serious-faced men. At Cape Vincent, still more men boarded the steamer carrying nothing but hand luggage and sober faces. The Patriot attack on the St Lawrence frontier of Upper Canada was underway.

Just before the steamer was to leave Cape Vincent, two schooners heading down river requested a tow from the captain. This was not an unusual request, especially when the winds on the river were not favourable. He agreed, and one schooner was lashed to each side of his steamship. As soon as the flotilla was again underway, all pretence was abandoned. The two schooners were full of Patriot troops who had been ordered to remain below deck until well out in the river. These men now clambered on deck and broke open cases of arms on the decks of the schooners and the steamship alike.

The total number of Patriot troops on board was variously estimated at between 400 and 800 men.[1] They included Nils Von Schoultz and a few of the Polish patriots that he had recruited, while Bill Johnston, the notorious river pirate, captained one of the schooners. As

---

1 K.F. Scott, PRESCOTT'S FAMOUS BATTLE OF THE WINDMILL, NOVEMBER 13 - 18, 1838, Prescott, 1970; see also Edwin C. Guillet, THE LIVES AND TIMES OF THE PATRIOTS, Toronto, 1938 & 1963, and George F.G. Stanley "Invasion 1838" Ontario History, vol. 54, December 1962.

The steamer United States provided transport to the Patriots.
METROPOLITAN TORONTO REFERENCE LIBRARY, J.ROSS ROBERTSON COLLECTION T-16107

soon as the flotilla left Cape Vincent, Johnston went below deck and reappeared moments later wearing the uniform of an admiral in the liberation navy. Bill Johnston was no longer a river pirate; he had become the Commodore of the Lower Division of the Patriot Navy.

Once the Patriots were in control of the steamer, Birge identified himself as the general and commanding officer, and changed into his self-designed dress uniform replete with brass buttons and gold braid suitable to his station. He, after all, was the Supreme Commander of the Eastern Division.

Von Schoultz, the only person on board with any substantial military training, had developed a detailed plan of attack. No one else seemed to have bothered preparing the specific objectives of the invasion. He suggested that the Patriots attack, seize, and hold Fort Wellington located at Prescott. If successful in this objective, the Patriots would then effectively control all shipping on the St Lawrence River and provide a secure rallying point for the citizens of Upper Canada.

To attack the fort, he proposed landing the Patriot troops at the most westerly town wharf at Prescott. The men would divide into three parties: the first would sweep along the waterfront of the town, the second would clear the centre by moving in a northern direction from the waterfront, while the third would proceed in a circling manoeuvre through the outer fringes of settlement. Once the town was securely in Patriot hands, the three groups would regroup in the east end of town and from there attack the fort.

Most of the regular troops ordinarily stationed at Fort Wellington had been redeployed to strengthen the British garrisons in Lower Canada. Having regard to the skeletal guard left at Fort Wellington, Von Schoultz's plan had some prospect of success.

Von Schoultz stressed that the element of surprise was essential to the success of the attack. The British must have no advance knowledge of the invasion. They must be denied the opportunity of organizing a defence or of sending for reinforcements. With this in mind, the Patriots seized the ferry that operated between Cape Vincent and Wolfe Island. Wolfe Island sits off the coast of Kingston, and another ferry connected the island to Kingston itself. The ferrymen had noticed the large numbers of men on the steamer and the two schooners heading down river towards Gananoque and Brockville and would undoubtedly see that the alarm was raised on the Upper Canadian shore.

The Patriot flotilla steamed onwards, down the main American shipping channel, hidden from any inquiring Canadian eyes by the river mists and the Thousand Islands. Just before Brockville, the St Lawrence River narrows and the camouflage provided by the Thousand Islands ends. It was no longer possible for the Patriots to hide. As the three vessels approached the sleeping town of Brockville, their presence was noted.

If the *United States* had steamed full ahead to Prescott with the two schooners in tow, it is doubtful that any alarm raised at Brockville would have been received in Prescott before the Patriot arrival, and Von Schoultz's plan might conceivably have had some prospect of success. But, Von Schoultz was not in command of the invasion and, as the Patriot flotilla approached the Three Sisters Islands between Brockville and Morristown, New York, the problems of an indecisive Patriot command began to appear. From the security of his cabin on the steamer, General Birge ordered his troops onto the two schooners and severed their tow lines. The schooners would proceed by sail. In this way, he reasoned, they would be less conspicuous as they approached the wharf at Prescott.

At Brockville the river narrows, as shown in this sketch from the American shore across from Brockville, looking down river towards Prescott.

Even more inexplicably, Birge ordered the steamer to set in at the village of Morristown, directly across the river from Brockville. As soon as the ship docked, the American authorities ascertained the full details of the impending attack on Prescott and, following the Neutrality Laws, they promptly advised their Upper Canadian counterparts at Brockville.

The alarm bells of Brockville shattered the stillness of the November night at two o'clock in the morning. In the pre-dawn cold of November 12, 1838, the Leeds Militia, including Gowan's Brockville Invincibles, answered the call and assembled on the green before the court house. Before the sun rose, Brockville's men were on the march to assist in the defence of Prescott and Fort Wellington.

The initial hesitation and indecision of General Birge were compounded when the Patriot schooners approached the intended battlefield. At the last moment, Birge, who had by then left Morristown and proceeded down river, decided that the steamer should set in to the port of Ogdensburg for reinforcements prior to the attack on Prescott. As soon as Birge set foot on the wharf at Ogdensburg, he developed a mysterious illness, which the uncharitable might associate with cowardice, and which, in any event, effectively removed him from the battle.

One of the two schooners, the *Charlotte of Oswego*, commanded by Admiral Bill Johnston, soon grounded on a sandbar. Her sister ship, the *Charlotte of Toronto*, with Nils Von Schoultz now in charge, slowly drifted through the night towards the upriver wharf of Prescott where Von Schoultz hoped to put his plan into action.

Von Schoultz's plan called for complete surprise. He had hoped to find Prescott's defenders soundly sleeping. That was no longer the case. The alarm had long since been given and Alpheus Jones reported later:

> Word came about one o'clock about suspicious schooners lying between here (Prescott) and Ogdensburg. Accordingly, the call to arms was sounded in our streets and a general muster made of all who could procure arms, pitchforks, or anything which would repel the midnight assassins.[2]

Von Schoultz's schooner approached McMillan's wharf but, before he could tie up and land troops, they were spotted by the

---

2 Scott, p. 14.

militia. It was reported later by eighteen year old Price Senter, who was on board the schooner:

> As we were about to land, a cannon shot was fired on the Canadian shore and the Royalists of Prescott rushed to their guns to meet our attack. We were not inclined to wage battle against such a superior force and retired down river.[3]

The schooner *Charlotte of Toronto* made good her escape from the Prescott shore and faded quickly into the November night. Sailing at night, fully loaded, and without power, however, proved to be an equally dangerous undertaking. As she proceeded down river, the schooner grounded on another sandbar off Windmill Point about a mile to the east of Fort Wellington. Desperate to float the schooner off the sandbar before daybreak, Von Schoultz ordered his men into the lifeboats to lighten her. Von Schoultz was first into the boats and led his men towards the shore. As he gained his bearings and surveyed the immediate topography, he began to realize the advantages of his position. The windmill for which the point was named loomed on a steep bluff above the river bank. It stood a full eighty feet tall with stout stone walls three feet thick, and small windows which would lend themselves for use as rifle slits. The windmill itself was flanked by stone outbuildings and fences, which together turned the site into a veritable fortress. It was virtually as defendable a position as Fort Wellington itself. Von Schoultz quickly decided that this was the place for the Patriots to make their stand for Canadian liberty.

The lull before the storm. With Prescott and Fort Wellington in the background, a lone paddler passes Windmill Point.

As Von Schoultz and his troop of 192 Patriots established their base in the windmill, the British steamer *Experiment,* under the command of Lieutenant Fowler, RN, arrived at Windmill Point from Brockville. Little more than a launch, the *Experiment* was armed with one eighteen-pound cannon and a three-pound carriage gun. She carried not only her crew, but Colonel Duncan Fraser and his troop of Brockville militia volunteers.[4]

The *Charlotte of Toronto,* now floating free of the sandbar, saw the British steamer as she approached and, rather than stand and fight, she simply sailed away. Von Schoultz and his Patriots were now stranded on the Canadian shore. They had no choice but to fight.

In Prescott, Colonel Young, commander of the British regular forces, prepared for the worst. The morning light revealed the *Charlotte of Oswego,* her decks swarming with armed men, grounded on the sandbar towards the American side of the river. Colonel Young reasoned that the landing of the Patriots at Windmill Point to the east of town might simply be a diversion so held his regular forces and the loyal militia at the ready in Prescott. He posted pickets around the town and ordered the removal of the bridge across Honeywell's Creek on the post road to Brockville. Only surveillance parties were dispatched to the windmill. They reported that Von Schoultz was preparing the place for war.

In the mid-morning, the *United States* steamed out of Ogdensburg harbour in an attempt to pull the *Charlotte of Oswego* off the sandbar. The attempt failed. Initially, the steamer attached a short chain to the schooner, but the schooner would not budge. The steamer put back into Ogdensburg for a longer chain. This time, when she steamed out of the harbour, the *Experiment* met her and opened fire. The *United States* beat a quick retreat back to the safety of the American harbour but, during the action, another American steamer, the *Paul Pry,* a shallow draft ferry, managed to slip out and successfully towed the *Oswego* off the bar. Together, the two ships headed down river towards Windmill Point. The *Experiment* moved quickly to cut them off. There was an exchange of canon fire with some of the shot landing in the streets of Prescott before the two American ships retreated to Ogdensburg. There would be no immediate reinforcements for Von Schoultz and his band of Patriots.

The *Experiment* continued her patrol of the river in front of the

---

3 Ibid.
4 Leavitt, p. 50.

town of Prescott. To the east, small craft crossed and recrossed the river to the windmill with impunity. The *Experiment* was concerned with a major frontal attack on the town itself and would not be diverted by the delivery of supplies to the Patriots at Windmill Point. The Patriot navy made one more attempt to break out of Ogdensburg harbour. The *United States* steamed out once more, but this time there was no attempt at evasion. The larger American vessel headed for the British steamer full-steam ahead. It was apparent that the Patriots were attempting to ram the British steamer. The *Experiment* held her fire until the *United States* was well within range and then let fly with a single blast from her eighteen-pound cannon. The cannon ball hit the wheelhouse of the American steamer, smashed it to smithereens, and decapitated the pilot. The *United States* limped back to Ogdensburg and was not seen for the balance of the action.

By noon, Ogle Robert Gowan and his two companies of Brockville Invincibles,[5] part of the Ninth Battalion of the Incorporated Militia, had arrived from Brockville. They had slogged through the mud in the cold November rain and were further delayed when they had to bypass the bridge at Honeywell's Creek just to the west of town, which had been demolished earlier in the day.[6] Gowan's men were soon joined by the 120 men of the Glengarry Militia who arrived on foot from Cornwall just as night began to fall. The Glengarrys, with blood in their eyes from their recent defeat of the rebels in Lower Canada, set up a bivouac in a field just to the north of the windmill.[7] In the early morning, they were joined by seventy-four regular troops and two officers of the Eighty-Third Regiment of the Royal Marines, who had sailed from Kingston aboard the steamer *Cobourg*. The British also dispatched the armed steamer *Victoria* to the scene. A feeling of security began to envelop Colonel Young.

The morning of November 13, 1838, dawned clear and bright. Colonel Young, his junior officers, and the assembled militia officers had met during the night and made the decision to attack the rebel stronghold. Captain Jessup and the militia under his command would

---

5 Scott, p. 21, suggests that the Brockville Invincibles arrived at noon. They were also referred to as the Royal Borderers.
6 Mary Beacock Fryer, VOLUNTEERS AND REDCOATS, REBELS AND RAIDERS; A MILITARY HISTORY OF THE REBELLIONS IN UPPER CANADA, Toronto and Oxford, Dundurn Press, 1987, concludes that it was a party of rebels that had been dispatched from the windmill to block the road from Brockville who destroyed the bridge. K.F. Scott in his work concludes that Colonel Young had the bridge destroyed to protect Prescott from an attack from the west.
7 Scott, p. 21.

remain in Prescott to guard the town from any attack or insurrection. The balance of the available attack forces would be split into two assault columns. The right column, under the command of Colonel Ogle Robert Gowan, was composed of a blend of British regular forces and Upper Canadian militia. Lieutenant Johnson from Fort Henry led the forty-four British regular troops of the Eighty-Third Regiment of Foot. They were joined by Gowan's own Brockville Invincibles and the balance of the Ninth Battalion of the Johnstown Militia, under the immediate command of Captain Edmonston, and half of the Stormont militia. Gowan's column was to sweep east from Fort Wellington along the waterfront and assault the Patriot position from the west. The left column, under the command of Colonel Duncan Fraser, was composed of the thirty men of the Royal Marines under Lieutenant Parker, augmented by the Lancaster and Glengarry Highlanders and supplemented with some of Captain Jessup's militia company under the command of Captain George Macdonnell. The balance of the column comprised companies of troops from the Grenville Militia, the Dundas Militia, and the balance of the Stormont Militia, under the command of Captains Dunham Jones, S. Fraser, and Henderson respectively. Fraser's column was to circle through the bush to the north and assault the windmill from the east. The two British steamers now on site would patrol the river and lay down a barrage against the Patriot position. Colonel Young, as the ranking British officer, had overall command of the operation and accompanied Gowan's column.[8]

Shortly after nine in the morning, both columns set off; once they were in position, the firing began. The Patriots, using the defensive perimeter of a stone wall and the outbuildings surrounding the mill, were able to withstand repeated British attacks. At the peak of the skirmish, Lieutenant Johnson and his men of the Eighty-Third, the spearhead of the right column, succeeded in forcing the Patriots to retreat from their outer perimeter. Johnson and his men managed to obtain the protection of the stone wall then, wishing to press the attack, Johnson rose and led his men onwards in a charge over the wall towards the outbuildings and the mill beyond. His immediate objective was to seize control of one of the few pieces of Patriot artillery, which the Patriots had momentarily abandoned in the retreat, and which now stood unmanned between the mill itself and an outbuilding. As Johnson advanced, he was fatally hit by a shot from a

---

8 Leavitt, p.50

Patriot sharpshooter hiding in one of the outbuildings. Patriot fire killed three more of his men who had made a futile attempt to recover his body as the British withdrew to the relative security of the wall.

Gowan himself was wounded in the assault, which he made the most of following the battle. This was the bloody proof of his courage, bravery, and loyalty to the queen and the constitution that he had always wanted. He wanted the evidence of his wound shouted from every rooftop in the district, but he settled for a vivid account in his newspaper, *The Statesmen*:

> As the left wing advanced, the fire of the enemy was so very galling, that Colonel Fraser, seeing so many of the brave marines, and their gallant companions of the 83rd falling, ordered the whole to charge. As we advanced many of our gallant men fell, among whom was the brave lieutenant Johnson, of the re. The ruffians were so securely planted behind the stone fences, that they stood the charge to the last moment. Colonel Gowan received the bayonet of one of the brigands in the left hip, at the moment they forced him and his men to retreat.[9]

Receiving a bayonet in the hip certainly sounded like a serious injury, yet the official return of killed and wounded referred to Gowan's wound as slight. In reconstructing the physical evidence of the assault, and the location of the wound, it is now accepted that Colonel Ogle Robert Gowan, the founder of the Loyal Orange Lodge in North America, the Member of Parliament for Leeds, and the self-proclaimed hero of the Battle of the Windmill, was jabbed in the arse with a Patriot bayonet as he turned and attempted to scramble back over the fence to escape the field of battle.[10]

The general retreat of the British regular and militia forces was sounded at three o'clock in the afternoon. Colonel Young withdrew all troops to Prescott and Fort Wellington while Gowan and the Brockville Invincibles were ordered back to Brockville later that day.[11] The Patriots remained in control of the windmill, but they were surrounded by hostile British forces, and British steamers controlled the St Lawrence River.

---

8 Leavitt, p.509 McLeod, p. 258, quoting Gowan's account of the attack in his newspaper, THE STATESMEN.
10 Akenson takes this position in both THE ORANGEMAN and THE HISTORY OF THE IRISH IN ONTARIO, his two books that deal with the subject. McLeod, in his BRIEF REVIEW OF THE HISTORY OF SETTLEMENT IN UPPER CANADA, takes the same position.
11 Leavitt, p. 50.

The battle rages, as seen in this view from the American shore.

Across the river on the American shore, a large crowd had gathered to watch the unfolding battle, but made no real move to get involved. The American infantry was now fully in control of the American shore and the town of Ogdensburg. The authorities had seized all available ships, men, and munitions that could be used to assist the Patriots. They were strictly enforcing the Neutrality Law.

During a lull in the battle, the American steamer *Paul Pry* managed to elude the American authorities and cross the river to the windmill. Von Schoultz and the Patriots might have considered escape, but the British laid down a barrage of fire on both the windmill and the *Paul Pry*, quickly driving her off. It was clear that the Patriots would have to fight on alone without hope of reinforcements from the American shore.

It snowed during the night of Tuesday, November 13, 1838, and Wednesday dawned wet and gloomy. During the night, one young Patriot had managed to cross the river by paddling a plank to advise General Birge of the urgent need of reinforcements and munitions. There was nothing that Birge could do from his bed at Ogdensburg other than attempt to pass the buck. That night he wrote to the old river pirate turned commodore, Bill Johnston:

> Dear Johnston: The fate of the men on the other side of the river is in your hands. Nothing is expected of the British above Prescott; and if you can rally your men and go to Jones' Mill and kindle some fires, you will save the men and save Canada. Start fires also at Gananoque and the British will think Kingston is being attacked. Do for God's sake, rally your men and start immediately.[12]

No diversionary attack on Jones's Mill,[13] or elsewhere ever took place. Dawn revealed the freshly snow-covered fields surrounding the mill and the bodies of the fallen men. During the day, the British appeared under a flag of truce, and it was agreed that both sides could remove and bury their dead. As the battle turned towards inevitable defeat, Levi Chipman, the lad from Bastard, "crept away through the middle of the field . . . and . . . put up at Stone's Tavern all night."[14] Unfortunately, Chipman had sought refuge in an inn owned by someone with no sympathy for traitors to the queen. During the

---

12 Scott, p. 29.
13 Jones' Mill was located at the mouth of Jones' Creek, approximately five miles above Brockville.
14 Public Archives of Canada, MILITIA GENERAL COURTS MARTIAL, trial of Martin Woodruff, RG5 B41, Vol. II, File 17.

night, the innkeeper became suspicious of the shivering renegade and, levelling his musket at Chipman, took him prisoner. In the morning, Chipman was marched to Prescott with the innkeeper's musket pointed at his back, where he was delivered to the British troops.

The stalemate continued over Thursday. The British had the Patriot position surrounded and were clearly in control of the situation. Colonel Young could afford to wait for reinforcements. He was not prepared to risk another frontal assault without the benefit of heavy artillery. He had sent to Fort Henry at Kingston for additional troops and canon large enough to demolish the windmill if necessary. Colonel Dundas of the Eighty-Third Regiment immediately dispatched a strong detachment of regular force infantry and artillery that, by morning, arrived by steamer at the windmill.

The artillery officers surveyed the site. They quickly discovered that they had underestimated the size of cannons necessary to reduce the windmill and returned the six-pound field pieces that they had brought from Fort Henry for heavier artillery. Colonel Young and his men polished their muskets for the final assault, which would begin with the arrival of the larger canons.

The American authorities did not want to witness the inevitable slaughter of the Patriot rebels, most of whom were young American men. The commander of the United States Infantry at Ogdensburg, Colonel Worth, brought together a group of influential citizens, including a personal friend of Colonel Young, his British counterpart. Under a flag of truce, Worth sailed across the river with his party aboard the American steamer *Telegraph* and anchored off the Canadian shore. That evening, Colonel Young accepted their invitation and came on board. The Americans agreed that the Patriots had to surrender, but suggested that they surrender to the American military and be dealt with as criminal violators of the American Neutrality Laws. Colonel Young listened attentively, but firmly stated the unequivocal position of the British government. The Patriots had now committed acts of murder on British soil, making it a British matter. Unofficially, however, Young advised the Americans that the British gunboat *Experiment*, which had been patrolling the shore diligently since the start of hostilities, would not be on patrol that night due to engine trouble. Young quietly hinted that if the Americans sent boats for the Patriots that evening, it would be virtually impossible for the British to prevent their escape back across the river.

To the Americans this was an obvious invitation to arrange an escape for the Patriots and they immediately proceeded to do so. The *Paul Pry* was again made ready to cross the river. Under cover of darkness, she made the brief run and was soon at anchor off Windmill Point. It was, of course, anticipated that the surviving Patriots would scramble quickly on board. They, however, refused to do so. The Patriots took the arrival of the *Paul Pry* as proof that the British blockade had been broken and that reinforcements would now rally to the cause. Postmaster King of Ogdensburg, selected as an emissary to the Patriots because of his credibility with them, attempted to explain the true facts and implored Von Schoultz, in vain, to get his men on board. In the end, the *Paul Pry* crossed the river with only seven of the 150 remaining Patriots.[15] The rest chose to fight to the end.

At roughly one o'clock in the afternoon of Friday, November 16, 1838, Colonel Dundas himself arrived from Fort Henry with two, eighteen-pound cannons, one howitzer, and the necessary gun crews under the command of Major McBean, Royal Artillery, to man them. To augment the regular forces and the militia already assembled, Dundas also brought four additional companies of the Eighty-Third Regiment of Foot.[16] These reinforcements supplemented the 2,500 men already in position.[17] With everything now in readiness for the final assault, Colonel Young sent a flag of truce to Von Schoultz offering one final opportunity to surrender.

"In what character?" Von Schoultz demanded to know.

"As rebels," came the reply.

The aftermath of battle.

"Never," declared Von Schoultz. "We prefer dying with our arms in our hands."

In the afternoon, the British steamers were ordered to move in and commence firing on the Patriot position. The British heavy guns were hauled into position four hundred yards from the windmill and summarily ordered to commence firing.[18] For a full three hours, the Patriots defended their position against the massive British firepower with nothing more than small arms.[19] Shortly after dusk, their ammunition exhausted, the Patriots surrendered. Von Schoultz managed to escape capture in the mill, but was forced to surrender shortly thereafter in a clump of cedars bordering the St Lawrence River.[20]

As the smoke from the guns cleared, the body count began. Of the Patriot forces, between fifteen to seventeen men lay dead – among them James Phillips the innkeeper from Bastard Township – while approximately twenty were severely wounded.[21] On the British side, some 268 men and officers had been killed.[22] At the moment of surrender, it was all the regular forces could do to prevent the militia from engaging in the wholesale slaughter of the surviving Patriots. In consolation, the British put the torch to four houses and two barns in the vicinity of the windmill owned by suspected Patriot sympathizers.

Lashed together two-by-two, the Patriots were paraded from the windmill down the post road and through the streets of Prescott, where the residents lined the streets to taunt and jeer. Placed on board the steamer *Brockville*, they set off up river for Kingston.

Landing at Scobel's Wharf at Kingston, the prisoners were again paraded through a hostile crowd. As they stumbled up Brock Street on their way to the dungeons of Fort Henry, the band of the Eighty-Third Regiment struck up "Yankee Doodle Dandy."

---

15 Scott, p. 30.
16 Leavitt, p. 51.
17 Ibid.
18 Ibid., p. 51.
19 McLeod, p. 257.
20 Public Archives of Canada, MILITIA GENERAL COURTS MARTIAL, RG 5 B40, Reel C1560. Trial of Von Schoultz, evidence of Ensign Smith who testified that he was with the party that had captured Von Schoultz and delivered him to Colonel Young.
This version is clearly more accurate than that provided by McLeod in his romanticized history where he describes Von Schoultz escaping the windmill to a stone house at the time of the surrender, and where he fought alone until the house itself was stormed and Von Schoultz finally taken. p. 257.
21 Scott, p. 32, relies on the evidence of Daniel Heustic to state that seventeen were killed. D. McLeod, at p. 258, relies on affidavit evidence filed at the trials or courts martial of the patriots at Fort Henry to conclude that only fifteen had died.
22 McLeod, p. 258.

CHAPTER XII

The Dark Days and the Light: from Repression to Reform

HE PATRIOTS TAKEN prisoner at the Windmill were lodged in the dungeons of Fort Henry to await their trials. Outside the prison walls, the public demand for speedy and rough justice grew. "The Tories evidently thirst for their blood," wrote P.P. Morgan to his friend Andrew Norton Buell. ". . . (The) opinion . . . in Brockville is, that they will all be executed forth with, and such will undoubtedly be the case if the Tories have the strength of nerve to do it."[1]

The Prescott *Sentinel* echoed the public mood in its editorial:

> The prisoners are to be tried by Militia Court Martial, forthwith and as a matter of course, death must be their doom. Whether Government will commute the sentences of any who may be considered culpable (an extension of mercy that none of them have a right to expect) still remains to be seen. We are not vindictive, but we do think it is high time examples should be made, that a firm and decisive stand should be taken by our Government if we are to remain British Colonies.[2]

The official British position was far more conciliatory. Shortly after the initial rising in 1837, the Colonial Office had dispatched Lord Durham to act as Governor of the Canadas and to enquire into the causes of the troubles. From the outset, it was apparent that Durham's approach would be one of conciliation and reconciliation. His principal concern was the pacification of the French population

---

1 Public Archives of Canada, WILLIAM BUELL PAPERS, MG24 B75, letter from P.P. Morgan to A.N. Buell, November 28, 1838, Morristown, New York.
2 John A. Morris, PRESCOTT, 1810-1967, Prescott, 1967, p. 56, citing the PRESCOTT SENTINEL.

in the province of Quebec. Durham correctly noted that the troubles in Lower Canada, imbued as they were with the inherent linguistic, religious, and racial overtones, were far more severe than in Upper Canada. The problems in Lower Canada required almost all of his time and attention and Upper Canada would simply have to wait.

Durham made only one brief trip to Upper Canada. His official party travelled by coach and steamboat up river to Lake Ontario and the settlements beyond during ten days in July of 1838. At Prescott, Durham spoke briefly and was well received. The governor and his party then re-boarded their steamer and resumed their voyage up river.

Durham was aware of Brockville's reputation as a hot bed of ultra-Loyalism. He had also heard of Ogle Robert Gowan and was aware of the views of the Orange Lodge and the effect that those opinions had on any rational political debate. He considered the Tories of Brockville both misguided and dangerous. Durham sought the reconciliation of the various factions of Upper Canada, and a public argument with the Tory faction in Brockville would not be conducive to any process of peaceful constitutional change. Nor could Durham allow Gowan or the other Brockville Tories to make outlandish statements in his presence without a strong rebuttal for fear that he be seen to endorse their position. For those reasons, Durham refused even to land at Brockville. "It is considered the Head Quarters of the Orangemen, or Ultra Loyalist party, and he fears an address to which he would feel himself obliged to give a strong answer,"[3] wrote Durham's aide and brother-in-law, Lieutenant Colonel Charles Grey, in his diary on July 11, 1838.

On his return passage, Durham again refused to stop at Brockville. A group of Brockville citizens, however, learned of his itinerary and travelled to Prescott to meet with him and make submissions. Durham was pleased to note that the inflammatory address he had feared never materialized.[4]

Even before he embarked upon his Upper Canadian sojourn, Durham had come to the conclusion that the cause of the rebellions in Upper Canada was the domination by those in the power elite over the general citizenry. It was Durham's belief that Upper Canadian disaffection could best be alleviated by the introduction of democratic principals and not by repression. As soon as the Tory power structure realized Lord Durham's political orientation, it viewed his mission as misguided and his writings as seditious.

---

3 Ormsby, ed., p. 72, diary of Charles Grey, July 11, 1838.
4 Ibid., p. 81, diary of Charles Grey, July 20, 1838.

He was back in Montreal at the time of the further outbreaks of rebellion in Lower Canada and at Prescott. Despite the renewal of the rebellions, his thesis did not change. When advised of the details of the Patriot invasion at Prescott and the Battle at Windmill Point, he noted that there were fewer than a dozen Upper Canadians among the rebels and, even more significantly, not one Upper Canadian settler had gone over to the enemy during the action.

The militia courts martial of the 180 Patriots captured at the windmill began in late November of 1838. In anticipation of the American-sponsored insurrection, the Upper Canadian government had enacted legislation making it an offence, punishable by death, for any citizen of a foreign state at peace with the United Kingdom of Great Britain and Ireland to assist or conspire to assist any of Her Majesty's subjects "traitorously in arms." This was the legislation under which Von Schoultz and his followers would be tried. From the Crown's perspective, the prosecution for violation of this statute was far easier than under the traditional laws against treason. To succeed in a prosecution for treason, the Crown was required to provide a minimum of two witnesses to the treasonous act, each corroborative of the other. Under the new legislation, this strict requirement of proof was not necessary. The prosecution did not even have to establish any specific act in order to obtain a conviction as the essence of the crime was to aid or abet. All that the Crown needed to prove was that the accused was a foreign national and that he had assisted or conspired to assist a Canadian engaged in acts of violence against the government.

In addition to these substantive provisions, The Act to Protect The Inhabitants of the Province Against Lawless Aggressions From the Subjects of Foreign Countries at Peace with Her Majesty established a code of summary procedure. The accused would be tried before a panel of military officers in a court martial. In addition, the code of procedure precluded legal counsel and each accused appearing before the court was obliged to do so without a lawyer. The trials were to be conducted with the appearance, but with none of the substance, of due process. The attitude of the British military commanders and of the government itself was to conduct the trials with all semblance of fairness and then proceed promptly with the executions.

While the accused were denied counsel at their trials, some did have the benefit of legal advice. The family of Daniel George, the Patriot paymaster and former American school teacher, contacted a relatively young Upper Canadian barrister by the name of John A. Macdonald and retained him to provide whatever legal assistance he could to George and the other Patriots.

The George trial is interesting from a legal perspective because of the evidentiary issues inherent in the prosecution and because of the legal strength of the argument that George advanced in his own defence. It seems that John Macdonald was a good teacher as well as a competent lawyer, and George was a keen pupil of legal principles.

The evidence against George was scanty but damning. Daniel George had been captured by Lieutenant George A. Leary, RN, the commander of the steamer *Cobourg*, in a rowboat in the middle of the St Lawrence River in the vicinity of the windmill. Lieutenant Leary testified that he had the *Cobourg* a little above Windmill Point in the early afternoon of Tuesday, November 13, 1838, when he saw a small boat with five persons on board pulling hard for the American shore. He captured the boat and all five passengers including the accused, Daniel George. He seized two muskets, two pistols, and a pocketbook which he found in the possession of the accused. The book, filed as an exhibit, contained the following notes:

> Boat will leave Oswego 6 o'clock Friday morning, leave Sackets Harbour at noon Friday. At Cape Vincent Friday evening 6 o'clock. Get all the men on schooners that can be – then let the schooner go down near Alexandria Bay.

There was also a receipt tucked into the notebook which read:

> Rec'd from W.D. George one hundred dollars for towing two schooners from Carleton Island to Ogdensburg and for transportation of men to Psyched's Harbour (Sackets Harbour), French Creek, and Cape Vincent by steamboat.[5]

The British also discovered a letter on the accused from one John H. Jones to Charles Smith at Fort Independence. The letter advised that if ". . . there is not ropes enough to hang the tories, you can buy more."[6]

Daniel George was arraigned, entered a plea of not guilty, and conducted a full trial on his own behalf. The accused did not testify at the trial, however, in a well-reasoned argument he noted that there was no evidence of his American citizenship and that the evidence of his

---

5 Public Archives of Canada, MILITIA GENERAL COURTS MARTIAL, trial of Daniel George, November 28, 1838, RG5 B41, Vol. 1, File 18.
6 Ibid.

involvement in the battle was weak and inconsequential. He pointed out that the act under which he had been charged made it an offence for foreign nationals to aid Canadian or British subjects, but the Crown had failed to offer any evidence of his nationality. On that basis alone, he argued the case against him must fail. He also argued that the legislation was unfair and fatally flawed in that it worked an injustice on those who were proved to be foreign nationals. British subjects charged with treason were afforded the protection of having the case against them proved through the testimony of two eyewitnesses. The same standard of proof ought to apply in the legislation under which he was charged. Unmoved, the Court immediately found the accused guilty and did not bother to offer reasons.

Once the trials were actually underway, it became apparent that the court, composed of a panel of regular army officers, would have no difficulty in convicting anyone who was found at the windmill. The accused were brought up from the dungeons to be tried either singularly or in groups of up to twelve at a time. Regardless of their defences and pleas, all were convicted.

Nils Szolteocky von Schoultz, the commander of the Patriot forces at the windmill, was brought before the Militia General Court Martial to stand trial on November 26, 1838. The court was composed of thirteen officers presided over by Lieutenant Colonel John Kirby. Like the other Americans, he was arraigned on a charge that on the twelfth day of November, 1838, and on divers other days between that day and the sixteenth day of November, 1838, he, being a foreign national of a country at peace with Great Britain, had conspired with British subjects to bear arms against Her Majesty, contrary to the Act to Protect the Inhabitants of (Upper Canada) Against Lawless Aggression From Subjects of Foreign Countries at Peace With Her Majesty.

While John A. Macdonald was at Fort Henry advising Daniel George, he had been introduced to the Patriot leader. Von Schoultz had listened to the legal advice offered by Macdonald, but would not argue his guilt. When asked for his plea, Von Schoultz replied, guilty. He added, reflectively, that he had been deceived, but that it was useless to deny that he was the leader of the party. Again he stated, "I plead Guilty." To substantiate the plea, the Crown called witnesses of the battle and produced an inculpatory sworn statement that Von Schoultz had given to justice of the peace while a prisoner at Fort Henry. The evidence was clear. Von Schoultz had indeed been in command of the Patriots at the windmill.

The prosecution quickly established that the rebels had arrived by ship from the United States. It followed that they must be presumed foreign nationals of a country then at peace with Her Majesty. They called Ensign Edward Smith who had served with the Prescott Militia under Captain Jessup and had been on the wharf in Prescott when the schooners approached. He had watched as they went on downriver and had seen the troops land at the windmill. Smith also provided the identification evidence. He had been with the party that had captured Von Schoultz in the cedar grove by the river edge.

The Crown then called Lieutenant Charles A. Parker of the Royal Marines who gave particulars of the battle from which it must be concluded that someone must have been in command. Parker had arrived with thirty men aboard the steamboat *Queen* and reported to Colonel Young. On the initial assault, he had been assigned to Colonel Fraser's column and had marched to "an eminence" inland from the village surrounding the windmill. As the rebels advanced against this position, he had been ordered to counter-attack and did so with his own men and those of Captain McDonnell's company of militia. In the skirmish, the rebels were driven back into the houses surrounding the windmill, at a cost of thirteen wounded amongst his own detachment. Parker and his men had then joined the right column commanded by Colonel Gowan for the duration of the action.

Following this evidence, the Crown had established all of the necessary elements of the charge. Von Schoultz was a subject of a foreign country and he had been part of the invasion. He had violated the act and the penalty was death. Everything else that the Crown proved was superfluous to the charge. But the Crown wished to prove much more about Von Schoultz's role.

The prosecution wished to establish that Von Schoultz had been the officer in command of the rebels. To do so, they called three Canadian rebels, John Baptiste Raza, Laurent Melhuit, and Levi Chipman, all of whom identified Von Schoultz as the leader, general or commander of the Patriots. Prior to doing so, however, the prosecutor chose to introduce evidence that would colour not only Von Schoultz's trial, but all of the others as well. The Crown called William Gardiner, Surgeon of the Eighty-Third Regiment to the stand. Gardiner testified that following the battle, he had examined the body of Lieutenant Johnson, the young British officer who had been killed in the assault on the Patriot position. His examination revealed that Johnson's corpse had been mutilated. Specifically, Gardiner testified that Johnson's penis had been excised.

The sole purpose of the evidence was to inflame the passions of the court against Von Schoultz. The evidence was not directly relevant to his prosecution since at no time was it suggested that Von Schoultz had been a party to the mutilation. Further, while the evidence led against one accused was often repeated over and over again against the others, the evidence of the mutilation of the body of Lieutenant Johnson by cutting off his penis was introduced only against Von Schoultz. The intention of the prosecution was clear: Von Schoultz as the officer in charge must bear responsibility for the actions of his men.

To close its case, the Crown produced the inculpatory statement of the accused as taken down in writing by Magistrate George Baker. In his statement, Von Schoultz related that he had emigrated to America from Poland and had taken up residence in Salina, New York. He deposed that he had some military experience, his father had been a Major in the Regiment of Cracow, was killed, and Von Schoultz had assumed his rank in the Polish army.[7] This, of course, was not true, and why Von Schoultz would represent himself to the Court as a Pole instead of as a Finn remains a mystery.

His deposition went on to state that in early November, 1838, he heard of the intended new government of Canada from a group of Patriots then being formed in Salina. At their urging, he agreed to travel to Ogdensburg to meet with General Birge of the Patriot army. He embarked on the steamer *United States* at Oswego on Sunday, November 11, 1838, not knowing of the invasion plan. He simply wanted transportation to Ogdensburg to discuss his potential involvement with General Birge. On his arrival at Ogdensburg, he was met by Birge who directed him to the Canadian shore saying that he would meet him there. Von Schoultz did so, still expecting to meet with Birge to discuss whether he would in fact join the Patriot forces. At no time did he formally join the Patriot forces or take any oath of service. Once in Canada and under siege, he had assumed command of the Patriot forces for the sole purpose of leading the insurgents back across the river to the American shore. He acknowledged, in his deposition, that two of his countrymen had accompanied him

---

7 Public Archives of Canada, MILITIA GENERAL COURTS MARTIAL, trial of Von Schoultz, deposition taken from Von Schoultz by George Baker, Justice of the Peace, and filed at his trial. RG5 B40, Reel C 1590.

throughout, the majority of the details of the actual battle, and that he had been told that the men of Upper Canada would rise and join the Patriot cause.

Von Schoultz attempted to portray himself as a naive dupe. His version of the events and of his role in the invasion does not square with the balance of the evidence. It defied logic that Von Schoultz could be on the Patriot flotilla, among 400 zealots, and not be aware that he was part of the invasion force. What remains a mystery is his motivation to admit his guilt and accept the death penalty, but to misstate some of the details surrounding his involvement in the affair. In the end, it did not matter. The Court accepted his plea of guilty, and he was sentenced to hang.[8]

The vast majority of the accused simply entered pleas of guilty and, in their own words, threw themselves on the mercy of the court. The court had very little mercy. At the outset of his trial, Martin Woodruff, a fifty year old American from Salina, New York, declared, "I will throw myself on the mercy of the Court and government and plead guilty."[9] The court advised Woodruff that he had a right to a trial and that so far as the prospect of mercy was concerned there was ". . . little prospect that the court would do otherwise than pass the utmost sentence on him." Despite the warning, Woodruff allowed his plea to stand. The trial proceeded by way of a guilty plea and, in the end, the Court having heard the evidence of his complicity in the incursion, accepted the plea. Woodruff was found guilty and sentenced to suffer death by hanging.

As the trials progressed, common themes began to emerge. It was apparent that the weeks spent in pretrial custody had provided the Patriots with the opportunity to agree on the best possible story in the circumstances. The general approach of each of the accused was to portray themselves as naive dupes who had been tricked or forced to engage in the invasion. Almost all of the accused argued that they had been lured onto the schooners with promises of employment and with no understanding of the purpose of the voyage. Many argued that once on board they were forced to take up arms on penalty of death. Each in turn argued that he had never fired a shot. Those who had been captured with a smoking rifle in their hands argued that they had fired only once, or at most twice, without taking aim and only because they had been

---

8 Public Archives of Canada, MILITIA GENERAL COURTS MARTIAL, trial of Nils Szolteocky von Schoultz, RG5, B40, Reel C1560.
9 Ibid., trial of Martin Woodruff, November 26, 1838, RG5 B41, Vol. II, File 17, Reel C-15691.

threatened with death if they refused. The near universal claim was that they were either tricked or forced to participate in the rising, that they held no animosity towards the British, and that their role in the battle had been inconsequential. They attempted to persuade the court that they had merely gone through the motions, pretending to fight the British only to satisfy those in command of the invasion.

Public opinion found the Patriot claims difficult to accept. "It is most absurd! Clever, shrewd, calculating Yankees deluded – it is a farce and an insult,"[10] concluded one correspondent to Alpheus Jones. Their arguments had no greater effect on the officers of the court martial. If none of the captured Patriots had shot a British soldier, then how had 200 men been killed. The accused were all found guilty and sentenced to hang.

The most that the court would do in dispensing leniency was to include with the warrant of execution a recommendation to the lieutenant-governor for clemency. Whenever an accused succeeded in convincing the court that in fact his involvement was minimal and the result of youthful exuberance, the death sentence would be accompanied with the recommendation. Family and friends of the accused began to rely on the traditional method of influencing government policy in Upper Canada in order to give effect to the recommendation. They contacted the Tory elite and attempted to enlist its support as intervener on behalf of the condemned. "I have a son in confinement at Kingston for having engaged in the affair at Prescott," wrote a concerned American father from Sackets Harbor to Alpheus Jones in Prescott.

> May I presume so far upon your generosity and our former acquaintance . . . in behalf of my deluded son. I have since learned he was induced to go (to Prescott) through the infamous imposition of men who have been engaged in betraying others into the same difficulties . . . Permit me . . . to ask your interest in his behalf and if opportunity presents and you can do so without injury to yourself to speak a word in his favour.[11]

Not only the relatives of the captured Patriots sought the favours of Mr Jones. While the vanquished sought clemency, the victors sought rewards. Dr Chisholm, a young man with a solid background, had

---

10 Public Archives of Canada, ALPHEUS JONES PAPERS, MG24 B98, Vol. 1, letter from Donald Murray to Alpheus Jones, December 8, 1838, Montreal.
11 Ibid., letter from William Vaughan to Alpheus Jones, dated December 3, 1838, Sackets Harbor, New York.

played his part to defeat the rebels at the windmill and now sought his reward. Chisholm enlisted the aid of several leading citizens to advance his cause. To increase his support amongst the Tories, Chisholm drafted those who already supported him to enlist others.

> Dr. Chisholm stated to me that he had written lately to Colonel Young requesting the favour of him to address a few lines to Colonel Corbitt, R.A., mentioning what share the Doctor took in the affair,

wrote James MacFarlane to Alpheus Jones shortly after the battle.

> He intends at no very distant period to become a settler in this province and in consideration of his long service to apply for a grant of land. He thinks and I agree with him that a letter from Colonel Young stating that the Dr. was a volunteer on the occasion and the assistance he rendered in the affair would be a very essential service to him . . . I told him that I would write you a few lines on the subject and perhaps if you were to see the Colonel . . .[12]

It appeared that Upper Canada would conduct its business as it had in the past. Neither elections nor rebellion had altered the way political business was done.

As the government began to carry out the sentences, political consideration was given to the effect of mass executions on the stability of the province. William A. Draper, Solicitor-General of Upper Canada, expressed his concerns to Alpheus Jones in a letter written on Christmas Eve:

> Do write and tell me what you think is the public sentiment and feeling in your part of the country as to the extent to which capital punishment should be carried – and what effect the execution of the six criminals who have suffered provided.[13]

In the end, Durham's policy of conciliation carried the day. Of all the prisoners who were sentenced to death, only eleven were actually executed. The balance had their sentences commuted. The more serious offenders who were spared the death penalty were transported to Van Diemen's Land for the rest of their lives.

---

12 Ibid., letter from James MacFarlane to Alpheus Jones, Fort Henry, December 6, 1838.
13 Ibid., letter from William A. Draper to Alpheus Jones, December 24, 1838, Kingston.

Transportation for life was in many ways a more onerous penalty than death by hanging. Often the transported felon was never heard from again. The mortality rate of those transported, in irons and below deck, to the farthest corner of the world, was extremely high. Those that survived the crossing still had to survive the conditions of the penal colony. Many men ended their lives in unmarked graves on the far side of the world.

While the trials of the Patriots continued behind the walls of Fort Henry, Durham continued to assemble the material for his report and, in the counties and districts of Upper Canada, the Tories continued with their repression of suspected radicals.

By chance, Andrew Norton Buell had happened to be in Ogdensburg on business when the Patriot invaders seized the windmill below Prescott. Like hundreds of others, he had stood on the American shore to watch the battle unfold. Unlike those others, however, Buell was a well-known advocate of reform and he had been picked out of the crowd by some observant Canadian with a spyglass on the Canadian shore. Regardless of the fact that his brother, William Buell, had served with distinction as an officer of the Leeds Militia during the battle, Gowan subsequently charged A.N. Buell with treason.

There was no evidence whatsoever to implicate Andrew Norton Buell in the invasion and nothing of significance came of the charge. Buell, however, continued to tempt fate politically and remained in communication with William Lyon Mackenzie long after the battle. In December 1838, MacKenzie summarized his life in exile and the failed invasion in correspondence to A.N. Buell:

> You may suppose that I had my pecuniary difficulties this summer, but I don't mind them a bit, for the prize of freedom for the remainder of the new world is before us, & will take it yet. I expected all the success our friends have got – they should have organized, acted in unison, and with prudence, and success would have been theirs.[14]

The citizens of the Johnstown District embarked on a general witch-hunt of rebels. Men who before the troubles had expressed reform views now turned on their brethren accusing them of treason. The general theory of political survival was to attack one's neighbour

---

14 Public Archives of Canada, WILLIAM BUELL PAPERS, MG24 B75, letter from Wm. L. MacKenzie to Andrew Norton Buell, Esq., December 17, 1838, Boonville, New York.

and thereby establish one's own credentials as a loyalist. McCarthyism was born in Upper Canada in 1838.

P.P. Morgan, expressed his concerns in a letter to his old friend Buell:

> I have been persecuted by vile miscreants . . . ever since you left, endeavouring to implicate me in this patriot business – language and expressions that I never dreamt off, has been attributed to me, these vilest of the vile who a few days before the election were chanting their patriotism, are now hunting every patriot like starved wolves.[15]

Regardless of the local successes of the Tories, the political fate of Upper Canada was being decided in London. In 1839, Lord Durham released his "Report on the Affairs of British North America" in the *British Parliamentary Papers*. It was instantly apparent that he did not share the exaggerated fears of the Tories of Upper Canada. Durham was a radical Whig reformer dispatched to Canada by a Whig administration, so it should have come as a surprise to no one that his analysis would reflect his liberal philosophy. The Tories were outraged and commented publicly on the lack of Durham's exposure to the province and his obvious lack of insight into the recent troubles. Durham's Report was widely regarded as partisan, opinionated, and inaccurate. Nonetheless, it set the British Colonial Office irrevocably on the path of significant and fundamental political reform.

John George Lambton, Earl of Durham, was born in 1792 into one of the richest and most influential families in the north of England. On entering politics, he was a clear and unambiguous Whig and, in 1830, Radical Jack, as he had come to be known, was appointed to the Whig cabinet of his father-in-law, Lord Grey. He fought tirelessly for the Reform Bill and helped draft that legislation with Lord John Russell. Ill health forced his retirement from active politics in 1833 and subsequently caused him to relinquish his post as the Ambassador to Russia. In 1837, he was back in London and looking for new challenges. The Whig government of Lord Melbourne was clinging precariously to power attempting to steer a middle course between the radical Whigs and the conservatives. It was widely believed that Durham would join the radical Whigs and provide them with a champion to bring down the government in the cause of further reform. In persuading Durham to accept the appointment as governor

---

15 Ibid., letter from P.P. Morgan to A. N. Buell, January 2, 1839, Morristown, New York.

John George Lambton, Earl of Durham.

NATIONAL ARCHIVES OF CANADA, C-16751

and fact finder in Canada, Melbourne was not only obtaining the services of a respected politician, he was limiting the influence of a potential political enemy.

Lord Durham was easily the most highly placed British political figure to enter the Canadian political stage to date. He had been assured of Melbourne's support and had been given extraordinary powers to accomplish his mission. He stayed in Canada scarcely more than a year, yet his report stands as a landmark of Canadian constitutional development.

Following his assessment of the situation in Quebec, Durham pardoned the majority of the captured insurrectionists and ordered the leaders banished to the colony of Bermuda. The Tories in Britain were as outraged as their counterparts in the Canadas at the seeming light treatment the traitors received. Durham's handling of the situation seemed to be condoning anarchy and Melbourne lacked both the gumption and the votes in parliament to honour his promise of unqualified support. Parliament voted to disallow the ordinances decreed by Durham. As a man of honour, a concept long since abandoned by modern politicians, Durham felt that he had no alternative but to resign. In 1838, he returned to Britain and began the arduous task of drafting his report.

Durham's analysis of Upper Canada's problems that led to the insurrections of 1837 and 1838 read as if it had been lifted from a reformer's copybook. He commented negatively on the oligarchy that had been allowed to develop in Upper Canada and, when referring to it, he adopted Mackenzie's use of the pejorative term, Family Compact. He noted the utter lack of responsiveness of the administration to the citizenry and he criticized the government for continuing to favour the political elite regardless of the will of the people expressed at elections. He agreed that the elected members of the Legislative Assembly were powerless to influence decision making. "It was upon this question of the responsibility of the Executive Council that the great struggle has for a long time been carried on between the official party and the reformers," he wrote.[16]

Durham was equally scathing on the still seething issue of clergy reserves and the system of land grants. "In the opinion of many this was the chief predispositioning cause of the recent insurrection," he wrote in relation to clergy reserves.[17] He noted that the Methodists,

---

16 Gerald M. Craig, ed., LORD DURHAM'S REPORT, McClelland and Stewart Limited, Toronto/Montreal, 1963, p. 81.
17 Ibid., p. 93.

Presbyterians and Roman Catholics were all more numerous in the colony than were the adherents of the established church and that, "the Anglican (Church) . . . is the Church which, being that of the wealthy, can best provide for itself."[18] If there was to be financial assistance to any denomination, Durham was suggesting that it should go to those denominations actually in need. It was his strong recommendation to the government that all provisions that favoured one denomination over another be repealed and that both the clergy reserves and all funds that had been derived from their sale be turned over to the Legislature of Upper Canada, to be disposed of as it saw fit. Durham warned that, "The result of any determination . . . to give one sect a predominance and superiority would be . . . to endanger the loss of the colony."[19]

On the issue of land policy, he advised, "I am sorry but compelled to add, gross favouritism has prevailed in the disposal of public lands."[20] Durham deplored the practice and listed the amount of land that had, over the years, been given to government favourites, pointing out that the land so granted amounted to one half of the surveyed land of the province. These lands in large part stood idle, a hindrance to the development of viable communities, as only ten per cent of these grants and reserves had actually been settled, while the balance remained uncultivated and unimproved.

Durham's report was a scathing indictment of the status quo. His recommendations followed logically from his observations of the facts. Upper Canada needed a system of government that would respond to the wishes of the people. This could only be accomplished if the Executive Council enjoyed the support of the Legislative Assembly and if the lieutenant-governor was obliged to follow the advice of the Legislative Council. In short, Durham advocated responsible government. In due course, his recommendations were followed, and the country would move on as a democratic and, ultimately, independent nation.

The political development of Canada would parallel, but not duplicate, the American experience. By 1840, the British colonies in North America were marching down a distinctive path from that which the United States was taking. The form of democracy followed by Canadians would closely follow the British concept of

---

18 Ibid., p. 97.
19 Ibid., p. 96.
20 Ibid., p. 110.

parliamentary democracy. Canadians, by the time of the advent of responsible government, had over half a century of historical experience as British North Americans, and Canadian Tories and Reformers alike now differed politically from their American brothers. With reflection, Reformers came to appreciate that they shared common beliefs with Tories and that they, like it or not, differed significantly from Americans.

William Lyon Mackenzie, during his period of exile in the United States, reluctantly came to this same conclusion. In correspondence to his old friend, Andrew Norton Buell, in Brockville, he wrote:

> It is very fortunate that we rebels of Toronto failed. It has given some of the constitution makers, that would have been, a taste of the working of free institutions, so called, where they are in practice – and has convinced me that the weak part of the American Constitution lies here. The Fathers of this republic are famous for having established constitutions nearly on this plan suggested by Pain – they provided against a nobility – a state church – primogeniture and halfblood laws – monarchy and so on, but corporations, monopolies, banks, of issue, they either left untouched, or, if they did not, the judges have so expanded their acts. And this inlet to Knavery is unsettling everything and giving a mercenary character to a people formed to be an example to the world.[21]

While not usually noted for his insight into political philosophy, MacKenzie correctly identified what would become the fundamental difference between the Canadian and American approach to political organization and the role of the state. Canadians would recognize the potential danger of this inlet to Knavery and attempt to curb its appetite, while Americans would revel in its excesses.

---

21 Public Archives of Canada, WILLIAM BUELL PAPERS, MG24 B75, letter to A.N. Buell from William Lyon Mackenzie Rochester, October 12, 1839, N.Y.

Epilogue

HAT DO THE POLITICAL battles of the 1830s and the rebellions that ended the decade tell us about who Canadians were becoming as a people?

At first blush, it might be said that by refusing to join the insurrection, Canadians demonstrated that, fundamentally, they were a peace-loving people who eschewed violence. That would not explain the alacrity with which the Canadian militia rallied to the British standard. The actions of Gowan and his Orangemen and the other militia forces at the battle of the Windmill are not indications of pacifism. Nor were the actions of the Highland troops from Glengarry cutting and burning a swath six miles wide through the province of Quebec as they marched home. Following the defeat of the Patriots, the major difficulty faced by the British regulars was in preventing the militia from burning and looting the area and murdering the prisoners.

In the end, Canadians opted to defend the status quo. But their earlier actions indicate that the majority was not totally resistant to change. Reform candidates enjoyed considerable success during the 1830s. Mackenzie had run successfully, again and again, on a platform of radical reform. He had withstood his expulsion from the Assembly on four occasions, while his only electoral defeat came in the general election of 1836. Other Reformers had done as well. In Grenville County, William B. Wells had successfully advocated Reform as had Buell and Howard in Leeds.

Are we left with the typical Canadian muddle? Was this nothing more than an early manifestation of a national split personality later to be encapsulated in the campaign slogan of the consummate Canadian politician, Mackenzie King, and his call for "Conscription if necessary, but not necessarily conscription"?

We see a populace torn between competing fundamental values. Ultimately, by an overwhelming margin, they opted to remain Canadian, whatever that might mean. Canadians wanted change. They wanted democratic structures. But, they were bound and determined that they would not become Americans. When Bond Head defined the issues in this way in the campaign of 1836, the Reformers were trounced. The people were faced with the choice of being Canadian, with all that entailed, or becoming Americans. For the vast majority, the decision was instantly and irrevocably made. When the Reformers allied themselves with the Americans and attempted to invade Upper Canada, the choice was even clearer. By their actions, the Reformers confirmed Bond Head's successful campaign theme. These people and all reform were treasonous.

Considering the three principal groups in society, it is not surprising that once the issues were defined in this way, the status quo would have near-universal support.

Quite aside from the favoured position of the few at the social and economic pinnacle of the High Church and Tory system, which was an obvious inducement to support the status quo, the old Loyalist blue bloods had compelling emotional reasons to reject Americanization. They thought that their forefathers had done something heroic in standing up for the king many years before. To change course now would be a rejection of the fifty years they had invested in creating their history – a history of a new colony as an integral part of the British Empire. It would mean that for half a century and two wars they had been wrong. This, naturally, they could not and would not admit.

Who then would opt for rebellion? Certainly not the Irish. The Loyal Orange Lodge had phenomenal success in recruiting members during the 1830s, precisely because it filled a real need within the Irish community. By and large, the Protestant Irish were the "poor white trash." Emotionally, they had a burning fire in their bellies to succeed and be accepted in the new world. That was coupled with the fear and anger that comes with the realization that one is looked down on. The result was the ultra Loyalist position taken by Gowan: All reform was treason.

That left only the non-aligned. People who did not identify or define themselves as Loyalist or Irish became susceptible to the call for radical reform. These included the late Loyalists who came from the United States looking for cheap land, the person with a Loyalist background who had lost his affiliation, and the Irish Catholics, whom Bishop Macdonell and his priests could not persuade that the key to acceptance lay in subservience to the status quo.

There simply were not enough of them for revolutionary reform to succeed.

Change did come eventually to British North America, but once more, it was legislated from above. In 1840, the British parliament established a new constitutional regime for Upper and Lower Canada. The Act of Union merged the primarily French Catholic Lower Canada with English and largely Protestant Upper Canada. Henceforth they would be known as Canada East and Canada West; two different peas placed within the same pod. Even though, at the time the majority of the population resided in Quebec, the act gave equal representation to Upper and Lower Canada in the legislature. Influenced by Durham's views on the subject, the British plan was to absorb the population of Quebec into English Ontario. That plan obviously did not succeed.

Durham's views in other areas had a more lasting effect. Parliament adopted his recommendations on responsible government. The role of the Executive Council was strengthened. The members of council would assume responsibility for government departments and become accountable to the elected representatives of the people in the Assembly. There would be further arguments concerning the balance to be struck between imperial control and independence, and over the form of democratic structures. But the die was cast. Canadians were about to embark on the task of moulding their own, independent, democratic nation on the northern half of the continent. The musket shot and cannon fire at Windmill Point marked the passing of an era. The blue blood and rednecked forces of reaction, while successful in battle, ultimately could not win the war.

Schedule A

INSTRUCTIONS to the Returning Officer of the County of Leeds

As soon as conveniently may be after the Receipt of the Writ and Warrant the Returning Officer is to give Public Notice of the time and place when and where he means to hold the Election not giving less than Eight Days between the date of his Notice and the day of Election.

The Notice may be in the following Form

To the Freeholders of the County of Leeds

WHEREAS His Majesty's Royal Proclamation hath been issued for the purpose of calling together a Legislative Council and House of Assembly for the Province of Upper Canada, and whereas by a certain Act of the Province passed in the Forty Eighth year of his Majesty's Reign intituled "An act for the better representation of the commons of this Province in Parliament and to repeal part of an Act passed in the Fortieth year of His present Majesty's Reign intituled "An Act for the more equal Representation of the Commons of this Province and for the better defining the Qualification of Electors," it is declared and appointed that the County of Leeds shall be Represented in the said House of Assembly by one Member and whereas by a certain Instrument under the Sign Manuel and Sealed with the Seal of His Excellency Francis Gore, Esquire, Lieutenant Governor, I have been nominated and appointed Returning Officer of the County of Leeds and whereas by a certain Writ under the Great Seal of Upper Canada by me received I am thereby directed to cause the most fit and discreet to be freely and indifferently chosen to Represent the said County of Leeds in Assembly by those who shall be present at the day of Election.

Now know ye that by virtue of the said Nomination and appointment and in obedience to His Majesty's said Writ I shall attend on   the   day of next at 10 o'clock in the forenoon and proceed to the election of one Knight to represent the said County of Leeds in the said House of Assembly and here of all Freeholders of the said County of Leeds are to take notice and attend accordingly.

N.B. as many of these Notices as can be conveniently disposed of should be affixed at Churches Taverns Etc. within the said County

A.B. Returning Officer of the County of Leeds

At the day and place specified in the Notice, the Returning Officer is to attend, and having ordered Proclamation of Silence to be made whilst His Majesty's Writ is Published, The Writ is to be produced and Read, a nomination of some Candidate is then usually made by a Freeholder which nomination being seconded, the Candidate may if he thinks proper step forward and make an Address to the Freeholders. If there is no opposition the Returning Officer is to declare that is duly Elected and the Indentures transmitted with the Writ to be executed by some four or five of the Freeholders who are to Sign and Seal the same in both parts, one of them to be annexed to the Writ and returned with it. If more than two candidates are proposed the Returning Officer is to name them to the Freeholders in the Order in which they are proposed, and is to call for a show of hands. If no opposition is made to this Declaration of the Returning Officer he may declare such candidate to be duly elected, but if a Poll be demanded for any other Candidate by himself or any two Freeholders the Returning Officer is bound to grant it. If a contested election is certain the Returning officer may erect at the Expense of the Candidates such a Booth or convenient place for taking the Poll as they shall require and shall appoint Clerks to take the Poll who are to be paid by the Candidates. Before the Returning Officer proceeds to the poll, he shall take and subscribe the following oath to be administered by a justice of the Peace or any three freeholders.

I, A.B. Do solemnly swear that I have not directly or indirectly taken any sum or Sums of money, office place or Employment, Gratuity or reward or any Bond, Bill or Note or promise of Gratuity whatsoever either for myself or any other person to my use benefit or advantage for making any Return at the present Election of a Member to serve in Parliament and that I will return such Person as shall to the best of my knowledge and judgment appear to me to have the majority of votes of such persons as shall be possessed for their own use and benefit of Land and Tenements within the said County of Leeds, such Lands being by them holden in Freehold or in Fief or Roture or by Certificate derived under the authority of the Governor and Council of the Province of Quebec and being of the yearly value of Forty Shillings Sterling or upwards over and above all rents and Charges payable out of or in respect of the same -

If the Election shall not be determined upon a view with the consent of the Freeholders present, The Returning Officer shall proceed to take The Poll and shall not adjourn the Court to any other place Nor shall he delay the Election but proceed therein from day to day, but that the said Returning Officer shall not continue the Election more than six days, but shall (if it is not sooner determined) at the expiration of that time close the Poll.

The Return is to be made by Executing the Indentures as above mentioned.

Dated York the Twenty third day of May 1808 and in the Forty Eighth year of His Majesty's Reign.

To the Returning Officer

of the County of Leeds.

Schedule B

RETURN OF DISBANDED TROOPS AND LOYALISTS SETTLED IN THE NEW OSWEGATCHIE TOWNSHIPS MUSTERED ON OCTOBER 13, 1784

TOWNSHIP NO. 6 (EDWARDSBURG)

Adams, G., Lieut.
Adams, James
Adams, Joel
Anderson, Henry
Armstrong, Thomas
Bolton, Abraham
Bolton, George
Bonesill, Jacob
Boyde, Thomas
Bush, John
Cameron, D.
Curry, Ephrem
Curry, James
Dayel, Charles
Drummond, P., Capt.
Dulmage, Phillip
Dulmage, T., Lieut.
Ferris, Wm.
Fraser, F., Capt.
Fraser, John
Fraser, Thos., 1st
Fraser, Thomas, 2nd

Jackson, Henry
Kilbreth, John
Lamson, Wm., Ensign
Lester, Thos.
Lukes, Nicholas
McAlpine, Duncan
McIlmoyle, Hugh
McIntosh, Duncan
McIntosh, Alex
McKenzie, John
McKinley, Wm.
McLean, Arch.
McNight, Thomas
Moore, H.
Moore, J.
Munro, Hugh, Capt.
Nix, John
Robertson, Joseph
Rudderbank, John
Saunders, Abraham
Saunders, Henry
Saunders, Wm.

Fraser, W., Capt.
Fraser, Wm., 1st
Fraser, Wm., 2nd
fraser, Wm., 3rd
Froom, James
Froom, James, jr.
Gooseberry, Thomas
Humphrey, James
Hunter, David

Saunders, Wm., jr.
Sillick, Daly
Smith, John
Snyder, Wm.
Sorrells, John
Steers, George
Thompson, John
Weatherhead, Samuel
Weycoff, John
Whilley, John
White, Samuel
White, Wm.
Wormley, Jacob

Total settlement: men, 68 : women, 29: children, 58 : servants, 11 acres cleared, 122

TOWNSHIP NO. 7 (AUGUSTA)

Andrews, Wm.
Armstrong, Edward
Avery, Jos.
Barnard, Alex.
Bateman, Samuel
Beech, Heirs of Corpl.
Bernet, Stephen
Bottom, Elijah, Ensign
Bowker, John
Bradford, John
Brooks, Widow
Brown, Nathan
Brown, Thomas
Brown, Widow
Bryan, Rev. John
Campbell, Alex, Lieut.
Campbell, James, Ensign
Carley, Elijah
Carrier, John
Closson, Caleb
Clunay, James
Corbin, Nathaniel

Faulkner, John
Fridenberg, Isaac
Fuller, Andrew
Grant, Daniel
Hanbury, Wm.
Hard, James
Hard, Philo
Hawley, Abijah
Haynes, Godfrey
Hogadon, Peter
Hougletail, Isaac
Jessup, E., Major
Jessup, Edward, Lieut.
Jones, David, Lieut.
Jones, Ephrem
Jones, John, Capt.
Jones, Thomas
Kenyon, Charles
Seeley, Joseph
Seeley, Justis
Shagnesay, Widow
Sherwood, J. Capt.

Dawson, John
Dibble, Asa
Kilbourn, Charles
Knap, Jos.
Landing, A.
Landing, Asa
Landing, Herman
Leakys, Wm. jr.
Loup, Jos.
Loux, John
Lowerey, Joshua
McCahron, Daniel
McDonald, Allen
McNien, Jos.
Mallory, Elisha
Mallory, Enoch
Mallory, Jeremiah
Mother, Nicholas
Mother, Lewis
Mott, Henry
Nicholson, Robert
Pitman, C.
Racoul, Nicholas

Sherwood, Samuel
Smith, Benoni
Smith, Daniel
Smith, John
Sparkman, Thos.
Spicer, Daniel
Soicer, Ezekiel sr.
Spicer, Ezekiel jr.
Spicer, Whelham
Sweet, Oliver
Trevoix, Asa
Valentine, Herman
Wall, Michael
Watson, Major
Wheeler, Ephrem
Wicken, Jonath
Wiltsay, Benoni
Wiltsee, James
Wiltsey, Benone, Sergt.

Total settlement: men, 82 : women, 42 : children, 92 : servants, 12 acres cleared, 124

TOWNSHIP NO. 8 (ELIZABETHTOWN)

Alkenbeack, John
Allan, Theodosius
Allan, Western
Barten, Thomas
Benwell, Bentley
Benwell, E. Wm.
Butler, Trewlove
Cane, John
Clark, Thomas
Clough, Wm.
Cole, Adam
Cross, Henry

Griffin, Joseph
Kenny, Amos
Kine, Constant
Leaky, Wm.
Leonard, Chris.
Maclean, Alex.
Maclean, Robt.
McKew, Wm.
Manhard, David
Mitchell, David
Mitchell, John
Mott, Rubin

Cross, John
Dunproof, Frederick
Earheart, John
Early, Barth
Elliot, John
Elliot, Thomas
Fulford, John
Ferguson, John
Graham, Oliver
Gray, John
Gray, James
Grant, Allen

Paterson, Conrad
Sherwood, C. Thos.
Sherwood, Reubin
Tenter, Chris.
Thelmy, James
Thompson, Jacob
Weaterwak, Wm.
White, Joseph
Wolfe, Lodwick
Wright, Samuel

Total settlement: Men, 51 : women, 27 : children, 104 : servants
3 acres cleared, 39.5

Schedule C

LIST OF FREEMASONS 1786

William Buell	David Breakenridge	Elijah Bottom
Bemsley Buell	Caleb Clauson	George Campbell
Bartholomew Carley	Lemuel Caswell	Henry Cross
Daniel Dunham	Nathaniel Hillyer	John Jones
Jeremiah McArthur	Ziba Phillips	Thomas Sherwood
Justus Sherwood	Thomas Smith	Francis Scott
Asa Starkweather	William Samson	Samuel Wright
John White	Samuel Wilson	William Warn

Schedule D

GOURLAY DELEGATES FROM THE TOWNSHIPS

TOWNSHIP	REPRESENTATIVE	CLERK	DELEGATES
SOUTH CROSBIE	Chapman Pennock	Nathan Ketchum	Joseph Merriman Henry Halladay Aaron Pennock
KITLEY	Duncan Livingston	T. S. Root	Benjamin Lyman Timothy Soper William W. Brown John Arnold
BASTAARD	George Breakenridge	Silas Smith	William Stevens Daniel Terrie Sheldon Nichols Judson Stoddard
LANSDOWNE	Nathan Hicock	Oliver Eaton	William Parish John Struthers Allan Sweet Isaac Soper
YONGE	Benoni Wiltse	Andrew Teed	John Dickson Squire Mott

Daniel Phillips
William Thompson
Walter Adams
Thomas P. Kenyon

ELIZABETHTOWN
    Thomas Smith   John Kilborn   Truelove Butler
                                                        Vincent Booth
                                                       Edward Howard
                                                        John Ketchum
                                                        Abraham Dayton

LEEDS COUNTY DELEGATION TO PROVINCIAL MEETING

REPRESENTATIVE   John Hicock
SECRETARY   John Kilborn
TREASURER   John Smith
COMMITTEE   Abraham Dayton, Thomas Smith,
                        Edward Howard, John Kilborn

Schedule E

MEMBERS OF THE LEGISLATIVE ASSEMBLY

ELECTED IN THE COUNTY OF LEEDS

Year	
1792	
1797	
1801	William Buell
1805	Peter Howard
1809	
1810	
1817	Jonas Jones
1821	Levius P. Sherwood and Charles Jones
1825	Charles Jones and David Jones
1829	William Buell (Jr.)
1830	William Buell and Mathew Howard
1834	Ogle R. Gowan and Robert S. Jameson
1836	Ogle R. Gowan and Jonas Jones

ELECTED IN THE COUNTY OF GRENVILLE

Year	
1792	
1797	
1801	Samuel Sherwood
1805	Samuel Sherwood
1809	
1810	
1817	Peter Howard
1821	Walter F. Gates and Jonas Jones

1825	Hamilton Walker and Jonas Jones
1829	
1830	Richard D. Fraser and Edward Jessup (died 1830)
1831	Hiram Norton replaces Edward Jessup (bi-election)
1834	Hiram Norton and William B. Wells
1836	Hiram Norton and William B. Wells

ELECTED IN BROCKVILLE

1831	Henry Jones
1835	David Jones
1836	Henry Sherwood

Credit, Thad. W. T. Leavitt, HISTORY OF LEEDS AND GRENVILLE, p.63,64

The Battle of the Windmill

On Tuesday morning we marched out,
In command of Colonel Fraser.
With swords and bayonets of steel
As keen as any razor.

Unto the Windmill Plains we went.
We gave them three loud cheers.
To let them know that day below
We're the Prescott volunteers.

Oh we're the boys that feared no noise
When canons loud did roar.
We cut the rebels left and right
When they landed on our shore.

Brave Macdonnell nobly led
His men onto the field.
They did not flinch, no not an inch,
Till the rebels had to yield.

He swung his sword right round his head
saying "Glengarrys follow me,
We'll gain the day without delay,
And that you'll plainly see."

The rebels now remain at home.
We wish that they would come.
We'd cut them up both day and night,
By command of Colonel Young.

If e'er they are return again,
They'll see what we can do.
We'll show them British play me boys,
As we did at Waterloo.

Under Captain Jessup we will fight,
Let him go where he will.
With powder and ball they'll surely fall,
As they did at the Windmill.

If I were like great Virgil bright,
I would employ my quill.
I would write both day and night
Concerning the Windmill.

Lest to intrude, I will come luck,
And finish off my song.
We'll pay a visit to Ogdensburg
And that's before its long.

Traditional folk song of Grenville County sung to the tune of "The Girl I Left Behind," recorded by George and Violet Dawson.

Bibliography

PRIMARY SOURCES

Public Archives of Canada:

Adjutant General's Office Correspondence for Grenville

Upper Canada Sundries

Trials of the Rebels at the Militia General Courts Martial, RG5 B40; Reel C1560: RG5 B40 C1590: RG5 B41 vol.I & II; Reel C15691

Report on The Queen v. Thomas D. McCormack, RG1 E3 vol. 54, Reel C1197

Correspondence of the Provincial Secretary's Office

Haldiman Papers, B.126

William Buell Papers, MG24 B75

Alpheus Jones Papers, MG24 B98

Charles Jones Papers, MG24 B7

Queens University Total Archives, Wells Family Papers

Appendix to the Journal of the House of Assembly of Upper Canada, Fifth Session, Thirteenth Parliament

Upper Canada Gazette

Notes of the Local Architectural Conservation Advisory Committee of Prescott, 1982.

Minutes of the Board of Police for the Town of Prescott, 1834 to 1838.

Brockville *Recorder*, 1833 to 1838.

SECONDARY SOURCES

Akenson, Donald Harman. *The Irish in Ontario, A Study in Rural History*. McGill-Queens University Press, Montreal/Kingston, 1985.

Bliss, J.M., ed. *Canadian History in Documents, 1763-1966*. Ryerson Press, Toronto, 1966.

Cartwright, C.E., ed. *Life and Letters of the Late Honourable Richard Cartwright*. Toronto, 1876.

Careless, J.M.S. *Canada: A Story of Challenge*. MacMillan of Canada, Toronto, 1963.

Clark, S.D. *Church and Sect in Canada*. University of Toronto Press, Toronto, 1940.

Craig, Gerald M., ed. *Lord Durham's Report*. McClelland and Stewart Ltd., Toronto/Montreal, 1963.

Cruikshank, Brigadier G.E. *The Settlement of the United Empire Loyalists on the Upper St. Lawrence and Bay of Quinte in 1784*. Ontario Historical Society, Toronto, 1934.

Cruikshank, Brigadier G.E. *"The Activity of Abel Stevens as a Pioneer."* Ontario Historical Society Papers and Records, vol. 31, Toronto, 1936.

Dawson, R. MacGregor. *The Government of Canada*. University of Toronto Press, 1948.

Dunham, Aileen. *Political Unrest in Upper Canada 1815-1836*. McClelland and Stewart Ltd., 1963.

Fraser, Robert L., ed. *Provincial Justice, Upper Canadian Legal Portraits from the Dictionary of Canadian Biography*. University of Toronto Press, 1992.

Guillet, Edwin C. *Pioneer Days in Upper Canada*. University of Toronto Press, 1973.

Guillet, Edwin C. *The Lives and Times of the Patriots*. Toronto, 1938 & 1963.

Hawke, H. William. *Historic Gananoque*. Mika Publishing, Belleville, 1974.

Head, Sir Francis Bond. *A Narrative*. London, 1839.

Henderson, J.L.H., ed. *John Strachan Documents and Opinions*. Carleton Library No. 44.

Houston, Cecil J., and Smyth, William J. *The Sash Canada Wore: A Historical Geography of the Orange Order in Canada.* University of Toronto Press.

Kilbourn, William. *The Firebrand, William Lyon Mackenzie and the Rebellion in Upper Canada.* Clarke, Irwin and Co. Ltd., 1964.

Larabee, Leonard Woods. *Conservatism in Early American History, Cornell University Press.* Ithica, New York, 1948.

Leavit, Thad W.H. *History of Leeds and Grenville, Mika Publishing Company.* Belleville, 1986 (reprint of original published by Recorder Press, Brockville, 1879).

Lockwood, Glen J. *Kitley 1795-1975.* St. Lawrence Printing Co. Ltd., Prescott, 1974. Copyright of G. Lockwood & J. Munro.

Lower, Arthur R.M. *Colony to Nation, A History of Canada.* Longmans Canada Limited, Toronto, 1946.

Lower, Arthur R.M. *Canadians in the Making.* Longmans Canada Ltd., 1958.

Lyons, Marjorie E. *Elizabethtown, A Typical St. Lawrence River Township.* Queen's University M.A. Thesis, Kingston, 1935.

Mackenzie, William Lyon. *Sketches of Upper Canada and the United States.* London, 1833.

MacPherson, Ian. *Matters of Loyalty: The Buells of Brockville 1830-1850.* Mika Publishing, Belleville, 1981.

MacRae, Marion. *The Ancestral Roof, Domestic Architecture of Upper Canada.* Clarke Irwin Co. Ltd., 1963.

McKenzie, Ruth. *Leeds and Grenville: Their First Two Hundred Years.* McClelland and Stewart Ltd., Toronto, 1967.

McLeod, D. *A Brief Review of the History of Upper Canada.* Reprint edition by Mika Publishing, Belleville, 1972.

Milani, Lois Darroch. *Robert Gourlay, Gadfly: The Biography of Robert (Fleming) Gourlay 1778-1863, Forerunner of Rebellion in Upper Canada.* 1837, Ampersand Press, 1971.

Moodie, Susanna. *Roughing it in the Bush, or, Forest Life in Canada.* McClelland and Stewart Ltd., New Canadian Library Series No. 13, 1961.

Morris, John A. *Prescott 1810-1967.* Prescott, 1967.

Nelson, W.H. *The American Tory.* Oxford, 1961.

Ormsby, William, ed. *Crisis in the Canadas: 1838-1839, The Grey Journals and Letters.* MacMillan of Canada, Toronto, 1964.

Pierce, Richard A. *"Nils Von Schoultz - The Man They Had to Hang."* Kingston Historical Society, No. 19, 1971.

Pipping, Ella. *Soldier of Fortune, The Story of a Nineteenth Century Adventurer.* Gambit Inc., Boston, 1971.

Raddall, Thomas H. *The Path to Destiny, Canada from the Conquest to Home Rule: 1763-1850.* Doubleday Canada Ltd., Toronto, 1957.

Read, Collin and Stagg, Ronald J., ed. *The Rebellion of 1837 in Upper Canada, A Collection of Documents.* Champlain Society, Toronto, 1985.

Robertson, John Ross, ed. *Simcoe Diary.* Toronto, 1911.

Sabine, Lorenzo. *Biographical Sketches of the Loyalists of the American Revolution, 2 vols.* Boston, 1864.

Sanderson, C.R., ed. *The Arthur Papers.* Toronto, 1957.

Saunders, Robert E. *"What Was the Family Compact?"* Ontario History, vol. 49, 1957.

Scott, K.F. *Prescott's Famous Battle of the Windmill, November 13 - 18, 1838.* Prescott, 1970.

Shelton, W.G. *"The United Empire Loyalists: A Reconsideration."* Dalhousie Review 45, (1965).

Stanley, George F.G. *"Invasion 1838."* Ontario History, vol. 54, 1962.

Stuart, E. Rae. *"Jessup's Rangers as a Factor in Loyalist Settlement."* Three history theses, Ontario Department of Public Records and Archives, 1961.

Vidler, Alec R. *The Church in an Age of Revolution, 1789 to the Present Day.* Penguin Books, London, 1961.

Index